More Praise for **Learning to Lead**

"In *Learning to Lead*, Ron Williams has given us an indispensable guide to leadership. Whether you are seeking ways to jump-start your career, lead others, or lead an organization, the book offers actionable tips and tools, from reframing issues, to the importance of honest and transparent communications, to creating a high-performance culture in the face of leadership challenges. Ron manages to distill what he's learned throughout his extraordinary career, and the book should be on every professional's must-read list."

—Julie Sweet, Chief Executive Officer–
North America, Accenture

"Ron Williams has written an exceptional book that seamlessly blends his amazing personal journey with keen business insight. In today's world, where leadership is often associated with bombast and antagonism, his commitment to empathy, ethics, diligence, and belief in the innate good of others offers an alternative vision of how to lead businesses that is extraordinarily compelling."

—Troyen Brennan, Executive Vice President
and Chief Medical Officer, CVS Health

"Ron Williams reveals how to turbo-charge your quest for success with this honest roadmap for all who want to thrive in their careers . . . starting on day one! Everyone from front-line managers to CEOs will find lessons that will help them unlock their potential and avoid needless mistakes when they read *Learning to Lead*."

—Jerri DeVard, Executive Vice President,
Chief Customer Officer, Office Depot

"*Learning to Lead* is an expert tutorial in leadership and management, with lessons that are applicable to all levels of leaders, from new business leaders to Fortune 500 CEOs. The stories and insights are clear and come alive with rich examples applicable to anyone who leads a team or organization. Ron Williams aptly identifies many of the attributes we look for in successful executives. *Learning to Lead* is accessible, practical, and inspiring. Its lessons will help you become a better leader and may help you become a better person."

—**Rusty O'Kelley,** Global Leader of the Board Advisory
& Effectiveness Practice, Russell Reynolds Associates

"I've known Ron Williams for many years and I've followed his career with admiration. We all can benefit from Ron's vast leadership experience. Now that he has written *Learning to Lead*, many other people—especially young men and women who aspire to leadership roles in organizations of every kind—can take inspiration and guidance from his experiences and his wisdom."

—**Bernard J. Tyson,** Chairman and CEO,
Kaiser Permanente

"Ron Williams's life story and business experience are inspiring, and the lessons he imparts about leadership apply across all sectors. His advice is personal, practical, and profound. *Learning to Lead* offers valuable insight for those seeking to grow and thrive in the workplace."

—**Roger W. Ferguson, Jr.,** President and
Chief Executive Officer, TIAA

"Ron Williams represents the kind of leader we need in every sector of society today—a person of integrity, focused on solving problems and building organizations that serve human needs with both efficiency and compassion. *Learning to Lead* offers wise counsel on every page."

—**Steve Odland,** President and CEO,
The Conference Board

"A prominent investor recently told me that his fund 'doesn't invest in companies, it invests in leaders.' That's one key reason why *Learning to Lead* is a must read. It embraces the notion that only a few great leaders are born that way—most must learn the DNA of leadership. Ron Williams is a proven leader and teacher, and reading his book is a great way to start learning to lead!"

—**Dennis Carey,** Vice Chairman Korn Ferry
and Founder, CEO Academy

The Journey to

LEADING YOURSELF,
LEADING OTHERS, AND
LEADING AN ORGANIZATION

LEARNING
to **LEAD**

RON WILLIAMS
with Karl Weber

GREENLEAF
BOOK GROUP PRESS

Published by Greenleaf Book Group Press
Austin, Texas
www.gbgpress.com

Distributed by Greenleaf Book Group

For ordering information or special discounts for bulk purchases, please contact Greenleaf Book Group at PO Box 91869, Austin, TX 78709, 512.891.6100.

Design and composition by Greenleaf Book Group
Cover design by Greenleaf Book Group

Publisher's Cataloging-in-Publication data is available.

Print ISBN: 978-1-62634-622-2

eBook ISBN: 978-1-62634-623-9

Part of the Tree Neutral® program, which offsets the number of trees consumed in the production and printing of this book by taking proactive steps, such as planting trees in direct proportion to the number of trees used: www.treeneutral.com

Printed in the United States of America on acid-free paper

21 22 23 24 25 26   11 10 9 8 7 6 5 4 3 2

First Edition

*To my wife, Cynthia, who has supported me
throughout our journey together.*

CONTENTS

Introduction

I BEGAN WRITING THIS book shortly after retiring from the chairmanship of Aetna Inc., a Fortune 100 company that is one of the world's largest diversified health-care benefits providers. But the origins of this book go back a lot further. In fact, I can recall quite vividly the conversation that first sparked my desire to share my story in writing.

It was in 2002, shortly after I'd been named president of Aetna. I'd been recruited to join the company a year earlier by Dr. Jack Rowe, a distinguished physician and medical researcher who had just been appointed to the position of CEO by Aetna's board.

At the time, the company was deeply troubled. It had been growing rapidly through a series of poorly planned mergers and acquisitions. As a result, Aetna's service culture had seriously deteriorated, its reputation among both patients and health-care providers had plummeted, and the corporation was losing almost a million dollars a day. With Aetna on the verge of collapse, the board had made the desperate decision of turning to Jack Rowe—an outsider with no business training and little knowledge of the insurance business—in hopes that he could somehow spark a turnaround. Jack, in turn, had called on me to help. I'd helped to run a major managed care company and developed a knack for the kind of analytical systems thinking Aetna needed. Jack and I hoped that our very different talents would make us an effective, complementary team to lead Aetna back to profitability.

The conversation I'm recalling took place one day early in our partnership. Jack and I were engaged in a crucial fence-mending campaign during which we would visit the headquarters of 150 of America's biggest and most powerful corporations—all of which were major clients of Aetna. Our mission was to reassure these important customers that Aetna was now in good hands and that the managerial problems that had plagued the business were finally on a correction course. To facilitate these vital meetings in cities across the country, Jack and I had used the corporate plane. Our whirlwind tour was scheduled to end when we returned to Aetna's corporate headquarters in Hartford, Connecticut, to conduct the regularly scheduled quarterly announcement of our financial results and hold a crucial conference call with nervous Wall Street analysts eager to hear the details of our turnaround plan.

In the midst of this multiday journey—I don't recall which city we were flying to—Jack and I decided to take a break from reviewing reports and discussing business strategies. We stretched our legs and poured a couple of cups of coffee. As we chatted, we began sharing our individual histories in a more personal way than we'd ever done before.

Before joining Aetna, Jack had been a professor at Harvard Medical School, had founded the school's Division of Aging, and had served as president and CEO of the then Mount Sinai–NYU

Medical Center and Health System, one of the nation's largest and most important medical research and training institutions. No one familiar with Jack's humble origins would have predicted such a career. His dad had been a professional soccer player in Britain, and then moved to the United States where he got a job working in a pencil factory in Jersey City, New Jersey. Jack's mother was a hospital clerk. Jack attended Canisius College, a small Jesuit-affiliated institution in Buffalo, New York, before going to medical school at the University of Rochester. From there, his innate talent, his dedication to the craft of medicine, his leadership instincts, and his tireless work ethic combined to bring about his remarkable rise to prominence.

As for me, I was a black man from a family in which no one had ever attended college. My dad was a parking lot manager who later became a bus driver; my mom was a manicurist in a neighborhood beauty parlor. I grew up on the South Side of Chicago and attended the kind of public school where almost every high school graduate immediately went to work or joined the military. I knew almost no one with a white-collar job or who had attended college; I couldn't imagine what a business career would be like, and to top it off, I stuttered, which made me hesitant to speak in public.

Yet in some ways I was relatively lucky. My dad helped me get my first job, washing cars after school. Though it was not my dream job, it kept me off of drugs and out of gangs. When people ask me what I learned from that first job, I tell them that washing three hundred or so cars a day, soaking wet, in temperatures of twenty below zero, taught me pretty darn fast exactly what I didn't want to spend my life doing. I recommend a stint of washing cars to everyone!

Jack Rowe laughed when I told him the story. "Did you ever

imagine that one day you'd be flying in a corporate plane on your way to meet with America's top CEOs?" he asked.

"Never in a million years," I told him.

"Neither did I," Jack confessed. And we agreed that ours was an amazing American story—the kind of tale of overcoming obstacles and conquering barriers that more people, especially young people, needed to hear about.

Then and there, I resolved to one day share my story with the world, along with the lessons I'd taken from it. The book you're reading is the result.

My goal in writing *Learning to Lead* has been to present the tools that have worked for me in a form that will allow readers to use them in their own lives and careers. It's not a book about competitive strategy, corporate finance, or other nuts-and-bolts skills like those you might study in business school. It's about principles of leadership that apply to life and that work in any arena, from the biggest company to the smallest mom-and-pop business to nonprofit or government organizations. The presentation is structured to reflect the real-life progression that most aspiring leaders will face, starting with learning how to lead yourself, moving on to leading others, and finally achieving the highest goal—leading an entire organization.

Along the way, I'll offer examples from my own story and from the lives of other successful leaders that I hope will illustrate and illuminate how the principles can be used to solve the kinds of practical challenges leaders face every day in life—turning seemingly impossible problems into opportunities to grow, achieve, and excel.

I've written this book not for my fellow CEOs—though if some of them find it interesting and thought-provoking, I'll be very pleased. Instead, this book is for people like those I grew up with in Chicago and those I frequently meet and talk with to this day—people who feel they're facing tough barriers to success and wondering whether there's any realistic hope that they or their children can truly achieve the kind of fulfilling, rewarding life they dream of.

I'm thinking of people like the friend I chatted with recently, a middle-class guy of black American heritage with a son who is struggling to make a life for himself. My friend's son hears companies tout their "diversity" message but wonders whether that message includes everybody but him. Having graduated from a good state university, he finds himself saddled with two daunting burdens—a crushing load of student debt and a seemingly unpromising entry-level job that barely pays enough to cover his rent. Now factor in the messages he is constantly receiving—from cynical friends, discouraged relatives, and society at large—that tell him the cards are stacked against him and that the American dream doesn't apply to people like him. It's easy to see why that young man is tempted to give in to helplessness and despair.

"You've been very successful, Ron," my friend said to me. "What can you say to my son that can help him become successful too? He hasn't found his passion and doesn't know where to start."

I wouldn't want to minimize the challenges that the young women and men of today are facing. There's no doubt that the tough economy, the ultra-competitive business environment, and the unrelenting pace of change all pose real problems that will take toughness and intelligence to solve. For young people who may lack some of the advantages that come with a privileged personal background—wealth, connections, a prestigious education—the game may even feel rigged. But I hope I can give them reasons to believe in themselves.

The best reason for hope is the fact that our society has a greater need than ever for talented, effective leaders. Given the enormous social and economic challenges we face, organizations of every kind—for-profit businesses, nonprofit organizations, and government agencies—are desperate for people of every background with the ability to formulate a compelling vision of the future and to inspire others to help make that vision a reality. By tackling an increasingly tough series of personal and organizational challenges, I gradually developed many of the skills that effective leaders need. Those skills enabled me, even under the most difficult circumstances, to create the kind of positive, high-performance culture that generates consistent excellence—along with rewarding outcomes for everyone else whose lives the leader touches. And I'm convinced that anyone who is willing to work hard and continually learn can master the same leadership skills.

If you do that, you may or may not make it to the CEO's office. But I promise that you and your talents will be in demand, no matter what field of work you enter. You'll have plenty of opportunities to tackle meaningful challenges, to create value for society and for yourself, and to grow as an individual, now and for years to come.

I've also come to believe that the principles offered in this book are even more important today. We live in a time when too many of the role models visible in the media represent styles of leadership that are far from ideal. We've seen too many self-proclaimed leaders—on Main Street, on Wall Street, and even at the highest levels of government—who seem to be willing to cut ethical corners, to bend and distort the facts, and to substitute bullying for persuasion—all in service of self rather than to benefit the organization and the people whose lives are affected. We can all use a reminder about the deeper values that experience shows represent the true path to long-term success.

I hope that reading *Learning to Lead* will help you master a more creative, positive, and honorable way of leadership that will enable you to solve problems that appear unsolvable and to achieve levels of success you may never have previously imagined.

Ronald A. Williams
September 2018

PART

1

LEADING
YOURSELF

Find Your Challenge:
Launching Your Career Quest

*Many successful people have started their careers
without a plan or without even a clear objective in
mind. If that describes you, here is some advice on how
to transform the twists and turns of an unpredictable
journey into a satisfying road to achievement.*

SOME HAVE CALLED ME the least likely person ever to lead a $34 billion corporation.

I grew up in the 1960s in a working-class family in one of the poorer neighborhoods of Chicago, then one of the most segregated cities in the nation. The cultural, educational, and economic opportunities around me were sparse. But I inherited a strong work ethic from my mom and dad, and I was determined to make something of myself. After graduating from high school, I made my way to

Southeast Community College of Chicago, then to Roosevelt University, where I majored in psychology. After a brief stint working in the office of Illinois Governor Richard Ogilvie, I launched a business career—first as a consultant, then as an entrepreneur, and then as an executive at Control Data Corporation, Blue Cross of California, and WellPoint Health Networks.

By the time one of America's biggest insurance companies was foundering, I'd established a reputation as a go-to guy—someone with a knack for making things happen in tough situations where others struggled. I was recruited to help turn around Aetna in 2001. After a year as executive vice president, I was named president and a member of the board, and in 2006 I added the titles of CEO and chairman. Aetna had recorded an annual loss of $292 million in 2001. However, by the time I stepped down in 2011—thanks to a tremendous amount of hard work and creative thinking by thousands of dedicated Aetna employees—that loss had been transformed into an annual profit of $1.97 billion, and the company had become one of the most admired in the industry.

As even this brief summary shows, my background and experiences are definitely unusual for the head of a Fortune 100 company. But much more important are the philosophies, methods, and principles that helped me achieve success. I've tried to be both a dedicated student and a successful practitioner of the art of leadership.

I've practiced that approach to life challenges for a long time. At one of my early jobs, I was tested for various traits and discovered that, according to science, I am a strong introvert. At first, I assumed that my introverted personality, combined with the difficulty of crashing through the glass ceiling that keeps many black Americans (and others) from positions of leadership and authority, might rule out business as a viable career for me. But then I found myself fascinated by organizations—what makes them work, how people relate to one another, why some succeed and some fail—and I realized that my different upbringing and background presented an opportunity. The world and its people were a puzzle for me to solve. Despite the fact that I hadn't grown up in the privileged environment of many future CEOs, my inquisitive mind and the search for understanding that it engendered gave me a chance to succeed once I had an opportunity to lead.

Along the way, I learned lessons that have helped me succeed—and that, I suspect, many other people may find valuable.

Here's the first lesson I'd like to emphasize: Growing into leadership begins with *self-leadership*—which starts with discovering and nurturing the inner drive that will spur you to seemingly impossible achievements. That drive may be moving toward your passion, if you're lucky enough to know it. Or it may be moving rapidly away from what you don't want to do—moving out of the cold and toward the sun.

Most young people find it hard to define a career path that excites and inspires them. It's especially challenging in tough economic times, when the opportunities that beckoned previous generations seem to have disappeared. The temptation is to seek out a well-trodden path in hopes of a comfortable route to success. Unfortunately, this is the road most people follow—and the most crowded trail is never the way to achieve extraordinary success.

The zigzag nature of my own early career demonstrates that there's more than one path to any goal. Fortunately for me, I managed to turn every job I had into a learning experience and a stepping-stone on the route to my greatest challenge. Along the way, I discovered that my unconventional background—including a working-class family and a degree in psychology rather than business or economics—could be turned to my advantage, offering lessons about perseverance, hard work, empathy, and understanding that profoundly enhanced my leadership skills.

I also discovered some other truths about the path to leadership, including a few that you may find surprising. For example, I've learned that the transition from being a follower to a leader doesn't necessarily involve any dramatic transformations or revelations. Looking back on my career, I'm hard-pressed to define any single turning point when I suddenly realized what it takes to be a success. Instead, I experienced a slow, steady growth in knowledge and understanding, fueled by a wide range of work experiences, most of them completely mundane. In the end, I found myself in a quite different place from where I started. But the ascent was so gradual that it never felt shocking or miraculous, but rather quite natural.

I've also learned that having an overwhelming personal passion that guides and shapes your life isn't essential to business success. Some accomplished people know from childhood the kind of work they want to pursue—as physicians, attorneys, high-tech entrepreneurs, movie directors, bankers, or what have you. But many more are like me: interested in a wide array of topics, willing to learn a variety of skills, and ready to try their hands at a number of job assignments. My experience suggests that being flexible can lead to a career that is just as successful, rewarding, and enjoyable as climbing to the pinnacle of a selected field based on a single-minded passion and dedication. Two things are essential: a deep personal commitment to excellence in everything you do and a commitment to continual improvement.

Finally, I would suggest that rising to the top in the world of business doesn't resemble winning a reality TV contest like *Shark Tank* or *The Apprentice*. It isn't about being anointed by some higher authority figure who recognizes and rewards your potential. Bosses, mentors, and advocates can be helpful, of course. I worked with a huge variety of bosses over the years, some good and some bad, and I learned useful lessons from all of them. But in the end, no boss or mentor drove my success—although they did open doors for me. My success came about through a combination of hard work, continual learning, fortunate career choices, and a bit of luck—by being in the right place at the right time.

SOAKING UP LEARNING, WITH NO SPECIFIC GOAL IN MIND

I grew up in the 1950s and '60s on the South Side of Chicago in a community called Englewood. I watched communities going through the phenomenon dubbed "white flight": When families of color would move into a neighborhood, the older white families would begin to move out, fearful that crime and decay would erode their property values and make life unlivable. The departure of stable middle-class families would help make the dire predictions come true, and vast swaths of Chicago—along with other northern cities—experienced significant economic decline during those postwar decades.

As a result, I grew up surrounded by a fair amount of crime, violence, and gang activity. There always seemed to be a handful of crazy guys in the neighborhood everybody worried about—guys who were prone to lashing out if they felt their dignity or power had been challenged. Early in life, I learned one of the basic lessons of life in a danger zone: The best way to stay alive is to try to remain on everybody's good side and pray you never get caught in the crossfire.

Unfortunately, that strategy doesn't always work. One time, a buddy and I were robbed by a kid wielding a .22 pistol. He got all of fifty cents for his trouble. Another time, I went down the wrong street on my way to school and was beaten up by a gang of kids who'd taken it upon themselves to define that street as their turf. By wandering down it I had set myself up to become a victim.

As you can imagine, I made a point of never walking down that street again. But I also vowed that I would try to live my life going forward in such a way that I could gradually make a place for myself in a very different kind of environment—one in which I would be surrounded by good people, positive influences, and life-enhancing experiences.

My parents had been part of the great northern migration of black Americans that played such a transformative role in postwar US history. My mother had come from Oklahoma, while my father's large family had come from Alabama and spread out to several midwestern cities—Detroit, St. Louis, Chicago. When I researched my family history on the Internet, I found that, around the turn of the twentieth century, my maternal grandmother and her parents were listed on the so-called Cherokee Rolls—the official register of people accepted as members of the tribe. Historians say the rolls include both some runaway slaves who became members of the tribe as well as formerly enslaved people who traveled west after emancipation. My ancestors on my father's side, meanwhile, were enslaved people in the Carolinas. They went on to experience the kinds of tough challenges known to millions of other black Americans. Some tilled the land as sharecroppers, while others found work as domestic servants, cooks, factory hands, or railroad laborers.

By the time I came along, my father was working as a parking lot attendant and as a manager/supervisor at parking garages in some of the high-rise buildings along Chicago's Lake Shore Drive. Later, the guys he worked for got into the automated car wash business, and my dad became a manager at one of their facilities. He didn't even have a high school diploma. But he was willing to work hard, to take orders, and to provide the extra effort needed to become a valuable employee. This helped him become a successful supervisor until the business was sold and he was forced to find another line of work.

Dad ended up getting a job as a bus driver at the Chicago Transit Authority. He must have shown some innate leadership abilities because when he got involved in the labor union, he was elected an officer. After that, he only drove the bus around half the time. He spent the rest handling union business—representing workers when they got into trouble with management, arguing on their behalf when they became embroiled in disputes. I like to think his hard work and compassion saved the jobs of more than a handful of his fellow workers.

My mom was a manager in a local beauty shop where she worked three days a week. While I didn't grow up in a home where big business was discussed, hard work was very much on the agenda, and it never occurred to me or my older brother that we would ever do anything but work hard, every day, for as long as we lived.

A strong work ethic wasn't the only valuable thing I inherited from my parents. They also set the example of powerful moral values derived, in their case, from religious faith. We attended a local branch of the African Methodist Episcopal (AME) Church, which was founded in 1816 by several black Methodist congregations in the mid-Atlantic states in response to discrimination in the mainstream United Methodist Church. I remain a member of the AME Church to this day, although I'm not a regular attendee at Sunday services. The biggest impact of my religious upbringing has been on my sense of commitment to ethical behavior, which I try to express through my business-related decisions, my participation in volunteer and charitable efforts, and the ways in which I treat those I come into contact with every day.

As for my brother, the two of us had different interests. Whereas I was always an avid reader (especially of science fiction), my brother was more interested in practical pursuits—working, making money, and enjoying life. He ended up moving to Las Vegas, where, like our dad, he got a job as a bus driver. Sadly, he is no longer with us—he died of pancreatic cancer at a young age.

But I loved school, and early on I started being rewarded for my efforts. After scoring high on a standardized exam, I skipped a grade in elementary school and found myself learning advanced subjects in a class with kids who were a year older than me. Then I started going to summer school, where I had the chance to take accelerated classes like biology. I enjoyed it a lot, especially when compared with the only real alternative, which would have been to hang out on the street with the other neighborhood kids. There was no such thing as camp or summer vacation. (To this day, I smile when I hear people talk about their two-week or three-week vacations as a kind of necessity. I still think of those things as a luxury reserved for upper-class people . . . not ordinary folk like me.)

In high school, I took advantage of a program that allowed high-scoring students to transfer from their neighborhood school to a better one in a nearby district. I ended up in a high school that had fewer than a hundred black kids among a thousand white kids. (The Chicago public schools had been legally desegregated only a couple of years earlier, in 1964.) I continued to enjoy my classes and do well in them, but it was pretty obvious that there was a difference in the way the black students were treated. There were only a handful of teachers who behaved as if they cared, including the two black teachers—a history instructor and a physical education teacher. But most of the faculty seemed utterly indifferent. No one ever talked to me about going to college; the help of the guidance counselors was reserved for the white students. So I learned to find my own path, making mistakes along the way—a pattern that would continue throughout my life.

Meanwhile, the habit of working at a job had already become a regular part of my life. I never played sports or participated in clubs in high school. I used my spare time to earn money—for clothes and for anything else I might need beyond the basics of life, which my mom and dad provided. (It never occurred to me that I might be entitled to an allowance or to spending money from my parents.) When classes ended at two or three in the afternoon, I'd take the bus to my dad's car wash/gas station and put in three hours or so pumping gas and washing cars. On weekends, I did the same thing all day Saturday and half a day on Sunday.

I worked with an interesting group of guys—grown men who didn't have much of a future beyond pumping gas. They used their paychecks not for discretionary things but to support themselves and their families—or, in some cases, to support their bad habits. I remember one guy who would get paid every Friday, go out drinking and partying, and pick up ladies in the neighborhood. By the time he came back to work on Sunday morning, he would need to borrow a couple of bucks from me to buy lunch.

Looking back, the single most important thing I learned from that first job is what I *didn't* want to do with my life. My specialty was cleaning the inside rear windows of cars. On a busy day, we would wash six or seven hundred cars, and I helped wash about half of them. Now remember that this was Chicago, which means that on a winter day it might be twenty degrees below zero—and when you wash cars, you spend the entire day sopping wet. You soon realize, as a fifteen-year-old, that this is not the kind of work you want to do for the next fifty years.

Working alongside my dad gave me a useful measuring stick for calibrating the problems that my colleagues and I had to deal with in the business world. Whenever I was tempted to complain about a particularly thorny management challenge, I would pause and remind myself: *I'm being paid a nice wage. I'm indoors. It's warm. It's dry. What the heck is there to complain about?*

For many years after launching my business career, I often thought back to my time in the car wash, but it eventually faded into a distant memory. Just a couple of years ago, however, I experienced a vivid flashback.

My business success has given me a degree of financial security I never imagined as a youngster. It has enabled me to do many good things for my family and my community, for which I'm very grateful. And although I'm not terribly concerned about the accoutrements of wealth, I do have a weakness for beautiful cars. So after retiring from my role as CEO of Aetna, I got a big kick out of being able to buy the kind of car I dreamed about as a kid—a beautiful sports car with a powerful engine. It was a pleasure to drive.

I'd been driving the sports car for a couple of weeks when I realized it was time for a wash and a detailing. As I pulled into the local car wash, a black teenager stepped up, chamois cloth in hand, gave my car an appreciative smile, and began sloshing soapy water over the hood. A moment of recognition flashed across my brain—*that was me when I was his age!* And I wondered whether that young man ever dreamed of owning a beautiful car of his own . . . and whether he realized that, with hard work, good decisions, and some luck, it could happen.

Maybe one day he will come across this book and discover that my story could also be his.

FINDING A CAREER PATH ONE TWIST, ONE TURN AT A TIME

When I graduated from high school, I followed the same path as many of the other black students I knew: I enrolled in the Southeast Community College of Chicago, taking nine to twelve hours' worth of classes at a time. It was affordable, and I enjoyed it. I had no great career plan in mind. My mom and dad knew a total of just one person with a college degree—a schoolteacher. So I had no idea what opportunities might exist for me after I finished college. But I knew I needed to keep learning if I was going to get out of the car wash—and stay out.

Sure enough, a different kind of job opportunity quickly came along. I knew somebody who'd gotten a job at the Federal Reserve Bank in Chicago, so I went down and applied for a job of my own. I was what was called a "checker." In those days, the Federal Reserve cleared all the checks processed by banks around the country. We checkers would be delivered big bundles of checks that we had to verify for "integrity"—to make sure the checks in each bundle and their total value matched the data shown on a printed tape. We did this by checking the first and last check in each bundle and spot-checking a few checks in the middle. I did that job for a couple of years while in school.

It's funny—while working at the Fed, I never developed any interest in the financial industry, and honestly, I don't think I even realized I was playing any role in that industry. It was just a job like any other, and a lot more comfortable than sloshing soapy water over car windshields.

After completing community college, I moved out of my parents' home and rented a small apartment. With the income from my full-time job and the help of student loans, I went to Roosevelt University, a school for adult learners in Chicago. This was a place where people with day jobs could attend classes on evenings and weekends to fill in the cracks of the courses they hadn't completed in community college. I signed up for as many classes as I could, and I graduated with my BA in psychology at age twenty, four years to the day after my high school graduation.

I worked for a while as a counselor in a program set up to train young people for manufacturing jobs, then got a position as a junior aide in the office of Richard Ogilvie, the Republican governor of Illinois. This would be my most intimate glimpse into the world of politics until many years later, when I was asked to serve as an advisor to the administration of President Barack Obama and to play a role as a thought leader on health reform and business growth, as well as serve as a public spokesperson during the national debate about health-care reform.

I discovered, to my surprise, that many of the cabinet-level people in the governor's office were business executives who were doing a public service stint in government. For example, the head of the Illinois Department of Employment Security had run the human resources functions for one of the major corporations in the area. Meeting people like him helped me gain a broader view of the universe. I began to discern the kinds of career paths followed by ambitious people who'd grown up in better circumstances than I had—paths that included graduate degrees, managerial business jobs, and a range of other positions that hadn't been available to people like me in past generations.

I set to work on a master's degree in clinical psychology, hoping this might open some interesting career doors for me. But when I reached the point in the program when I had to do a one-year, unpaid internship in a mental hospital, I stopped short. I'd been earning money for my work ever since I was thirteen years old, so the notion of working for free simply didn't compute for me. I like to joke that that was the day I discovered I was a capitalist. I decided to set my sights on the business world instead.

However, my psychological studies turned out to be helpful to me throughout my entire career. Probably the single most important insight I gained came from something called *attribution theory*, a part of the then-new discipline of social psychology. Simply stated, attribution theory captures the common experience that if people like you, they attribute good things to you and bad things to your environment, but if they don't like you, they attribute bad things to you and good things to your environment. (A simple example: An avid Republican is likely to blame a Democratic president for everything that goes wrong during that administration, while claiming that anything that goes right can be credited to outside forces—a strong economy, Republicans in Congress, or other factors. An avid Democrat, naturally, will do the same thing in reverse.) Understanding this common psychological dynamic helps to explain a lot of the conflict one encounters in business and elsewhere—and makes it much easier to depersonalize that conflict and therefore deal with it more effectively.

While I still didn't have any career vision in mind, I was moving further away from washing cars, which in itself was pretty satisfying.

In fact, by the time I was twenty-two, I had accomplished everything I had ever envisioned in my life: I'd earned a college degree and I'd bought my first house, a two-bedroom townhouse on Chicago's South Side that cost me $16,000, which seemed like a fortune at the time.

After I'd spent almost two years in the governor's office, Richard Ogilvie lost his reelection bid. I decided to leave before the new administration of Democrat Dan Walker took office. I started working for Greenlea Associates, a consulting firm whose customers were state and local governments. My knowledge of how state government worked turned out to have value in this new job. I spent about a year working on contracts in North Dakota, living in places like Bismarck, Fargo, Grand Forks, and Jamestown. It was a unique learning experience to meet people from such a different world than the one I had grown up in.

I also learned that, while I was a pretty good salesman, I knew absolutely nothing about business. I didn't know how to price products, didn't know how to organize and manage budgets, and didn't have a good idea about how a business actually operated.

I concluded that I needed to gain some business experience, so I set out in search of a major corporation that I could join to get some solid management experience. I ended up being interviewed and hired by Control Data Corporation, a giant technology firm that, at the time, was one of the major players in the field of computing. And that was when my career as a business leader truly began.

PAT RUSSO: FIND YOUR HIDDEN ADVANTAGE AND RIDE IT TO SUCCESS

A successful executive whose leadership talents I admire is Pat Russo, the former CEO of Lucent Technologies (and its successor company,

Alcatel-Lucent). Like me, and like many of today's top-level female executives, Russo comes from an unusual background for a high-tech CEO. Her story, like mine, illustrates how you can take a set of personal experiences and a background that might appear ordinary and turn them into stepping-stones to success.

Russo grew up as one of seven kids in a middle-class family in a New Jersey suburb. She was a talented athlete—co-captain of her high school basketball team and captain of the cheerleading squad and a good student. After graduating from Georgetown University in 1973 with a degree in political science and history, she was uncertain of what to do next. She considered a traditional "woman's career" as a teacher or nurse, but neither appealed to her. At the same time, she'd never studied business or thought seriously about working in the corporate world.

But she needed a job. So Russo applied for, and got, a job in Cranford, New Jersey, as one of the first female sales representatives in the eastern region for IBM, then near the height of its dominance in the world of corporate computing.

As you might imagine, Russo encountered a fair amount of sexism in her pioneering role. Surprisingly, she hadn't expected this at all. "I couldn't believe that some of IBM's customers didn't want to have me as their account representative!" she recalls. "It made no sense to me. After all, they didn't even know me! What could they possibly have against me?" Today, Russo chuckles at her naiveté. "Maybe it's because I grew up with four brothers who treated me as a complete equal. We skied and played tennis together, and I always held my own. So when I went to IBM, it was the first time anyone had treated me as less capable than a man."

Russo quickly discovered that the success hurdles were set higher for women than for men, particularly in the male-dominated world of technology. She decided not to let it bother her. "I've found that every job has both advantages and disadvantages. My approach is to start by figuring out which is which. Then I try to make the most of the advantages—and as for the disadvantages, I don't waste any time complaining about them."

Russo doggedly set about doing a better job as a sales rep than any of her IBM colleagues, male or female. She discovered that her gender could even be an advantage in certain circumstances. One of the corporate clients assigned to her was Revlon, the major cosmetics company. The fact that Russo was a woman—like the vast majority of Revlon customers—gave her a cultural edge that earned her access to higher-level executives within Revlon, even including the company's chief information officer (despite the fact that these executives were male). Russo's natural talent, combined with the unique visibility afforded by her gender, attracted favorable attention inside and outside Revlon. She soon became a star member of the IBM sales force.

Having discovered an affinity for business, Russo began climbing the corporate ladder. IBM loved her. But Russo wasn't sure she felt the same way. She recalls a conversation with a member of the company's human resources staff. "I know I'm on the fast track here," Russo told her, "but I'm not sure I *want* to be! If I become a member of IBM's A team, what will my life be like? Will I spend my career being moved from city to city, never having a chance to settle down and live a normal life?" (Those were the days when IBM was famous for transferring its managers from one facility to another every few years; employees joked that the company's initials stood for the words "I've Been Moved.")

Worried, like millions of women then and now, about how she could achieve a comfortable work-life balance, Russo made what felt at the time like a very risky move. It happened when she got a call from an old IBM colleague who had made the jump to AT&T, then the overwhelming telecommunications giant. "Come join us at AT&T!" he said. "A few of us from IBM are here, and we've been talking you up. We could use someone exactly like you!"

At the time, in the early 1980s, AT&T was in the midst of a challenging transition from a big but staid company protected by its near monopoly over the telephone industry, into one of many players in a rapidly evolving, extremely competitive high-tech environment. That's why AT&T had been luring key people from IBM—and why it now wanted to snatch up a star saleswoman, Pat Russo.

Russo recognized this as an exciting opportunity. "It was flattering to have my old colleagues reach back to me at IBM to recruit me for their new company," she says. "It taught me a lesson I've never forgotten—that you should always maintain good connections with the people you work with, because you never know who is going to bring you the next big break." And Russo imagined that the leap to AT&T might also give her a chance to achieve a more satisfactory balance between the demands of work and her personal life.

"That turned out to be completely false!" Russo now says with a laugh. "My career at AT&T was as intense and high pressure as you can imagine—probably a lot more so than staying at IBM would have been. Moving to AT&T turned out to be the right move for me, but for totally different reasons I could never have imagined at the time."

I'll return to Pat Russo's story in a later chapter. But for now, notice the role played by serendipity—unpredictable good luck— in her rise to success. Her start at IBM . . . her connection with Revlon . . . her wooing by AT&T—all came about not through deliberate planning but through happenstance. The key was that

Russo recognized the opportunities when they arose and did what she needed to do to take advantage of them. It's a pattern I've seen in the careers of many of the world's most successful people.

In my own case, my career advantage is my willingness to take a chance and to move into unfamiliar situations. I didn't realize this at first, but over time it has proven to be my true north.

CAREER STEP ONE: TAKE A CHANCE!

If you hope to be one of the leaders of tomorrow, I urge you to embark on your career journey in the same spirit of dauntlessness and self-discipline demonstrated by people like Pat Russo. If you're like them—or like me—you'll find it can take time to discover the challenge you were born to tackle. I can promise you that the journey will amply repay the effort.

Here are some specific suggestions to consider as you tackle some of the early career decisions that will shape your lifetime path:

Reject stereotypical thinking. Don't let other people define who you are, what you can become, or what you can accomplish. Feel free to disregard the familiar assumptions that define the characteristics of a business leader. For example, many people would probably assume being an introvert would be a handicap for a leadership role. But over my years in business, I've found that being introverted has helped me to develop a leadership style that is consistent, stable, and predictable—qualities I've used to help fuel my effectiveness.

Break out of your comfort zone. In every job, look for opportunities to stretch yourself. As a natural introvert, it took me a long time to learn that a certain amount of social interaction was necessary for a leader; otherwise, people felt neglected or unappreciated and didn't feel that I cared about them. Fortunately, doing things that make me uncomfortable is what I've done all my life. In fact, I believe that if you're comfortable with every activity in your life, then it's probably time to start doing some new things. The sense of discomfort is a good sign—it means you are trying a fresh route that offers potential rewards far greater than those you'll enjoy on the path of least resistance.

Take a calculated risk. Which is the better choice for a young person coming out of school—a job with a big, established company, or one with a tiny startup? If both job assignments appear equally appealing, my counsel is to take the job that you perceive as carrying the bigger risk. That's probably the job where you'll face the greatest challenges—and therefore learn the most.

Pick jobs with quantifiable results. Pat Russo urges ambitious young people—especially women—to look for work in line management (i.e., helping to run operating departments or divisions) rather than staff jobs (such as human resources or public relations). She advises: "Staff jobs can be challenging and valuable. But I suggest you seek out jobs that have results that are measurable—jobs where you're held responsible for sales revenues, customer growth, new product introductions, profit margins, or other specific metrics. Jobs like this give you a chance to build up a track record of results that no one can question or argue with, and that create opportunities for your future. People who produce results rise to the top."

Keep your future options open. When making any career choice, think in terms of increasing the number of options you will have in the future. Ask yourself: If I take this job, will I have more choices at the end of the day? Avoid choices that you sense may be leading toward a dead end or simply repeating more of what you have already done. And do your homework to identify sectors of the economy that are growing rather than shrinking. That's where the best and most numerous future job opportunities are likely to be found.

Exceed your job description. One strategy that is likely to stall your career growth is to take a transactional view of your current job—in other words, to think of it strictly as a *quid pro quo* arrangement in which you give the company exactly what you are paid for, no more and no less. Team members who never provide any extra value— who avoid special assignments, ignore opportunities to take on new challenges, and never offer ideas for improving the organization— are asking to be passed over when promotions are being considered. If you think about it, it makes perfect sense: By sticking strictly to the tasks listed in your job description, you are refusing to demonstrate your ability to perform at a higher level. Why should anyone think of you as a potential leader when you've provided them with no evidence to suggest it?

Be patient. As you're working your way to the higher levels of an organization, avoid trying to force the process. My experience tells me that most companies are hungry for leadership talent, which is always in short supply. They're unlikely to ignore someone who is gifted with that talent or to leave them buried in the mail room. So if you think you are being unduly delayed in your journey to the top, think again! It's more likely that you are in need of additional seasoning—that, as skilled as you may be in some aspects of the work, there are other talents you have yet to fully demonstrate. As I've advised more than one eager beaver hungry for a chance to prove themselves, "Take it a little slower. If you focus too intently on the when in your career, you may end up sabotaging the if."

Of course, there are exceptions. Sometimes you may find yourself working for a company whose fundamental values and culture are markedly different from your own. If you feel consistently uncomfortable with things you are asked to do, it may be necessary to make a break and seek work elsewhere. In other cases, you may be working in a company or an industry that is slowly dying—one that has been rendered obsolete by shifts in technology or market preferences, where every year the resources for personal growth and learning become scarcer. That's another sign that it may be time to move on.

But when there is no fundamental problem with the company—when you are enthusiastic about the business but antsy about the speed at which you personally are rising, my advice is not to worry too much. When you're ready for the next job, it will come along, right on time.

TAKEAWAYS FROM CHAPTER 1

- Many successful people didn't start with a career plan—so don't worry if you don't have one. You'll find that your future will reveal itself one step at a time, as varied experiences deepen your knowledge about the world and about yourself.

- In every life situation, look for opportunities to learn. You may discover personal talents you never knew you had...or at least

continued

develop a stronger sense of the kinds of work you *don't* want to spend your life doing.

- Take calculated career risks—but with every decision, strive to broaden your future options rather than limiting them. Avoid job choices you suspect may lead to dead ends, and instead look for positions that will increase your store of knowledge and skills, so that the next job will be an even more interesting and rewarding one.

- Seek out jobs in sectors that are growing. When I chose health care, it represented just ten percent of the economy; it has now grown to eighteen percent, while other industries have shrunk, leaving more people chasing fewer jobs.

- Don't be afraid to break out of your comfort zone. Learning and growth are often painful...but also beneficial.

- Try to get a job with results that can be measured—and that you can be rewarded for. Being able to quantify your accomplishments (customer wins/retention, sales made, projects completed, profits earned) gives you credentials that no one can argue with or ignore.

- Be patient! Climbing the success ladder takes time. Worry less about when you will get the next promotion and more about making yourself the best possible candidate for it.

2

Redefine What's Possible:
The Art of Reframing

*Many times, the barriers that hold us back
are mental walls of our own construction.*

*Reframing is the art of seeing familiar problems in a
new light. Practice this skill and you'll find yourself
achieving goals you assumed were unattainable.*

EVERY WORTHWHILE LEADERSHIP JOURNEY encounters roadblocks and detours. Unfortunately, far too many people succumb to frustration and give up the quest prematurely. Often they blame themselves: "I guess I just don't have what it takes to be a leader." Sometimes they blame a business world that seems to throw up barriers for leaders who don't fit the traditional mold, like women, people of color, or those with unusual educational and career histories.

In either case, they fail to recognize that most of the limitations we experience in business and in life are self-created and therefore capable of being overcome. The ways we think define the box in which we find ourselves. Often our mindset makes it impossible for us to escape that box, magnifying short-term setbacks into insurmountable obstacles.

Reframing is about creating a new mental landscape with a larger scope of freedom, a greater degree of flexibility, and a set of alternative ways of approaching any problem—which can often lead to new and unexpected solutions.

A NEW FACE IN THE MIRROR: REFRAMING AS A CAREER TOOL

Sometimes reframing is about seeing *yourself* in a new light. As I've noted, during my early years I didn't see myself as a potential business leader. After working my way through community college, I studied clinical psychology with an eye toward a job in health care. I figured that I could be a counselor or therapist of some kind, doing work that would help people and provide me with a steady, if modest, income.

Partly because of my personal background, I hadn't really considered a corporate career. I came from a minority-group heritage and an inner-city neighborhood; I didn't match up in an obvious way with the conventional image of a leader. I remember being surprised and impressed whenever a black person appeared in a leadership role on television—for example, when Vernon Jordan Jr., then a prominent figure in the civil rights movement, popped up during the six o'clock news in the early 1960s, when I was thirteen or fourteen years old. (After that, I followed his career over the years. I remember being shocked when, in 1980, he was shot and seriously wounded by a sniper during a visit to Indiana, a crime to which serial killer Joseph Paul Franklin later confessed. I couldn't have imagined then that, years later, Jordan and I would become fellow business executives and good friends. In fact, Jordan was the one who encouraged me to write this book, believing that my story could help others.)

The influence of leaders reflecting our whole society led to a leadership gap, especially in the world of business. There was a dearth of business role models in my immediate family, and back in the late '50s and early '60s when I was growing up, you didn't see black faces on the cover of *Business Week* or *Fortune*. Black leaders in government were equally rare. And the fact that psychological testing identified me as a dyed-in-the-wool introvert complicated the picture for me even further.

In retrospect, the stereotypes that influenced my thinking back then—the assumptions that future business leaders come from privileged backgrounds, attend high-ranked suburban schools or fancy preparatory academies, and are naturally gregarious, back-slapping extroverts—were all highly dubious, rigid beliefs that severely limited the pool of candidates our society drew on in seeking the next generation of leaders. In other words, our culturally reinforced concept of business leadership was a false one that was badly in need of reframing.

Thankfully, over the past fifty years, social changes driven by the civil rights movement, the women's movement, and the gay rights revolution have done much to broaden the way we think about leaders. Youngsters today are lucky to have role models of all genders and ethnic backgrounds—and not only in sports and the arts, but also in business, science, technology, and politics, including, of course, a two-term black president. There must have been quite a few small kids in America who saw their first white president of the United States on inauguration day in January 2017.

America has acknowledged the terrible unfairness and waste involved in denying opportunities to millions of people based on their color or ethnic background. And while there is plenty of work still to be done to make good on our national commitment to equality, the continuing social evolution of the past two generations is making young people of today much more open-minded about their futures than most of us were a generation or two back.

When I was a child, those changes were just beginning—which meant I was positioned to take advantage of opportunities that older people couldn't enjoy. In 1954, when I was four years old, the US Supreme Court ruled in *Brown v. Board of Education* that racial segregation in public education was illegal. In 1964, when I was fourteen, the Civil Rights Act barred segregation in public accommodations and employment. So by the time I graduated from high school in 1966, I was able to enter a world that was completely different from the one my parents had grown up in.

Still, we are all shaped by the social mores of our time. So despite the advances triggered by the civil rights movement, during my early college years I assumed that business leadership was out of the question for me.

Luckily for me, my college studies brought me fresh insights that dramatically reframed my understanding of the world—and of myself.

I discovered that I was fascinated by the field of organizational dynamics. I learned that there existed an entire cadre of specialists who devoted their lives to studying what makes organizations tick—how the cultures and norms of companies are shaped, enforced, and changed; why some organizations are productive, creative, and progressive, while others are inefficient, slow-moving, and stagnant; and how the best leaders develop and communicate a vision that inspires people, enabling them to achieve results beyond their own expectations. I realized it was possible to think of organizations as living organisms, shaped by processes, people, and technologies linked together in delicate and complex relationships that could be studied scientifically in the same way as an ecosystem like the Brazilian rainforest or the coral-dwelling denizens of the Great Barrier Reef. And I discovered it might be possible to dedicate a lifetime to mastering the art of leading teams of people from chaos to order.

It was an amazing realization, and it developed into a full-blown passion that would fuel my career in business.

Most important, studying organizational dynamics offered me an entirely new way to think about business leadership. A corporate manager or executive didn't have to be a charismatic member of the "boys' club" who led his colleagues using the power of personal charm, social status, or flamboyant oratory. He (or she) could also be someone deeply analytical, with a scientific bent, a gift for accurate observation, a strong sense of logic, and patience and determination. Someone like me.

Suddenly, I found I could see the traits that had shaped my self-definition as an introvert through fresh eyes. They didn't have to be weaknesses that relegated me to the role of a spectator in the arena of life. Instead, they could be strengths that I could parlay into a career as an active participant, and maybe even a leader, in that arena. Without realizing it, I had reframed myself—and, as a result, doors I had assumed were locked began swinging open.

URSULA BURNS: "AN ENGINEER LOOKS LIKE ME— AND YOU!"

As the story of Pat Russo from the previous chapter shows, I'm not the only executive to take an unconventional route to the top. Another example is my friend Ursula Burns. She was raised by a single mom in a New York City housing project. She went on to become the CEO of Xerox, a position she held from 2009 to 2016, and one of the most effective high-tech executives in the world. Her career is, among other things, a testament to the power of reframing to open amazing opportunities in life.

Burns's mother worked as a child care worker, gratefully accepted blocks of government surplus cheese to help feed her family, and cleaned a local dentist's office in exchange for having her kids' teeth cared for. When Burns was old enough, her mother somehow managed to pay the $650 yearly tuition charged by Cathedral High School out of an annual income that topped out at $4,400.

"I look different from most other business leaders, and I came from a different background than most of them," Burns says. "But in other ways, I have a lot in common with other leaders. My siblings and I were ragtag only on the outside. Inside us, there was never any question who was in control of our destiny."

Burns was surrounded by great role models—her mom and her aunts and uncles. These were not people with impressive educations or high-paying jobs, but people with self-discipline, inner strength, and high aspirations—"look-up people," as Burns calls them. They helped her avoid getting caught up in the problems in her community—crime, drugs, gang violence—and taught her to stay focused on education and personal growth. She also learned to define achievement not in monetary terms but in terms of bigger, deeper values. "My mother always reminded me, 'You have to leave behind more than you take away.'"

Burns did well in high school. She says it helped to attend Cathedral, a Catholic girls' school with no boys to distract her, and to this day she is an advocate for the value of single-sex education. She excelled at math, and as graduation approached, she was determined to attend college. Even the application process was daunting. The fifty-dollar fee required by each college was simply impossible for her to afford. But the state-funded Higher Education Opportunity Program (HEOP) stepped up with help. "If your mom can find the money to pay for one application," Burns's counselor told her, "HEOP will pay for the others." (Decades later, when Burns's own daughter was a high school senior, she applied to eleven colleges without giving the cost a second thought, as most middle-class kids today will do. It's an example of the kinds of barriers that the less fortunate among us face that are so easy for many of us to overlook.)

Burns was accepted to Brooklyn Polytechnic Institute, a college that has since become part of the New York University system. She was excited about the opportunity, but she had no clue about basic career-planning strategies like choosing a major, and no one in her family or her circle of friends knew how to advise her. She chose chemical engineering simply because she spotted it on the top of a list of high-paid careers in a student guide at her school library. But when she took her first chemistry class, she discovered that she hated it. So she switched to mechanical engineering, which turned out to be "all about math—so I loved it!"

Engineering was a brilliant choice for Burns. "I later discovered that all of us in what we call the STEM fields—science, technology, engineering, and math—are the problem-solvers of the world. And I also discovered that women and minority-group members, like me, are rare and in demand in those fields. All we have to do is to walk into a room, and we stand out!"

Today, when Burns visits inner-city schools, she asks those bright young kids—many of whom have never imagined a career in technology—an important question: "What does an engineer look like? She looks just like me. And like you!" She teaches young people to reframe their self-image by discovering that being different can be an advantage—and a source of pride rather than embarrassment. Her goal is to help them get comfortable with the idea of "standing out" in a positive way—something that teenagers in general find difficult to embrace.

Burns's bachelor's degree in engineering, followed a year later by a master of science degree, opened career doors for her. She took an entry-level job at Xerox and spent several years working in product development and planning. She learned how corporate life works, honed her technical skills, and became adept at working with colleagues on complex projects.

One of the big turning points in her career came in January 1990, when the thirty-two-year-old Burns was asked by a Xerox senior leader named Wayland Hicks to become his executive assistant. "At first, I thought the job was below my stature," Burns recalls. "I didn't realize it was a position for what we call high-potentials." Burns took the job and soon found herself reframing the idea of being an "assistant" to actually being a high-powered, unofficial, one-on-one master class in leadership. Her daily work was filled with hundreds of small, important tasks: fielding communications for her boss, organizing his schedule, researching problems, developing presentations, and preparing him for meetings with government officials and international business leaders. In exchange, she got to observe the inner workings of a large corporation at the highest level, sitting in on meetings and phone calls that were typically restricted to a privileged few.

"Being the assistant to Wayland, and later to Paul Allaire, then Xerox's chairman and CEO, was an amazing opportunity for me to learn to lead myself," Burns says. "It's a job where you get very little direction, very little training, and practically no structure. Your boss is incredibly busy and relies on you to figure out what to do and how to do it. So, over time, you teach yourself how to set priorities and how to find ways to add value. And in the process, you learn, little by little, how a big organization works. It was an incredible education I could never have gotten any other way."

OPEN UP TO NEW PERSPECTIVES: HOW TO MAKE REFRAMING SECOND NATURE

Reframing is a way of thinking that seems to come naturally to some people. But it's also a learnable skill, as I've observed through years of helping colleagues and team members master it. When you find yourself surrounded by people who define problems using expressions like "Everybody knows" and "It's obvious that," your antenna should go up. It's a sign that you and your colleagues may be trapped in a box of your own making—one in desperate need of reframing. You may need to take steps to shake up your thinking and that of your team members.

One effective way to improve your talent for reframing is to deliberately open yourself up to new perspectives. Don't talk only to people from inside your own organization or even from your own industry. Meet, swap ideas with, and learn from people who come from different walks of life and apply quite different perspectives to the challenges and opportunities of life.

My friend Ken Chenault, who retired from American Express in January 2018 after a seventeen-year run as the company's CEO and chairman, is a regular practitioner of this technique. He makes a point of rubbing shoulders with people from many disciplines and learning to view the world through their eyes. For example, Chenault periodically visits with Wynton Marsalis, the famous jazz musician and composer who is the artistic director of Jazz at Lincoln Center, a New York–based nonprofit organization dedicated to nurturing appreciation for jazz. "I love hearing about how Wynton tackles the challenges of his life and work," Chenault says. "He tells me about his musical group, about the unique issues of managing a nonprofit arts organization, about how he prioritizes projects, and about how he identifies talent. In return, I share with him some of the problems I've tackled at American Express. I think we've both gained a lot from our conversations."

You can imitate Chenault's strategy even if you aren't fortunate enough to be friends with a Grammy-winning performer. Expose yourself to diverse sources of new ideas. And in time, when you become an organizational leader, you can look for opportunities to connect the members of your team to such sources. Some high-tech startups organize periodic field trips to movies, concerts, sports events, art exhibits, food festivals, and other off-the-beaten-track experiences simply to stir up their team members' thinking and suggest new contexts in which to view their work. Google invites authors to visit its headquarters to discuss their books—most of which deal with social and cultural topics that are seemingly unrelated to the company's web-based business activities. Of course, you should develop ideas that fit your company's culture. The goal is to be open to ideas from fields that may have an offbeat relationship to your work—or even no obvious relationship at all.

You can also swap site visits with well-managed nearby organizations from fields that are unrelated to your own. For example, if you work for a professional services company in a field like accounting, advertising, or law, you could visit a local craft brewer or fashion design house. If you work for a company that makes and markets consumer products, you could ask for a behind-the-scenes tour at a nearby hotel, theater, or science museum. Later, you can debrief your colleagues over lunch, chatting about such topics as: Did you notice any activities or practices that were relevant to the work we do? Are there things that our hosts are doing that we could adapt to our business? Are they serving customer needs that we've never thought about but that our customers might also share? Are they creating forms of value that we could create as well?

Finally, immersing yourself in business history can be a great way of developing your reframing skills. Study how innovative business strategies have been created simply through an adroit reframing of conventional thinking about an industry. Many of the famous breakthroughs by leaders of the past were the products of such reframing:

In the 1880s, Thomas Edison built a giant industrial empire by reframing the practice of invention, changing it from a haphazard activity engaged in by lone tinkerers into a methodical process conducted in big labs by teams of trained experts pursuing specific, pre-planned objectives.

In the 1920s, Alfred P. Sloan enabled General Motors to seize dominance of the auto industry from Ford by reframing the car from a uniform, utilitarian tool into a trend-setting consumer product available in an ever-changing array of styles and models to fit every family's budget.

In the 1950s, Walt Disney invented the modern theme park by reframing his company's business, transforming the firm from a movie maker into a creator of many kinds of entertaining and inspiring experiences for families.

In the 1980s and 1990s, Howard Schultz took a commodity sold cheaply, practically everywhere, and made it the basis for a high-margin, worldwide business—Starbucks—by reframing coffee as an affordable, everyday luxury and reframing the coffee shop as a neighborhood hangout where people can work, socialize, and hold meetings.

Studying the lives and thought processes of geniuses like these—and less-famous but equally creative innovators in many other industries—may spark insights in an area of your own business that is ripe for reframing.

When you learn and practice the art of reframing, you'll find that almost any situation, even one that may appear hopeless, can be transformed into a growth opportunity.

TAKEAWAYS FROM CHAPTER 2

- Reframing is about freeing your mind from false assumptions that hold you back.

- One powerful way to use reframing is by breaking free of stereotypical thinking about yourself. If you (or people around you) have pigeonholed you as a certain type of person, don't be afraid to push back. Countless people who were told, "You don't have people skills," "You're not well organized," or "You're not a leader" have proven the naysayers wrong simply by testing their own limits.

- Sharpen your reframing skills by exposing yourself to people, ideas, and perspectives that are new and mind-expanding— from creative artists, writers, and thought leaders to businesses and areas of activity you've never experienced before.

- Read the life stories of the great innovators of history— scientists and inventors, entrepreneurs and business founders, social reformers and political leaders. You'll find that many were masters of the art of reframing.

3

Start with Minor Miracles:
The Tougher the Challenge, the Bigger the Opportunity

Searching for that "dream job"?
It may look different than you expect.

The best job, especially early in your career, is often one that provides tough, unpredictable challenges and unexpected opportunities to learn valuable life lessons.

EARLY IN MY WORKING life, I realized I needed a broader and deeper understanding of how the business world worked—so I actively sought a job where I would have a chance to expand my business knowledge. Control Data Corporation offered me that opportunity.

Working for Control Data represented a huge change from everything I'd previously experienced. With around seventy thousand employees worldwide, it was a giant conglomerate, headquartered in

Minneapolis, Minnesota. It manufactured some of the world's fastest computers; had a dominant position in the market for computer disk drives; and owned such well-known companies as Commercial Credit, Ticketron, Arbitron, and a host of other businesses.

My job was in a division known as Control Data Institutes, a kind of technical school based in Minneapolis that the corporate leaders hoped to expand by offering training programs to corporations and government agencies. I enjoyed a successful year or so working out of Chicago for the Institutes' sales department, developing business for them.

I wasn't overly impressed by the leadership team in Minneapolis, however, and I didn't think the job was leading to any exciting growth opportunities. So I visited my boss, a guy named Elmer Haas, and told him, "I've enjoyed working with you, but I think I'm going to be moving on."

Haas had other ideas. "Don't leave, Ron," he told me. "I know you don't care much for our leadership team in Minneapolis. The fact is that we have some changes in mind. Please hang in with us for a while."

I'd already been offered a job by another company in the corporate training and development field, the major publisher McGraw-Hill, and I'd made up my mind to accept it. I explained this to Haas, and I even started work at McGraw-Hill.

But Haas had never officially accepted my resignation from Control Data. And less than two weeks later, he called me up. "We'd like you to take over our whole marketing operation, Ron," he said. "We'll move you to Minneapolis and let you run the business the way you see fit."

Well, this was an offer I had to take seriously—my first opportunity to manage an entire division within a big, successful corporation.

But I hesitated. I'd never lived anywhere but Chicago, except for a single six-month stint in Boston on a consulting assignment. Minneapolis felt remote to me, like the end of the earth—or like North Dakota, which to a big-city boy like me had not exactly seemed the most scintillating place to live.

Complicating matters further was the fact that I'd met a special young woman in Chicago named Cynthia whom I'd fallen in love with and who had a job of her own. I didn't want to disrupt our relationship for a job I wasn't sure I wanted.

But I recognized the potential in Haas's offer. And the more I pondered it, the more I realized that the downside was minimal. "What's the worst thing that can happen?" I reasoned. "If I don't like the job, or Minneapolis, I can move back to Chicago and be exactly where I started—except that I will have under my belt a year or two of experience running a division of Control Data. I won't be worse off than I am now . . . in fact, I'll be better off. So why not take a chance?"

I later learned to think of this type of choice as a *reversible decision*—one I could undo if it didn't work out. By contrast, an *irreversible decision* is one you have no choice but to live with, as when the Spanish conquistador Hernán Cortés scuttled his ships—and so irrevocably committed himself and his men to conquering Mexico. A reversible decision is much less risky, which means you can make it with little fear.

Happily for me, Cynthia saw it the same way. In fact, we decided to cement our relationship by getting married. We moved to Minneapolis as husband and wife. And the choice worked out quite well. I liked the city, I liked the job, and the Institute's staffers I worked with turned out to be great. The division grew successfully on my watch, and I ended up earning promotions and getting new responsibilities.

Taking a calculated risk had proven to be a smart career move for me. It wouldn't be the last time.

SEIZING THE OPPORTUNITY TO LEARN

In 1980, the world of electronic learning was in its infancy. Control Data was light-years ahead of everyone. It had commercialized an educational software product called Plato Systems, originally developed in the 1960s at the University of Illinois. Plato courses covered subjects from elementary school to higher education and managerial levels and were run over Control Data's virtual network, enabling students to take classes sitting at computer terminals, each working at their own pace. The company was selling this product to universities and corporations for use in their training programs.

I appreciated how cool Plato Systems was as a technological tool and as a commercial product. And I also recognized that it represented a learning opportunity for me personally. Control Data employees were required to invest forty hours per year in an educational program devoted to personal development. I went much further. During my four years at Control Data Institutes, I took the equivalent of an entire MBA program through Plato Systems—all at no cost to me. I spent four hours every Saturday morning and two hours every Sunday evening in the company's learning lab, studying the basics of accounting, managerial planning, control, supervision, and many other fundamental business topics. In addition, I took as many instructor-led courses as possible. I had a wonderful time and greatly sharpened my understanding of how companies worked.

But then I had an experience that altered my thinking about the self-education process. We were recruiting someone to fill an executive job and lined up several attractive candidates for interviews. It turned out that three of the candidates had worked in the same company; they were all in the job market simultaneously because of a major workforce reduction.

When I asked the first of the three, "What was your most important contribution at the company?" he enthusiastically replied, "The Alpha Project. I was the key catalyst that really got it going." (I'm using a fictitious name for the project, of course.) He went on to discuss in great detail the Alpha Project and its positive impact on the company.

Later, I asked the second candidate about her most significant contribution. "That would have to be the Alpha Project," she answered. "The whole thing was my idea, and I managed it from beginning to end."

You're probably already anticipating what happened with the third candidate. Sure enough, he claimed total credit for the success of the Alpha Project.

This experience got me thinking. As long as you're within a company, people know who really did what on a particular project—it's unlikely that the three candidates would have been able to get away with their mutually contradictory claims if their colleagues had been in the room. But once you leave the company, how can anyone know what you really accomplished? All an outsider can do is call somebody with personal knowledge and hope to stumble upon the truth.

The point is that personal claims of experience, expertise, and success are of limited value and don't travel well. Applying this truth to myself, I realized that the self-education I had been developing using the Plato System, while empowering to me, wouldn't stand up as a credential in my future career. I decided then to finish my formal education—to earn an MBA, preferably from a well-respected institution. That degree is a credential that is universally understood and has the same meaning wherever you go.

When two or more candidates for leadership have comparable credentials, a fine education can be the tiebreaker. Why not have that advantage on your side?

I applied for a grant called the Bush Leadership Fellowship, which had been created by Archibald Bush, an executive at 3M. Every year, the Bush Foundation selected about twenty people for leadership awards that permitted them to take a year and get a degree. I won the award, which would cover about half of my MBA tuition, and I was accepted by two prominent universities—MIT and Stanford.

I chose MIT. I thought it had the more rigorous program, and I wanted to go to a school that had a difficult, challenging curriculum. After all, I knew I would only earn one MBA in my life; I wanted to make it as meaningful as possible.

Once in a while, I wonder what my life would have been like if I had gone to Stanford. I'm guessing that, post-graduation, I would have followed a Silicon Valley track rather than a health-care career. I have no regrets, but it's fun to imagine where my journey would have taken me if I'd ended up at a company like Apple, Alphabet, or Amazon rather than Aetna.

I moved to Boston to attend MIT's Sloan School of Management, while Cynthia stayed in Minnesota, continuing to pursue her career in marketing. MIT was an amazing experience for me. The instructors were first-rate—world-class experts with up-to-the-minute knowledge of the worlds of business, finance, and technology. My classmates included some of the most promising executives from many of the leading organizations of that day—nine from IBM, eight from General Motors, plus others from United Technologies and other Fortune 50 companies. Today's equivalent would be a class full of executives from firms like Apple, Alphabet, Facebook, Netflix, and Amazon. Many of my classmates went on to become senior executives or CEOs, and their presence made the educational program even more valuable because of the real-life experience they contributed. When we analyzed the financial implication of the breakup of AT&T, we had nine people in the room who had been involved in it. When the topic was high-tech entrepreneurship, Mitch Kapor came to our class to describe his experience in developing Lotus 1-2-3, the first "killer app" to transform the personal computer business.

And of course there was no way to compare the technical, theoretical training I'd obtained sitting in front of a computer terminal with the hands-on, real-world teaching I received in my classes at MIT. As Lester Thurow—a noted economist and one of my professors at MIT—once observed, there are two common ways to go wrong in your thinking: to rely solely on theory and to rely solely on experience. The secret is to keep the two in balance. My MIT training helped me achieve that balance.

MIT agreed to defer the payments on the half of my tuition not covered by the Bush fellowship until after my graduation. By the time I finished school, I owed MIT what seemed like a fortune—between $25,000 and $30,000. I paid it off little by little over the next six to seven years, and it was the single best investment of my life.

MISSING THE TURN—AND BACK TO THE ENTREPRENEURIAL PATH

Having completed my degree, I went back to Control Data and found that I no longer had a job. I interviewed with the president and with several other members of the company's leadership team, and none of them had a clear idea of how best to use my newfound knowledge within the company. So for several months I sat on my hands, waiting to learn what my new assignment would be.

Meanwhile, I discovered that Control Data's business prospects had taken a serious turn for the worse. The company's cash cow was its eight-inch disk-drive business, which Control Data had used to dominate the market for computer memory. But somehow the company had missed the latest technology turn. The whole world had converted to smaller internal disk drives, leaving Control Data stuck with an obsolete technology. While the company engineers scrambled to get back on track, customers abandoned Control Data, and the corporation began a precipitous decline.

In retrospect, the missed technology turn was likely a symptom of more serious underlying problems. William Norris, Control Data's executive chairman, was a visionary. But he'd taken his eye off the ball. The company had overexpanded into too many different domains, many of them fundamentally unrelated to its technological expertise. This lack of focus may help to explain why the company failed to recognize the coming shift to internal five-inch disk drives until it was too late.

Many of us at Control Data had had a sense that trouble was coming. We'd been bemused by the diversion of company resources into hundreds of what I thought of as "hobby businesses"—interesting little operations that were irrelevant to the core innovations needed by the corporation. I had the feeling that the company might be heading for a spectacular crash-and-burn when I noticed one day that the roof of one of our buildings had been converted into a greenhouse for biofuel experimentation—a worthy activity, sure, but hardly within the daily mission of a computer hardware company struggling to stay in business.

Under the circumstances, I realized it might be just as well that Control Data didn't have an exciting new assignment for me.

I put feelers out for new businesses that I might join, and soon I heard from a group of guys who were building a health-care business in California. I didn't know much about health care, but I applied the analytical rigor I'd acquired at MIT to study the industry and its prospects. The projections for growth of the health-care sector were impressive: It already amounted to about eleven percent of the US gross domestic product, and forecasts predicted that, with the aging population and burgeoning new medical technologies, it would increase to fourteen percent over the next ten years—a significant slice of our national economy. That's a recipe for great business growth.

The company was called Vista, and it was located in Manhattan Beach, southwest of downtown Los Angeles. The partners invited me to meet with them at a hotel on Ocean Avenue in Santa Monica, overlooking the Pacific Ocean, where the beautiful, sun-drenched view was one of their best recruiting tools. I was favorably impressed by their presentation, and after talking it over with Cynthia, I agreed to join the company. I moved into a nearby place, where Cynthia soon joined me.

My first job in business had been with a small, entrepreneurial company (the consulting firm, Greenlea Associates), but returning to the world of entrepreneurship was quite a change for me after my years at Control Data. Forget about being one of seventy thousand employees. At Vista, it was three of us sitting around a living room drawing up our business plan and figuring out where we would get funding.

Here's a comparison to illustrate the difference. Suppose a Control Data manager wanted to hang a picture in her office. She would fill out a form and put it in her outbox, from which it would be automatically and effortlessly routed to a housekeeping office some-where in the bowels of the corporation. The next day, someone in a nicely pressed uniform would show up with a little toolkit, hang the picture for her, and ask her to sign another form indicating that the job had been handled to her satisfaction.

By contrast, at a startup company, if you want to hang a picture in your office—assuming you have an office in the first place—you get a hammer and do it yourself. If you don't, it'll never get done. And in fact, not only do you hang your own picture, you also brew your own coffee, staple your own photocopies, and vacuum the hall floor when it gets dirty.

Another big difference in an entrepreneurial setting is the chal-lenge of communication. In a large business, there's a hierarchy. The president talks to the division head, who talks to the regional man-ager, who talks to the district manager, who talks to the salesperson. At each level in the process, information and terminology get trans-lated into terms that that next person in the hierarchy will under-stand and appreciate.

When you're running a small business, there is no hierarchy to shield you. Instead of talking only to people who are one level from you, you talk to everyone connected with the business, from man-agers to salespeople to the people working on the factory floor. You have no choice but to learn how to tailor your language to people from many different backgrounds. It took me awhile to figure that out and to adjust to the varying demands of the job. But once I did, it was a great leadership lesson.

Vista's business model was to create health-care savings for com-panies by moving certain behavioral health issues that were typi-cally dealt with in an inpatient setting into an effective outpatient approach. We'd found that the research made clear that a segment of the population with problems like chemical dependency and substance abuse could be handled much more economically out-side of the hospital. So we built nine centers to serve these patients in the Los Angeles area. To generate revenue, we sold contracts to major aerospace companies such as Hughes, Rockwell, Lockheed, and Boeing.

It was a sound business concept, but strategically we couldn't achieve the scale we'd hoped for. And since my partners and I couldn't agree on an approach to solve that problem, we parted ways. Vista ended up being acquired by a large hospital chain, which produced a decent payday for all of us founders. My entrepreneurial stint with Vista had lasted about three and a half years.

Entrepreneurial experience is something that I would recommend to all ambitious people. Operating at the ground level—and taking personal responsibility for everything that happens—is a tremendous learning experience. Working for a time in an entrepreneurial startup can go a long way to providing young businesspeople with the hands-on experience they need to make the concepts they've learned in school more meaningful, thereby avoiding the trap that Lester Thurow warned about: failing to connect, and balance, the wisdom of theory with the wisdom of experience.

OFFICIAL AND UNOFFICIAL MENTORS

Some young people wonder whether having a mentor is key to career success. A mentor can be helpful, but I'd advise you not to spend time searching for one. Mentors come along without planning. Mentorship must arise naturally out of the situation rather than being forced. And above all, don't think of mentorship as something that someone owes you. You earn mentorship by demonstrating your value and your promise to someone in a position of leadership or authority. They may then choose to mentor you because of what they hope you can bring to the organization. The value and benefits must flow two ways, not one.

On the other hand, it is true that mentorship is an act of generosity. The mentor almost always gives more than they receive. Thus, the person who willingly takes on the responsibility of mentorship can be an enormous help to an aspiring leader. But from the mentee's perspective, there is much to be learned from what I call *unofficial mentors*—leaders who teach you what to do and what not to do, without being aware that they are doing so. In my career, I've learned a lot by observing a series of mentors, both official and unofficial.

After Vista, my next career stop was at Blue Cross of California. I'll never forget interviewing for the job. "You've been working with a tiny startup," the interviewer observed. "Blue Cross of California is quite a bit bigger—we have four thousand people working here. I wonder whether you'll be able to manage the transition."

"I'm not too worried about that," I replied. "My previous company had seventy thousand employees."

I got the job and worked for Blue Cross's CEO, Leonard D. Schaeffer, for fourteen years. I played several roles: chief of staff, vice president of corporate services, head of the health-care delivery business, chief of the California business, and finally head of national operations after a successful period of expansion. Schaeffer was both an official and an unofficial mentor to me. I learned from him how to run good planning, budgeting, and strategic processes. I also learned about accountability—the importance of creating lofty goals and leading people to achieve them. During my time with Schaeffer, we transformed the company from the worst-performing Blue Cross plan in the nationwide system into the best performing.

I also learned from Schaeffer what *not* to do. He was an expert at building a high-performance culture, but unfortunately it lacked some of the positive elements I believe are important, including a strong emphasis on talent development and effective use of the board of directors. Schaeffer was a demanding leader—although, to his credit, he was as hard on himself as he was on everyone else. I benefited greatly from the opportunities he provided me.

When I later got the chance to run Aetna, I tried to combine the high standards that Leonard Schaeffer insisted on with a culture that put its people at the center. The goal was to build a positive, high-performance culture—and I think we succeeded in doing that.

Building Your Board of Advisors

A mentorship relationship generally emerges naturally, without advance planning. But that doesn't mean you can't make a conscious effort to learn from the people around you. As you work on learning to lead yourself, you should also seek out others whose examples, experiences, and insights can be of value to you. They may be leaders in your organization with backgrounds similar to yours, in which case you may be able to imitate some of the career moves that proved successful for them. Or they may have backgrounds different from yours, which gives you an opportunity to discover skills and knowledge you currently lack but that you may be able to develop over time.

When you encounter people of achievement that you sense you can learn from, try to make a connection with them. It's as simple and informal as saying, "Would you be willing to have a brief phone call or a cup of coffee with me sometime? I'd like to hear a little about your career and how you've managed to achieve so much.

And I think there are times when I would benefit from getting your advice on an issue." Most successful people are flattered and happy to be asked for career advice, provided you're careful not to become pushy or demanding. If you ask for fifteen minutes of someone's time, be on your way after the fifteen minutes have passed, unless they are actively keeping the conversation going.

Once you've established a personal connection with someone you admire and would like to learn from, keep up the relationship and develop it. Look for ways to make yourself useful and interesting. For example, if you run across an article that's likely to be of interest to your new connection, send it along. If you have occasion to meet another person who might be useful to them, offer to provide an introduction. If you learn of a business opportunity they might find intriguing, pass it on. When you provide anything of value, you're nurturing a two-way relationship rather than simply seeking favors.

Over time, you may be able to build a kind of "personal board of advisors"—an informal collection of three to six associates whom you can call on from time to time for advice, counsel, or support. The ideal board would include people from various domains—colleagues within your own organization, people from other companies in the same field, people from different industries, and so on. They may or may not know one another; it doesn't matter, because you are not going to convene formal meetings of your board. Instead, you will make sure to touch base with each board member at least once per quarter, thereby ensuring that the relationship feels current and fresh. And when you face a career challenge—a tough decision about whether to pursue a particular job, for example—you will be able to call on them for advice and guidance.

KNOWING WHEN IT'S TIME TO GO

My years at Blue Cross were a period of learning and growth for me. And in financial terms, I benefited greatly from being a part of Leonard Schaeffer's team. When I joined the company, Blue Cross was a not-for-profit. After several years, we converted it legally into a for-profit business under the new name of WellPoint Health Networks. Then we took twenty percent of the value of the company, sold it in the form of shares of stocks available on the equity market, and gave two foundations the eighty percent of residual stock. (The foundations received the value of the twenty percent of shares through cash payments from WellPoint.) None of us as individuals got anything out of the conversion. But we did get options to buy company stock at fair market value, and in addition, I purchased additional shares.

By the year 2000, the options I had acquired had run up in value. I had made a lot of money. But it had become clear to me that, for all my success, I was never going to be WellPoint's CEO. Leonard Schaeffer and I had closely parallel skill sets—both of us were operationally focused and strategic thinkers. We were also fairly close in age, and he had no interest in leaving. Schaeffer and I had often discussed the possibility of my becoming president, but neither he nor the board was serious about succession planning. It was clear to me that if I was ever going to become a CEO, it would not be at WellPoint, so I decided that it was time to go. (Ultimately, WellPoint was sold, in part, I believe, because of the lack of a clear succession plan.)

I put the word out among a few close friends, past colleagues, and my personal board of advisors that I was ready to consider a move. I was intrigued by the idea of private equity investing—buying shares in companies, helping to turn them around, and then reaping a portion of the profits. I'd been on a few interviews and was weighing an offer from a private equity firm known as Essex Ventures when I got a call from a search firm. "We're recruiting a new leadership team for Aetna," the recruiter said. "We just hired a new CEO, and we'd like you to interview for a spot on his executive team."

At first, the prospect didn't excite me. The nearly one-hundred-fifty-year-old Aetna, one of the nation's largest insurance companies, was trying to shift to a new managed care paradigm. However, the company had spent nine billion dollars on acquisitions that it had failed to integrate. In the process, Aetna had developed a horrible reputation in the industry—it was losing a lot of money, morale was in the basement, and caregivers and customers alike were full of complaints about service. The company was being sued by hospitals, physicians, and customers, and it had turned over the significant senior leadership positions to the executives of one of its acquired companies. They were ill-suited to run a company with the size and complexity of Aetna successfully, and many of them belonged to the Attila the Hun school of management, viewing aggressive toughness and fierce internal competition as the keys to leadership.

Furthermore, I wasn't sure about the guy they'd recently hired to be the CEO—a physician named Jack Rowe. I'd never met him, but I knew he came out of a hospital background. I wondered, *What can a guy like that know about running an insurance company?*

Finally, Aetna was based in Hartford, Connecticut—a nice enough town, but Cynthia and I had come to really like California.

Based on all these factors, I was on the verge of turning down the opportunity. But to check my perceptions, I called one of my good friends, a guy named Jeff Weiss. He runs an industry discussion group that brings together health-care CEOs from many kinds of companies—pharmaceutical device makers, private equity health plans, hospitals, insurance companies, and more. I respected Weiss for his objective, above-it-all perspective on the health-care industry. He had no axe to grind and could be counted on to offer sound, thoughtful advice.

Weiss surprised me by recommending that I seriously consider the Aetna opportunity. "I know you're thinking about private equity," he said, "but you are an operations guy—one of the best, in fact. I have a feeling you're probably one of the few people in the country who could actually turn Aetna around."

So I went out to Hartford and talked to the people from Aetna. To my surprise, I liked the new CEO very much. I learned that Rowe was a brilliant physician and medical researcher who had developed his leadership skills as the director of New York's famous Mount Sinai Medical Center. When we met, I could quickly see that he was incredibly smart, which wasn't surprising. But even more impressive, he had a shrewd awareness of what he knew and what he didn't know. He sensed there were certain ways he could add great value to Aetna: improving relations with physicians, reshaping corporate strategy, and revitalizing the company culture. But he also knew he needed a lot of help in fixing the day-to-day operations of the company. "You and I can make a great team," Rowe told me. The more I thought about it, the more I agreed.

We negotiated a contract specifying that I would join Aetna with the title of head of health operations, and that if my performance warranted it, I would have a clear path to the president's position as well. If circumstances changed to make this impossible, I would leave Aetna with an attractive financial package, making this a highly reversible decision.

The big step I'd been hoping for—the opportunity to shape the future of a major corporation—was now within reach.

Perhaps the toughest part of the process was calling Cynthia to discuss the opportunity, which required a move to Hartford, Connecticut. It took her awhile to warm up to the idea, but she finally did.

Looking back on my transition from WellPoint to Aetna, I can see how fortunate I was. By this point in my career, I'd developed a clear sense of my major goal: to become CEO of an important company. Having that knowledge enabled me to take a clear-eyed, realistic look at my prospects working under Leonard Schaeffer and to make the hard decision that simply hunkering down in place was *not* the right choice for me. By contrast, I had several colleagues at WellPoint for whom remaining in place was the right choice. They did quite well for themselves and for the company and eventually retired from WellPoint.

That self-awareness, combined with the willingness to reinvent myself, made it possible for me to open a new door—one that led to both the toughest challenge and the most rewarding adventure of my entire career.

THE BENEFITS OF TAKING ON THE IMPOSSIBLE CHALLENGE

Most businesspeople don't want to go anywhere near a company or a division that's in trouble. They fear being overwhelmed by the challenges and perhaps being tainted with the label of "loser." Yet troubled businesses offer great opportunities for learning and growth, particularly to aspiring leaders who may not otherwise have a ticket to the fast track.

For example, watching Control Data flounder due to overexpansion into unrelated business fields taught me a valuable lesson about the importance of focus. That insight served me well when I took the helm at Aetna, which had also expanded beyond reason. Selling off the extraneous businesses Aetna had acquired would be one of the first survival strategies we implemented.

Troubled companies, compared to well-managed ones, also offer ambitious people better opportunities to gain hands-on leadership experience. When you're willing to take on the tasks others shun, doors begin to open for you. Those at the top of the corporate hierarchy are likely to give you responsibilities and opportunities far greater than those you might otherwise enjoy. That's how many leaders especially those from atypical backgrounds—get the chance to build a reputation as someone who gets things done, even when the company finances look dire, competitive pressures are intense, and employee morale is at its lowest.

The benefits of taking on a tough business challenge don't apply only at the very top of an organization. I've seen the same dynamic at work in the careers of my colleagues at various levels of the corporate hierarchy.

Elease Wright worked with me at Aetna as senior vice president of human resources. Years earlier, she'd been a rising star in the HR department when she dared to take on an incredibly challenging systems reengineering project that her boss warned her might be a career killer. "I got sympathy cards, because everyone thought I'd been demoted," Wright recalls. "I lost my office, got stuck in a temporary cubicle, and had to beg for an assistant. But through hard work and by picking the brains of everyone in the organization with a creative idea, I made the project work. It ended up being one of my most powerful learning experiences as well as a stepping-stone to quicker career advancement."

Actually, Wright's willingness to take on a reengineering job that no one else would tackle was characteristic of her personality. Years earlier, upon graduating from the University of Connecticut, she began her job search in the middle of a serious recession—not exactly ideal timing. She ended up becoming one of the first women to work in an all-male maximum security prison, serving on the psychiatric staff as an inmate intake specialist. Her job involved giving the new prisoners a psychological assessment and determining where to place them within the system. "When your first job is that challenging and depressing," Wright now says with a laugh, "you have no place to go but up."

When I became Aetna's CEO, I was involved in orchestrating a somewhat similar career epiphany for an outstanding young woman named Kim Keck. She'd been working in Aetna's finance department, managing relations with the credit ratings agencies, among other important tasks. I was impressed by what I saw of Keck's intelligence, strategic insight, and mental discipline. So I invited her to join my executive staff as head of planning. It was a demanding job, with long hours, enormous responsibilities, and complex requirements—much like most of the other jobs in the executive suite at Aetna, especially during those early days of the company turnaround. But I felt deep inside that Keck could handle it, and that she had the talent and growth potential to take full advantage of all she would learn by working side by side with me on some of the company's toughest challenges.

It soon became clear that Keck had never worked so hard in her life. To this day, she likes to reminisce about the fact that she started her new job on Good Friday, stayed in the office until eight o'clock that night, and then got a call from me asking for an update on some key projects the morning after next—that is, on Easter Sunday! Keck says that was the first indication she had as to exactly how tough it would be to work for me.

After a couple of months of this, Keck was feeling a bit staggered by the scope of the job. So she was relieved and grateful when her old boss, Aetna's chief financial officer, called, saying, "Kim, the person we hired to replace you here just left. Is there any chance you'd be interested in having your old job back?" She was on the verge of accepting the offer when I intervened. I called the CFO and put the kibosh on the plan. "I don't want Kim to go back to her safe cocoon," I said, "She feels as if she's struggling right now but that's because she's learning and growing faster than she ever has before. I don't want her to let this job defeat her!"

At the time, Keck was devastated and probably furious with me. But today she is grateful for my intervention. "I didn't realize what the next few years had in store for me," she now says, adding:

> First, I was exhausted and frustrated by the work I was doing. I wanted out of the pool, but I came to realize that Ron wanted me to learn to swim. Working closely with him—first as Aetna's head of planning, and then later as his chief of staff—opened incredible doors for me. I got to watch him making some of the biggest decisions in the company's history—and then I got to ask him about, and even to challenge, the thinking behind those decisions. I saw him in action as he negotiated huge deals with some of the toughest minds in the business world. And I participated in helping Ron shape and deliver his leadership messages, both to the thousands of Aetna employees and to individual executives with key roles in guiding the company's future. It was an education that no amount of money could possibly buy. As a result, I've had one fantastic job assignment after another in the years that followed. Even in my new job at Blue Cross, I can hear his voice as I work through issues, offering contributions to my thinking and strategizing process.

Suffering isn't worthwhile in itself. Not every tough job is guaranteed to be a great learning opportunity. But many are. If the first few days or months of an assignment feel exhausting, overwhelming, or even painful, don't jump ship. Hang in there. There's a good chance that one day you'll look back on that job as the most difficult yet worthwhile growth experience you ever had.

Kim Keck became one of my most valued and respected colleagues at Aetna, and her career has continued to flourish. She currently serves Blue Cross & Blue Shield of Rhode Island as its president and CEO.

SEAL or Sailor? Making the Choice

The Navy SEALs are the primary special operations force of the US Navy. They're trained to operate in all environments—sea, air, and land—thus the origin of their name. Their training is so rigorous that only twenty percent of the carefully prescreened candidates make it through the process. From the Vietnam War through the conflict in Iraq, the SEALs have been recognized as an elite corps of combat troops who take on the toughest assignments in the most dangerous conditions—hence their depiction in popular culture, from the novels of Tom Clancy to action pictures like *The Rock* and *Zero Dark Thirty*. The career of a Navy SEAL is exceptionally demanding—but it also carries with it an aura of heroism and honor that few other professionals command.

By contrast, a typical career Navy enlistee has a life that is less grueling. The mental and physical qualifications, while high, are less demanding than for an aspiring SEAL, and the training regimen is less strenuous. And while Navy officers, technicians, and corpsmen may spend time in harm's way when stationed in a combat zone—and many have paid the ultimate price in defense of their country—they are unlikely to experience the extreme, high-intensity, recurring danger that SEALs routinely face.

In some ways, however, the life of a SEAL and that of an average sailor are similar. Both contribute measurably to the safety and freedom of our country, and after a career in service, both can retire with full honors and the respect and gratitude of the nation.

You may never have considered serving in the US Navy as a career. But as you read the descriptions of these two paths, it's likely that one struck you as more immediately appealing. Can you picture yourself as a Navy SEAL? Or does the life of a regular sailor feel more natural to you?

This isn't merely an idle question. Most industries have the equivalent of SEALs and sailors—people who take on the high-risk, high-demand, high-prestige challenges, as distinguished from those who prefer more mainstream careers performing important but less grueling assignments. Both kinds of work are necessary and honorable. But the demands are different, the obligations are different, the daily expectations are different, and the rewards are different.

At some point in your life, you may find yourself asked to choose which of these paths you want to take. The answer will depend on many factors: your innate personality traits, your ethical and moral values, family and other obligations you've assumed, and even physical attributes such as your health and stamina. It is also important to know and communicate when you can no longer serve as a SEAL due to changing circumstances. Many organizations have a cadre of former SEALs who may go back to SEAL status when the time is right.

People can live happy, rewarding careers either as SEALs or as sailors. The most important thing is to avoid a serious mismatch. A person who is at heart a SEAL may never be content living the life of a sailor, while a natural-born sailor is likely to be ineffective and unhappy trying to fill the boots of a SEAL.

In the early years of your career, as you get to know yourself through a range of experiences, successes, and failures, pause from time to time to ask yourself: Am I a SEAL or a sailor? Making the choice that's right for you will help you discover the most fulfilling path for your future.

TAKEAWAYS FROM CHAPTER 3

- When you're weighing job options, especially early in your career, look for opportunities to learn, whether formal or informal. A job that gives you the chance to try new things and stretch your limits will be much more valuable to you in the long run than a less-challenging job, even one that pays a little better or may be more fun.

- In every job, seek ways to enhance your future marketability, especially by developing and practicing your value-creation skills—talents that help in producing goods and services that people appreciate and will pay for.

- If possible, over the course of your early career, expose yourself to differing *kinds* of businesses—large and small, startups and established ventures, in varying industries. This is the best way to discover the kind of environment in which you're most likely to thrive.

- Everyone you work with can be a mentor—because you can learn from them all, whether or not they consciously intend to teach you.

- Don't be afraid to take a job at an organization that seems to be foundering. A troubled business often provides huge opportunities for learning and achievement—particularly for the unproven leader in search of a chance to shine.

- Think realistically about your strengths, weaknesses, and personal inclinations. A few people are cut out for the high-stakes, high-demand career of a Navy SEAL, while others are better built for the life of a traditional sailor. Both paths can be rewarding.

4

Make Your Enemies Disappear:
Assume Positive Intent

Not everyone you meet in your career will be friendly.
Some may even be out to get you.

But the smart strategy is to assume that people mean
well until they demonstrate otherwise. Here's how
assuming positive intent can be a powerful tool for
disarming potential opponents.

EVERY LEADER, OR ASPIRING leader, can expect to encounter
people who appear to be standing in the way. They may include potential rivals, seemingly incompetent team members, overly demanding
customers, unfair bosses, or apparently hostile colleagues. The temptation to react with anger and defensiveness, or to blame institutional
or personal bias, may be enormous.

My advice: Resist the temptation. Instead, always take it as a given that those around you are motivated by positive intentions—until they make that assumption impossible to maintain. It's a strategy that I summarize with the rubric *assume positive intent*—and when practiced consistently, it can often turn potential enemies into allies and resources.

When people first hear about this motto of mine, they sometimes react with skepticism. "Am I supposed to be some kind of pushover—a patsy?" they wonder. "Don't you know it's a dog-eat-dog world out there? If you assume positive intent on the part of the people around you, all you're doing is making yourself vulnerable to their attacks. Business is a game of survival of the fittest . . . and the only way to be one of the survivors is to be bigger, badder, and tougher than everybody else—not to make nice with them."

This attitude sounds grown-up, hard-nosed, and realistic. But in fact it's shortsighted, narrow-minded, and usually counterproductive. A little thought about how the world *really* works makes it clear why this is so.

It's true that business is a competitive environment, in which everyone is motivated largely by self-interest. Of course, everyone wants to do things that will benefit them. They want to earn the most money, capture the biggest share of profits, get the best deal on the goods and services they buy, and win the largest slice of any marketplace in which they compete. So when your interests compete head-to-head with those of another person, usually there must be a winner and a loser . . . and having ended up on both ends of that deal, I can tell you that winning is better!

That doesn't mean that there's nothing going on in business *except* competition. Vast areas of activity are dominated by cooperation—by people helping one another to achieve shared objectives. After all, what is a company except a collection of people working together to reach goals they have in common—productivity, sales, profit, growth? What is a marketplace except a place where individuals and companies meet to make deals that will benefit *both* parties? And what is the economy as a whole except a vast network of people and organizations interacting cooperatively in countless ways—as suppliers, customers, marketers, distributors, partners, investors— thereby helping each other accomplish things that no one could achieve alone?

Of course, in their myriad economic activities, all these individuals and organizations are jostling one another for advantage. But they are also constantly finding ways to help one another—and to enjoy mutual benefit in the process. So when it comes to dealing with people in the world of business, assuming positive intent rather than relentless, cutthroat competition is actually *much more realistic*—not naïve or idealistic. In the vast majority of situations, this approach is also much more effective, leading to better outcomes— including more advantageous results for you.

When you're negotiating a business deal with a supplier who is pushing you to pay a little more than your company can afford— and a little more than you think is fair—you can conclude "they're trying to screw me," respond with anger, and likely make finalizing a contract impossible. Or you can assume that your negotiating partner is simply trying to get the best deal possible (as we all try to do) and use whatever tools are at your disposal to reshape the contract to make it fair to both parties. Those tools include the option of walking away from the table when necessary.

When your boss repeatedly drops the most difficult assignments on your desk while giving easier, more enjoyable tasks to a colleague with the same background and credentials as you, you can assume "she's taking advantage of me!" and complain to anyone who will listen about how rotten your job is. Or you can assume that your boss has some reason for allocating the work the way she does. She may regard you as the most skilled and responsible member of the team when it comes to tackling tough challenges. So you should make an effort to learn from every difficult problem you solve—and *record* the results, so you will be in a position at the end of the year to ask for a raise, bonus, or promotion commensurate with your accomplishments.

In these situations and others like them, you can choose how to respond to a difficult, unpleasant challenge. You can assume that others are "out to get you" and respond with anger and resentment. In the process, you can easily turn someone into a long-term opponent, even a personal enemy. Or, you can assume that others are simply behaving the way most people would, given their particular circumstances . . . and respond by doing whatever you can to manage the difficulty with skill and integrity.

In almost every case, the latter choice is the better one. When it is not, and you find that you are dealing with a real jerk, you can switch gears. That's when it's necessary to be firm about what behavior you'll accept and what you will not tolerate—and to stick to your guns.

THE OUTSIDER'S SECRET WEAPON

Assuming positive intent isn't always easy. It may even demand the ability to remain cool in the face of extreme provocations, when almost anyone would find it natural to explode in anger.

In the 1970s, I was a young management consultant pursuing business in the hinterlands of North Dakota. One October, a couple of potential clients took me to dinner at a country club on the evening of the club's annual Halloween party. Many people around the dining room were dressed in costumes—gladiator, princess, sorcerer, pirate. It was amusing to glance around at the fanciful outfits . . . until I saw that one of the revelers at a nearby table was costumed as a stereotypical ghetto hipster, complete with blackface, a giant Afro, and garish bell-bottoms.

As the only non-white guest at the club, I was intensely embarrassed. I felt as if every eye in the room was on me. How should I react? Was this a deliberate insult directed at me? Had my hosts knowingly brought me here to see how I would respond? If I said and did nothing, would they conclude that I was a "wimp"? Or that I found the racial mockery acceptable, maybe even funny?

Part of me wanted to blow a gasket at the affront—or at least to walk out of the dinner party. I would have derived a measure of satisfaction from sending a message of outrage to my hosts and to the other white people at the country club. After all, the civil rights movement wasn't only about voting rights or school desegregation. It was also about treating everyone, including black Americans, with a modicum of decency and respect. Apparently that was a lesson some white people still hadn't learned.

But rather than exploding, I took a deep breath. A glance at the face of my dinner partners quickly told me they hadn't anticipated, much less planned, this humiliating encounter. They were red-faced and tongue-tied, unable even to figure out how to apologize to me. And they were watching me closely, praying I wouldn't worsen their embarrassment by berating them or making a scene, even though I would have been totally justified in doing so.

I couldn't let the embarrassment pass without comment. "Some people have a peculiar sense of humor," I remarked. "The way they act belongs in the 1860s, not the 1970s." Then I went back to eating my dinner. Utterly relieved, my potential clients laughed shame-facedly and told me how embarrassed and upset they were by the idiotic behavior of their fellow guest. We all agreed to ignore the imbecile and get back to talking about business.

I ended up winning the contract.

As this story suggests, the strategy of assuming positive intent is especially useful for leaders who may be following an unorthodox career path or have nontraditional backgrounds—ethnic minorities, those with unusual educational or job histories, and women in male-dominated industries. Chances are good that you will encounter situations that make you feel awkward, uncomfortable, or intimidated: the conference room in which you are the only person who is not a member of the ethnic majority, the colleague or customer who makes an unthinking remark that embodies an offensive stereotype, the informal get-together at which everyone seems to be swapping stories about the upper-crust college they attended or the swanky club they belong to—neither of which you've ever set foot in.

When things like this happen, your feelings of self-consciousness and exclusion can intensify. The temptation is to take it personally—to assume that others are deliberately making you feel "less than" in order to assert their power over you or their superiority to you. You may even want to lash out verbally in an effort to reassert your sense of self-worth.

I'd urge you to resist that temptation. One piece of advice I often give to aspiring leaders: "If there's something that will make you feel really good to say—something you are *itching* to say—*don't say it*." Blowing up in the face of provocation is a way of *losing* power, not of claiming it. It shows that you are not in control of your feelings, and it reinforces many of the negative stereotypes ("hot-headed," "emotional," "angry," "radical") that are used to help keep outsiders down.

Instead, assume that the people who are behaving in exclusionary ways are simply uninformed, insensitive, and unaware—which is likely true—and look for opportunities to quietly and assertively educate and enlighten them. For example, you might ask a question like, "How do you suppose you'd feel if everyone around you was talking about places and experiences you hadn't shared—and they knew full well that was the case?" Starting a constructive dialogue can turn an unpleasant encounter into an opportunity to demonstrate what being inclusive is all about.

Don't misunderstand me—there are times when someone's behavior deserves and even demands a forceful negative response. If you hear a person in the workplace using racial slurs or witness an act of obvious sexual harassment on the job, you need to take advantage of the systems most companies have in place for lodging a formal complaint so that the misconduct can be addressed appropriately. I'm suggesting a way of defusing unpleasant incidents that don't cross that threshold—which covers most of the everyday conflicts we experience.

Assuming positive intent can be an empowering strategy that disarms defensiveness and turns potential enemies into allies. I've found it to be one of my most effective secret weapons.

LUBRICATING THE FRICTIONS OF BUSINESS AND LIFE

Assuming positive intent can also serve as an essential lubricant for overcoming the inevitable frictions of business and life. Here's a small but typical example from my career.

Early in my career, I spent quite a bit of time as a salesperson. I've sold almost everything under the sun, and I learned an awful lot about business—and about human nature—in the process.

If you're a salesperson, I'm sure you've had the experience of calling a potential customer—perhaps someone who has personally expressed an interest in your product—and leaving a message with a request for a call back . . . and hearing nothing in return, even after leaving a second message, and then a third. How should you respond to this behavior, which is at best careless and at worst extremely rude?

If you don't assume positive intent—if you take the customer's behavior personally—when you finally reach him on the phone, your instinct may be to say something like, "Hello, Tom! Where the heck have you been? I tried calling you three times, and you never got back to me. It was really frustrating!"

You can easily imagine Tom's feelings. His immediate response will be to go into defensive mode—to start conjuring up reasons and excuses, real or imagined, for his failure to call you back. He will feel guilty and uncomfortable. And like most people who feel bad, he will probably want more than anything else to end the conversation as quickly as possible. In this scenario, your chances of selling Tom anything are small, and quickly getting smaller.

On the other hand, if you assume positive intent, when you do get through to the potential customer, you will say something like, "Hello, Tom! I called and left you three messages last week. I can see how busy you must be. I'm glad we finally reached each other! Now, let me tell you about our product . . ."

Do you hear the difference? By making Tom's excuse for him, you are assuming positive intent—clearing away any sense of resentment, anger, or guilt, and turning the conversation in the direction you want it to go. That's a simple example of how assuming positive intent can serve as a powerful lubricant for business interactions. The same approach can be applied to all kinds of small irritants that can easily blow up into major sources of conflict—as when a colleague greets you with the remark, "Good morning! That's an interesting new hairstyle you're wearing!" You can choose whether to take this as a sarcastic dig and perhaps launch an extended feud with your coworker, or to assume positive intent and get on with your day.

In many circumstances, assuming positive intent is a two-way street. The best and most productive business relationships are those in which both parties have a degree of trust and respect that enables them to communicate freely and honestly. Both know that the other would never say or do anything to intentionally harm them—and because they can assume positive intent, they know they can share confidences with each other without fear or anxiety.

One time during my years at Aetna, I was engaged for several weeks with a group of mergers and acquisitions specialists in exploring and evaluating the details of a potential business deal. As the project unfolded, our group would engage in conference calls practically every day, with my chief of staff Kim Keck participating to help me gather and organize information and plan follow-up steps.

In the midst of the process, after the fourth or fifth of these telephone meetings, Keck came into my office. "You probably don't even realize this, Ron," she said. "But you've gotten into the habit of concluding every one of these conference calls by saying, 'Thank you, gentlemen.' There are plenty of words you could use that don't assume that everyone in the meeting is male—'people,' 'team,' 'guys.' This isn't about me—but for future reference you might want to change that habit."

Let's pause the story here to notice the courage that Keck exhibited in saying this to me. It's never easy to criticize the boss. In many organizations, doing so can be downright dangerous!

And the mistake I'd made that Keck wanted to call me out on wasn't a particularly egregious one—not something that could endanger the organization, like revealing business secrets or doing something unethical. It was an error in judgment that subtly minimized the role and importance of women, thereby harming, in a subtle way, Aetna's efforts to be a progressive, inclusive, and respectful organization. Minor? Arguably, yes—and so it would have been easy, and safe, for Keck to let it slide. But she cared enough about me, and about Aetna, to want us to be our very best, so she was brave enough to point out my mistake.

In so doing, Keck exemplified the principle of assuming positive intent. She could have said to herself, "Listen to the language Ron Williams is using! His talk about inclusiveness and respect is so much hypocrisy." Drawing this conclusion, she probably would *not* have said anything to me about my mistake.

But Keck didn't make this assumption. Instead, she assumed that my commitment to inclusion and respect was sincere . . . and that therefore I would appreciate an honest observation of one way I'd fallen short. She assumed positive intent on my part, and this gave her the courage to speak up. Bravo for her!

After Keck delivered her critique, it was my turn to practice the principle of assuming positive intent.

Nobody likes having their use of language criticized, and in using the word "gentlemen" to address the group, I certainly had no intent of ignoring or minimizing Keck's role—she was a wonderful chief of staff and an important member of our team. I could easily have responded to her critique by scoffing at it, dismissing its importance, or using sarcasm. I could have defended my behavior with a condescending explanation of how "gentlemen" can be considered a generic term that theoretically includes both men and women—a kind of behavior that is sometimes (rightfully) condemned as "mansplaining."

Fortunately, I resisted the temptation to react in any of these ways—strong as the temptation might have been! Instead, I did what I always try to do when I am feeling a little emotional: I paused and reflected before saying anything. That few seconds of thought was enough to create a mental space for a different reaction: "Kim is *not* trying to attack or hurt me," it said. "She is a loyal friend and ally who has always defended my best interests. And that's why she is trying to help me improve my way of talking with people. And you know, she's right."

"Thank you, Kim," I finally said. "Language matters." From that day forward, I tried to remember to use more inclusive language when addressing groups of people in the office and elsewhere. (I probably didn't always succeed. But I made the effort—and I think that Kim Keck, and the many other women who played such an important role in Aetna's success, appreciated that.)

Criticisms delivered by one businessperson to another aren't always motivated by positive intent. Occasionally they can be deliberately hurtful, especially when they are presented in a time, place, and manner calculated to embarrass. But in the vast majority of cases, they are intended to be helpful, even if the immediate emotional impact is a negative one.

When you're stung by a criticism, remember to assume positive intent. It can help you overcome the emotional reaction, examine the criticism objectively, and derive some educational benefit from it.

Remember, the pain you feel when criticized is often a measurement of how *accurate* the criticism is! The social commentator and satirist H.L. Mencken once remarked, "Injustice is relatively easy to bear; what stings is justice." When a comment from a colleague hurts the *most* is probably the time when you have the greatest need to practice forbearance, patience, and self-reflection . . . rather than indulging the natural desire to fight back.

TAKEAWAYS FROM CHAPTER 4

- The business world is marked by both competition and cooperation. It's easy to take the competitive attitude too far—which eliminates the possibility of cooperation for everyone's benefit. Don't assume that the person in the next cubicle, or the job applicant you are up against, or the salesperson from a rival company, is an enemy who is out to get you. In most cases, they're not.

- Assuming positive intent on the part of other people—at least until they provide clear evidence to the contrary—can help you avoid needless conflicts and turn potential adversaries into allies and partners.

- If you're from an unconventional business background—for example, if you're a member of an underrepresented minority group—assuming positive intent can be especially powerful. Treating everyone as though they are potential friends and supporters can reduce conflicts and help open doors that might otherwise be closed.

- Assuming positive intent whenever possible helps to lubricate the inevitable stresses of everyday business life, making teams more productive and successful.

- When assuming positive intent fails, you may find you are dealing with a genuine jerk—in which case, you'll need to take a strong stand against offensive behavior. But you'll probably find such moments are far more rare than you might expect.

PART

2

LEADING
OTHERS

5

"It Can't Be Done":
Meeting the Toughest Leadership Challenge

The biggest challenge any leader faces is the difficulty of changing people's perceptions of what is possible. This story from my early days at Aetna illustrates how a leader can help people discover capabilities they never knew they had, making unexpected levels of achievement possible.

A FRIEND OF MINE whom I greatly admire as a leader is Ken Chenault, who retired in 2018 as the long-term chairman and CEO of American Express. Chenault is often asked by interviewers to share his personal concept of leadership. He usually replies by quoting a definition of leadership once offered by the legendary French general and emperor Napoleon. The job of the leader, Napoleon said, is "to define reality and to give hope."

While both Chenault and I would acknowledge that there is much more to the leader's job than this, I think this simple, two-part formula is a pretty good place to start:

"To define reality" is to shape an understanding of the world, and of your place in the world, that you and your team share. Without an agreed-upon picture of reality, it's virtually impossible to formulate strategies and programs that everyone in the organization can support.

"To give hope" is to make it possible for your team members to believe in a better future—one in which your organization is growing and contributing to an improved way of life for all of its members as well as for the customers it serves. Hope energizes people; it releases their creativity; it encourages them to give their best efforts to all they do.

The leader who can achieve these two goals—simple sounding yet vast in scope—has created a solid basis for enormous achievements.

DEFINING REALITY—THE CRUCIAL FIRST STEP

There are plenty of obstacles to achievement in many organizations today. You've probably encountered a few of them yourself. They include complacency, lack of clear goals, flawed assumptions, poor communication, inconsistent incentives, dysfunctional teams, and many others. One of the worst is sheer blindness—the systemic failure to accurately define the real challenges confronting the organization and the steps needed to meet them.

That's the biggest problem I faced when I came to Aetna early in 2001.

As I've explained, I was recruited to join Aetna to help participate in a much-needed company turnaround. Aetna was losing money rapidly. Unhappy policyholders were abandoning us by the thousands, and service providers that Aetna customers relied on—physicians, hospitals, and health-care organizations—were refusing to work with us, angered by what they perceived as high-handed and incompetent service. The company's troubles were obviously serious—and the path to solving them was far from clear.

Like most executives joining a new team, I devoted my first few weeks on the job to getting the lay of the land—meeting key people, acquiring a sense of the corporate culture, studying the strategic position of the company, and asking managers from throughout the firm to share their perspectives on Aetna's strengths, weaknesses, challenges, and opportunities.

It was an eye-opening experience in many ways. Perhaps the most significant—and alarming—discovery I made was related to Aetna's rapidly changing business environment. Shifting aspects of that environment included everything from customer preferences and market conditions to health-care technologies and product trends. The impact of these changes was a big part of what we didn't know, and *couldn't* know, about the nature of Aetna's problems.

After that first month, it had become clear to me that the organization had tons of *data* but a severe shortage of *timely information*. Numbers? We had them aplenty. But they flowed across our desks too late, organized in ways that shed little light on the critical issues we faced and the choices we needed to make.

We were like pilots flying in a dense fog, relying on instruments with a built-in lag in reaction time.

So one of the first projects I undertook in my tenure at Aetna— while still learning everything I could about the nature of Aetna's troubles—was to spearhead the creation of a new management information system that could enable us to—finally—get a grip on the problems the company faced. You might assume this would be a purely technical challenge—a task we could delegate to a few of our top finance, actuarial, and IT experts. They'd use their expertise to design interfaces to all our source systems, standardize our data definitions, and add a presentation layer to bring it all together, and presto! The problem would be solved.

So you might assume—but the problem turned out to be much bigger and much tougher than that. It involved not only technical specifications and software design but deeply ingrained perceptions, attitudes, and relationships shaped by years of dysfunctional behavior at every level of the corporation. Fixing the system required hacking away at the roots of that dysfunction, including the sense of frustration, fear, anger, and helplessness that had gradually permeated Aetna, leaving thousands of bright, talented people sincerely convinced that our problems were simply too overwhelming to solve.

A technical problem? Sure. But it was also a matter of *transforming the way we thought.*

The creation of what came to be called our executive management information system (EMIS) proved to be a turning point in the history of Aetna and in the lives of many of us who participated in it. It was an opportunity for me to apply some of the most important leadership tools I'd learned and honed throughout my career—and to begin spreading the use of those tools throughout the organization. Together, my leadership team at Aetna discovered the effectiveness of asking questions that challenged deeply ingrained assumptions, the transformative power of fact-based decision making to inspire a vision of *shockingly* greater achievement, and the enormous value of investing time and effort in rigorous planning before tackling any crucial project.

Building our new information system didn't only revolutionize our ability to run the corporation effectively and profitably—though it did that, in spades. It also taught us that there was almost *nothing* we couldn't accomplish by applying some clear thinking, tough-minded and open communication, a lot of hard work, and a bit of creativity. It's a lesson confirmed by the years of turnaround, rejuvenation, and growth that followed the crisis—and one that I'm convinced can be applied with equal success in almost any organization.

In the course of my reconnaissance, I found that there were several elements to Aetna's information management problem. One element was the many business acquisitions Aetna had made in recent years. This had led to a proliferation of computer systems serving separate legal entities—as if Aetna were 150 separate insurance companies rather than one. Yet despite this, the corporation was being run on a top-down, centralized basis, and it closed its books on what we called a consolidated, aggregated basis. That meant that all the data—about revenues, policy sales, customer and member enrollments, health-care claims, personnel expenses, and much more—flowed in from a wide variety of sources around the country and was rolled together into a single giant mass every month. As you can imagine, this took time—even with the enormous computing power that Aetna, like every other big corporation, had at its disposal. The executives at headquarters received the numbers that indicated where the company stood as an enterprise some ten to fifteen days *after* the end of the month.

That wasn't very timely. But it got worse. I further discovered that data broken out by region and product line wasn't available until after twenty-eight days. If you were running a specific business within Aetna—let's say, our Northeast Region health maintenance organization (HMO) insurance business—you didn't know how you'd done in January until the end of February. The delay meant that you'd already made decisions during February purely by guesswork, with no way to know whether you'd improved your business or made it worse.

Talk about flying through fog! The situation had become so dire that it was entirely possible we might one day discover that the plane we were piloting had already crashed into a mountainside weeks earlier—without anyone even knowing it.

We couldn't allow things to go on this way. I invited a dozen of the best and brightest people in the company—representatives from finance, IT, actuarial, and other business departments—to a meeting in the Aetna boardroom. When the team was assembled, I explained our mission:

> To get started on fixing the problems Aetna faces, we need an information system that feeds all the data we get—the financial ledger, the membership ledger, and so on—into a single source system. This system should be prestructured so that our executives can see how all seven business regions are performing in real time. We need a report that reflects fully allocated P&Ls, changes in membership, actual revenues and expenses versus forecasts, and so on. When we click on a region, we need to be able to track the performance of every district within the region as well as particular customer segments—the individual customer business, the small group business, and the national accounts business. And finally, I'd like us to close our books every month within seven days, so we can make necessary adjustments in a timely fashion.

I explained that having this information within seven days would represent an eight-day improvement for the corporation as a whole but, more important, a twenty-one-day improvement for regional and district leaders struggling to run their businesses.

As I spoke, mapping out these ideas on a whiteboard, I could see heads nodding around the room. These were bright, experienced business leaders, and they well understood what I was proposing. "Gee," someone said, "that would really be terrific!" And someone else remarked, "This sounds like the system we tried to build a few years ago."

"What happened to that system?" I asked.

"Well, we worked on it for a while, and then we gave up."

"I see," I responded. "Well, here's the big difference between this system and that one. This one *will* be built."

I caught glimpses of people exchanging glances. Maybe they were a little unsure how to take my determined stance.

"All right," I continued. "We all understand what we need. Now let's talk about timing. It's now April, and we're about to launch our budgeting process for next year. Our goal is to have the budget mapped out by September or October, so we'll know how to price our policies before the customers sign up in January. We can't do that accurately without having real, up-to-date numbers to work with." More nods from around the room.

Encouraged, I asked the group to consider themselves the steering committee for this important project. "Meet among yourselves to map out a plan. We'll call the project the executive management information system—EMIS for short. We'll reconvene in ten days to review your ideas." The meeting broke up, and I was pleased to feel that I'd started us moving toward a solution to a major problem.

But when we gathered in the same room ten days later, it quickly became apparent that my expectations weren't exactly shared by the other members of the group.

"Let's take a look at the project plan you've come up with," I said.

The spokesman for the group cleared his throat. "Well, we got together and talked through the project requirements," he said. "We've determined that we should be able to create a detailed project plan for EMIS by September."

I was taken aback. "I don't understand what you mean," I said. "I don't want a *plan* by September. I want a prototype by then—a system that's up and running, feeding us the basic information we need to manage our businesses. It may be rough or imperfect—I understand that—but it should be better than what we've got, and we need to have it in operation by September."

Now it was my colleagues' turn to be taken aback. "That's impossible!" someone said. I felt a dozen pairs of eyes staring at me. You would have thought I'd asked them to grow wings and learn how to fly.

I could see that we'd arrived at a major turning point—not only for the future of the EMIS project but also for my tenure at Aetna. How would we deal with these conflicting visions of reality?

Most of the people at Aetna could conceive of only two possibilities.

First, there was the approach that would have been taken in the old Aetna. The company had long been known for its nurturing, conflict-averse, employee-coddling style. At our headquarters in Hartford, Connecticut, multiple generations of families had gotten jobs at Aetna right out of college, assuming that they'd be taken care of generously for a lifetime as long as they didn't screw up. Layoffs were virtually unheard of. Hence the affectionate nickname for the company, well known throughout the insurance industry: "Mother Aetna."

If a problem like this one had arisen in the old, maternal Aetna, everyone would have known how to handle it. After a bit of vague discussion about the problem, someone would have concluded, "We'll go away and think about it," and within a few weeks the whole concept of a new information system would have simply been forgotten. No one would have announced a change in direction or even have made a firm decision—instead, the issue would have quietly vanished. This approach to decision making—perhaps "decision avoiding" would be a better description—had even been given its own catchphrase: "Aetna nice."

It might have been "nice," but it wasn't especially effective at getting things done.

Then there was a more recent problem-solving model that some of Aetna's newer managers—especially the intense entrepreneurial types who ran some of the businesses that we'd recently acquired—might have applied in this situation. If one of these executives was told that his goal for EMIS was "impossible," he might have screamed, "You say you can't do it? Don't give me that BS! Of course you can do it! And if you say you can't, I'm going to fire your ass and bring in somebody who can!"

This approach was the extreme opposite from "Mother Aetna." And it wasn't likely to be any more effective. One thing I've learned over the years is that most people in business are interested in meeting *expectations*—but they're *not* interested in meeting *demands*.

What's more, screaming at folks when they deliver bad news usually guarantees two things. First, they will tune you out—and while they may agree with everything you say simply to get you to stop screaming, they'll find plenty of ways to sabotage your efforts in the weeks and months to come. And second, no one will ever deliver bad news to you again.

As far as I was concerned, neither of these models for problem-solving was acceptable. I was determined to map out a new, third way.

So I said, "Okay. I believe that getting a prototype for the EMIS system up and running by September is doable. You believe it's not. Let's talk about what you see as the barriers to achievability. Let's lay out the process in specific detail, attaching dates and time frames to each step." I took my place at the whiteboard and began mapping out the process, based on suggestions from my colleagues around the table.

Soon a major stumbling block emerged. "We're going to need the help of an outside vendor with expertise in designing and implementing complex software systems," someone observed, and we all agreed that this was true. "That's the first big problem," someone else chimed in. "There's no way we can negotiate a vendor contract and then design and implement the new system within just a few months."

"It would take a lot longer than that just to get a contract in place," agreed a third person. "First, we'll have to analyze the problem, benchmark the solutions being used at other companies, and map out a general plan for our system. All of that will take several months. Then we'll have to choose a vendor who can write and test the actual code for our new software. After that, it'll take a month to negotiate the contract. By that time, we'll already be into the fall. Practically all of the time you've given us would already be used up."

"I see," I said. "Well, let's think this through in more detail. How many vendors are there who could do this?"

"There are lots of companies that do this work," replied one of the information technology experts. "But realistically, there are just three with the size and experience to tackle a job this big." He named them—let's call them Acme, Basic, and Central.

"So there are three vendors to choose from," I said. "Let's narrow it a little further. Which *two* do you think are most likely to be our best choice?"

"Well, Acme has some plusses and minuses. The last time we worked with them, their work came in a few weeks behind schedule. I think Basic and Central are going to be our best bets." His colleagues nodded in agreement.

I said, "Very good. So what about considering a different approach. Instead of waiting until we have the project mapped out, what if we had our contract negotiation team start negotiating contracts with Basic and Central *tomorrow*? Of course, we'll have to be upfront with them. We'll tell them, 'One of you will get the deal and one of you won't. If you can't live with that, then don't engage with us.' Do you think they'd be willing to talk with us on that basis?"

The folks in the room with outsourcing experience exchanged glances with one another. Finally someone spoke up. "It's unorthodox," she said. "But this will be a big project, and I bet the vendors will be happy to send contract teams to talk with us on that basis."

"Okay," I said. "If we can have a contract ready to sign the moment the project is outlined, that will save us a month." I made a note on the whiteboard.

We then began to examine the other bottlenecks that threatened to delay the project.

"How many man-hours will it take to complete this project?" I asked. "Let's break it down into its component parts to come up with some reasonable guesstimates." The experts around the table tossed out estimates—three hundred hours for this piece of the puzzle, five hundred hours for that piece, and so one. The whiteboard quickly filled up with lists and projections; someone pulled out a calculator and added up the figures. Within a few minutes, we'd spit-balled a rough estimate of the time the project would require.

"Now let's divide the total into two portions," I said, "one portion containing the pieces that only we can do, the other containing the pieces that we can hire outside help to do."

We went down the list of project components, one by one, sorting them accordingly. We decided that Aetna's insurance experts were the best equipped to handle the task of performing actuarial calculations to adjust for nuances and anomalies in our existing data system. On the other hand, contract employees from a management consulting firm, provided they were equipped with accurate decision rules outlined by Aetna, could handle the task of sorting customers into various categories—individuals versus small groups versus large employers.

"That will cost us a few bucks," I commented. "But for the EMIS project, time is more important than money."

"Wait a minute," someone in the room objected. "Sorting customers can be tricky at times. There are gray areas that only an insurance expert can accurately assess. We might end up with customer lists that are inaccurate, which could reduce the value of our financial reports."

"That's true," someone else chimed in. "Maybe it's a mistake to outsource customer sorting."

"Let's talk about that," I said. "What percentage of customers do you think might fall into one of those gray areas?"

After a pause, someone ventured, "Maybe five percent." Another suggested, "Maybe less than that."

"And if our customer sorting was off by that amount," I asked, "would it make our financial reports too inaccurate to use?"

I saw heads shaking around the table. "Nah," someone remarked, "five percent isn't enough to make a real difference. We'll still have the control total at the top. Any variance below will get worked out over time. And timely data that's ninety-five percent accurate is still going to be a heck of a lot better than the outdated information we have now."

"All right," I said. "Then sorting customers can be outsourced without any big problems."

We went through the rest of the tasks in the same fashion. By the end of the session, we had discovered that a large fraction of the work could be delegated to outside suppliers who could work simultaneously with us, not only reducing the amount of work we needed to do but also dramatically reducing the total amount of time needed to complete the project.

Suddenly the idea of getting an EMIS prototype up and running by September wasn't looking so crazy.

We didn't iron out all the complications in a single two-hour working session. It took three meetings of our steering committee to develop a detailed plan—what I call a "glide path"—that spelled out all the decision points in the process, possible glitches, and alternative routes that we would implement if necessary. In between these meetings, subcommittees worked on specific issues—highly detailed but contentious problems like "How should we assign responsibility for broker commissions, and how will we match the commission paid to the product?" Any problem too thorny for these subcommittees to resolve would be brought to the steering committee for a final resolution. Piece by piece, the plan took shape.

During those first few meetings, as the plan was being created, one of my main jobs was to ask a lot of pointed questions. There's an art to asking such questions. When people protested that a particular deadline I suggested was "impossible," I would ask, "Can you help me understand how you determined that?" or "What are the factors that led you to conclude it's impossible?" I avoided starting my questions with the word *why*, having long ago discovered that "why" questions tend to make people feel defensive—and respond accordingly. By contrast, the more oblique wordings I used directed attention away from the blame game and exactly where I wanted it—toward uncovering the root causes behind their objections. That enabled us to jointly determine whether those objections were sound and, if so, what to do about them.

Similarly, when I had an idea for a creative approach that might overcome a supposedly insurmountable difficulty, I refrained from simply suggesting it. Instead, I might ask, "Have you considered X? How would it work out if we gave that method a try?" My goal wasn't simply to give people the answer to an immediate dilemma but rather to educate them in a new way of thinking about problems, knowing that if they mastered this technique, it would help them generate their own solutions for years to come.

Sure enough, my colleagues at Aetna soon began coming up with problem-solving approaches I could never have imagined on my own. Understandably so—after all, they'd had decades of experience in the insurance business. They didn't lack smarts or ability; they'd simply been lacking the opportunity to apply them creatively. As soon as I opened the spigot by letting them know that new ways of thinking were encouraged, the ideas began to flow.

The EMIS planning process was time-consuming, detail-driven, and arduous. We got to know the windowless walls of the boardroom (dubbed "the Bunker" by some) all too well. We spent many a dinnertime—including some on Saturdays and Sundays—scarfing down take-out meals as we debated the latest wrinkle in our program, sketching and re-sketching flow charts on easeled whiteboards.

People often get impatient during a planning process of this kind. "Another committee meeting!" they complain. "Can't we just get on with the work already?" But guiding the creation of a plan for a seemingly impossible project is one of the most critical things a leader can do—not because the plan will be executed in precisely the way you expect, but precisely because it *won't*. When the future differs from your forecast is when having a plan is most important. The plan enables you to recognize when an anomaly arises, to measure the magnitude of the variance, and to quickly devise corrective actions.

Having a plan lets you ask such key questions as: Are we on schedule to deliver results as needed? What are the barriers and issues that we've run into? What must we do to get back on the glide path? Is there a work-around we can use to make up for the time we've lost? Can we add more resources to complete the next step in one week rather than two? Without a plan, when unexpected problems arise, you're wandering in the dark. Once you have a plan in place—even if it's not perfect—your odds of reaching your goal, despite setbacks and problems, go way, way up.

Investing the time required to create a detailed plan is essential. And the quicker project participants check in, the better. I call this the "reporting cadence." When participants report their progress once a month, you have only twelve chances per year to fix any problems. If they report every two weeks, you have twenty-six chances. If they report weekly, you have fifty-two chances. Each additional chance to address any problems increases your chances of success.

The big issue then becomes getting people to communicate openly. You need a business culture that encourages your team members to deliver bad news openly and early. You also need to voice that expectation clearly, calmly, and—at least in the beginning—often. Building a culture of transparency is difficult—a five-year process, according to most expert estimates. It requires the will to do it and the self-discipline to deal with people consistently. When a problem arises, resist the temptation to get flustered, lose your temper, or point the finger of blame. Instead, focus on analyzing what has happened and finding a solution. If you behave this way *every* time bad news arrives, people will eventually realize that you're sincere about valuing honesty and openness.

Over time, my Aetna colleagues gradually realized that I was serious about wanting them to tackle problem-solving in a spirit of collaboration and realism. Little by little, fear gave way to creativity. Piece by piece, the plan for EMIS came together—and by the early summer we were implementing it. The steering committee members and I were working some of the longest hours we'd ever experienced—including plenty of evenings and weekends. We were constantly connected with our outside suppliers, reviewing and adjusting the details of our program specifications and ironing out last-minute complications. But bit by bit—somewhat to our amazement—the "impossible" project we'd launched in April was becoming a reality.

By September 2001, we had a prototype for EMIS in place. Each member of our executive team could log in from their desktop and access a host of vital data—membership figures by region, actual revenues versus budgeted figures, fully allocated expenses, and much more. Seemingly basic questions like "how many people actually work for Aetna?" could now be answered for the first time. I now had access to a vital tool for communicating with, training, and developing managers. Whenever I met with the head of a regional operation or a product line, I'd start by asking them to walk me through their business on the EMIS screen. I quickly learned how well they understood the details of the business, and together we'd be able to zero in on the key issues that were hampering growth and depressing profitability. The newly fledged EMIS wasn't a perfect information system—not yet—but it was a lot better than what we'd had before and maybe eighty-five percent to ninety percent of what we needed to run our business at maximum efficiency.

The day the EMIS prototype went online was a moment of great satisfaction for me and for the other team members who had worked so hard to accomplish it. I must admit that the satisfaction only lasted a few minutes, at least for me, since my colleagues and I were already deeply immersed in the many other challenges that were bedeviling us at Aetna, from transforming our relationships with physicians, customers, and members to restoring the sense of pride our employees needed to be fully engaged in the work of building the company.

In retrospect, EMIS was a transformative event in the evolution of Aetna. For the first time in years, the company had accomplished an effort critical to its turnaround. In the process, Aetna had overcome a significant cultural challenge, tapping the intellect, knowledge, and creative energies of its employees and proving that we were still capable of innovating in a truly impressive way.

I was lucky at Aetna. I quickly discovered that the people I was working with were much more talented than their business results suggested. The company's problems in the late 1990s and early 2000s weren't caused by any lack of talent, knowledge, or dedication, but rather by misaligned systems and unfortunate failures of leadership. Above all, as I soon came to appreciate, these were people who desperately wanted to win and were prepared—even eager—to do whatever was required to turn themselves into winners. As I began to say soon after arriving at the company, "Aetna was bent, not broken." That message served as an elixir of hope for the thousands of hardworking people who were eager to contribute to the turnaround.

Aetna isn't unique in this regard. Over the years, I've found that most organizations have their fair share of smart, hardworking, and caring people. This goes back to my leadership mantra about assuming positive intent. Practically all people *want* to do the right thing. If they can't or don't, it's either because they don't know how or because they haven't been given the appropriate tools. It's the leader's job to remedy those shortfalls—not to berate employees for skills or resources they may lack.

Sometimes, of course, personnel changes may be unavoidable. In a turnaround situation like the one we faced at Aetna, a few folks are usually so invested in the dysfunctional old systems—or incapable of making the mental adjustments necessary to participate in change—that you simply have to let them go.

One example was the information technology team I inherited from the previous regime. Having built our EMIS prototype in only a few months, we knew that we needed to further expand and improve our IT infrastructure in the years to come. In today's business world—especially in a knowledge-based business like insurance—technology is not only a cost, the way a lot of companies view it; it is close to the heart of your competitive strategy. So during our strategic planning process for the coming year, we developed a concept for improving our IT systems to further support our business needs, building on the success we'd enjoyed with EMIS.

In late January, the IT team visited me to discuss our jointly developed annual plan. "We've estimated everything," they told me, "and we figure we can probably do about seventy percent of what we have in the plan."

I was a bit confused about what they meant. "Do you mean you can do seventy percent of the 2002 annual plan this year?" I asked.

"Yes, that's what we mean," they replied.

I admit I was taken aback by this response. We'd developed our information technology plan for the year in close coordination with the IT team, and our financial and operating results were dependent on that plan. Since they'd never uttered a word of concern during the planning process, I'd assumed they were personally committed to achieving it. This offhand repudiation of the plan left me stunned and dismayed. It was suddenly clear that we had fundamentally different ideas of what business planning was all about. They thought the business plan was a wish list; I saw it as a solid commitment to produce the planned-for results.

Of course, there was no question about what we had to do next. We quickly reformulated our operating plan for the coming year, and we launched a strategy to retool our IT team. Meg McCarthy, an experienced IT executive, was recruited as the head of application development, and she took the lead in working with IBM. McCarthy later went on to become my chief information officer, leading the transformation of the Aetna IT area.

We downsized our IT organization while retaining the best members of that team and developed what we called a co-sourcing deal with IBM. Knowing we lacked the technical capabilities we needed, we brought IBM's people in to help us. They helped us recruit and train our own team, and worked with us for three years to professionalize our entire IT process. The end result was a transformed IT division that was fully capable of doing everything we'd asked for—and then some. Many of the best performers on this new IT team were junior staff members who'd been buried under the prior structure.

Sometimes retraining an organization to achieve the impossible does demand new blood. But in many cases the talent you need is already in-house, under your nose, just waiting to be unleashed.

In other cases, that talent is out in the world, looking for a winning team to join. During the next few years of our turnaround, we found that, as word began to spread about the new culture and the new leadership at Aetna, we were able to lure back many capable people who had left Aetna during the painful days of the old regime. Just as failure tends to breed failure in a downward spiral, so success breeds success—and once you start moving in the right direction, many other details begin to fall into place.

The story of EMIS is the story of a team of people who desperately wanted to improve their performance and that of the business they served. But they were trapped in a way of thinking that made them believe that the things we needed to accomplish were impossible. My job as a leader was to show them a new way of thinking—to demonstrate, through coaching, a clear articulation of my positions and my expectations, and through my own personal example, how they could think their way out of the box in which they felt trapped.

This, to me, is the essence of leadership—the art of helping people free themselves from the mental constraints that limit what they can achieve. In the chapters that follow, I'll share more of what I've learned about this art from my years of success—and failure—in striving to master and practice it.

TAKEAWAYS FROM CHAPTER 5

- In most organizations, people make assumptions about what is possible and what is not. These assumptions—often unfounded—play a huge role in limiting what the organization can achieve.

- When faced with attitudes that limit what your team can do, you can begin to challenge unfounded assumptions by ascertaining the underlying facts—which are often surprisingly difficult to uncover.

- Polite, probing questions are a powerful tool in the quest for hard facts. Be persistent—keep asking questions until the underlying reality emerges. In most cases, the *real* problem that keeps a team mired in underachievement is hidden under layers of misunderstandings and false beliefs.

- When tackling any big, complex project, a detailed plan with plenty of check-in points is essential to help keep the team on course. Resist the temptation to rush through the planning process!

- Honest, transparent communication is crucial to keeping any project on track. Early detection of problems makes it possible to return quickly to the glide path toward completion.

- Make sure all the members of your team are using the same terms with the same meanings. Hidden misunderstandings lead to confusion that can cripple a project.

6

When All Else Fails, Get the Facts:
Solving Problems in the Real World

You might assume that the importance of making decisions based strictly on facts would be taken for granted by most business professionals—yet experience shows that's not the case. Here are some ideas about how to make fact-finding a routine part of your leadership toolkit, and how to use hard data to improve your problem-solving capabilities.

IT'S A REMARKABLE FACT of life: Smart professionals with impeccable technical skills and keenly logical minds often flounder when called on to make tough business decisions, especially when time pressures are intense, conflicting values or interests are involved, and emotions are running high. And these are precisely the circumstances most likely to arise when especially important decisions must be made.

Over the years, I've faced my share of these troubled decision points—times when problem-solving meetings devolved into heated arguments full of confusion, finger-pointing, and defensiveness. At such moments, I like to call a halt to the debate and then invoke one of my favorite mantras, "When all else fails, get the facts!"

This appeal tends to lower the emotional temperature in the room and returns the focus to where it should be: on what is *really* happening (as opposed to perceptions distorted by anxiety and self-interest) and what can be done to get the organization back on the right track.

GETTING TO THE FACTS

Within a few weeks of my arrival at Aetna, I set about working with my leadership team to get at the realities underlying the crisis the company faced. We held a series of lengthy fact-finding sessions, attended by representatives of every company department and division. We worked our way through the status of the business, studying the numbers, drawing connections among systems, and identifying the problems that were draining us as well as the opportunities we were overlooking.

In the process, the information system I'd insisted on creating—EMIS, whose story I told in the previous chapter—emerged as a crucial weapon in the battle for clarity and accuracy. It provided, for the first time, a systemic breakdown of Aetna into its many business components, enabling us to see at a glance our revenue and cost experience in each of our market segments. EMIS became what I liked to call "the single source of truth"—the unimpeachable database that everyone could turn to for resolution when there were conflicts among individual accounts of what was happening in the company.

As the facts emerged, we realized that the helter-skelter growth by acquisition that Aetna had undergone had turned us into a vast, unwieldy collection of businesses—some profitable, some not, but with no rhyme or reason either way. Aetna was serving a wide array of customer types: individuals, small groups, middle-market businesses, large national accounts, government purchasers, and more. But no one had been looking at the business holistically in terms of customer segments. This resulted in a complete lack of logic in how decisions were made and resources allocated.

Here's a small but representative example. To sell insurance products to clients, you naturally need an array of sales and informational materials. But these need to be tailored to the type of customer you are addressing. If the customer is a giant enterprise that is buying insurance for forty thousand employees, clients expect a handsome array of four-color brochures spelling out various coverage options, pricing choices, and so on, to be used in big recruitment meetings held in giant company auditoriums. But if the customer is a mom-and-pop dry cleaner with three employees, then simpler, more cost-effective materials for your clients to scan over their morning coffee are a better option.

This simple, seemingly obvious principle of tailoring your offerings to match the needs of your customers applies to benefits design, service systems, and many other crucial business choices. The problem was that Aetna wasn't applying that principle. Instead, we were drastically overengineering some of our decisions while underengineering others. As a result, we were wasting untold sums of money on things no one needed or wanted—while failing to invest in things that were crucial to our growth and to our ability to serve customers well. We were also mispricing our insurance products because we simply didn't know what our costs were—and this was one of the big reasons for our financial problems.

Once we had EMIS and began mastering the steady flow of detailed data it provided about every nook and cranny of our business, we could recognize and fix mismatches of this kind. We knew for the first time where we were making money and where we were losing it. And we could finally start to identify what we needed to do to turn the red ink into black.

One department and product line at a time, we systematically started making the kinds of rational, fact-based decisions we should have been making all along. Some insurance products had their prices adjusted to better reflect their underlying costs. Other products had to be dramatically redesigned or even eliminated. In some cases, customer groups that had been costing us millions of dollars were allowed to leave us for other suppliers who could afford to serve them better. The chaotic non-system we'd built during the era of unplanned growth gradually gave way to a logical, strategically sound structure with the potential to be financially sustainable.

MAKING THE FACT-FINDING PROCESS
ROUTINE AND SYSTEMATIC

Of course, ascertaining the facts isn't important only in the midst of a company crisis. The facts concerning your business and the environment in which you operate are constantly changing. You need to create systems that will enable you to keep track of the facts and their evolution—and to recognize when *new* sets of important facts are emerging that will affect your business. That's what the EMIS system was all about. As the crisis ebbed, we worked on building practices and behaviors to make fact-finding and smart decision making into routine elements of corporate life at Aetna.

I instituted regular meetings dedicated to each of our various business markets. I'd sit across the table from the manager responsible for a particular market, and we'd go through the numbers together and ask these questions: Where do the numbers match those in the plan we developed before the start of the year? Where do they diverge, and why? What is working and what is not?

These meetings required significant advance planning. I spent hours poring over the numbers, highlighting figures that seemed irregular or troubling. Because we were operating in a low-margin industry—as opposed to a high-margin industry like software—a penny or two on the dollar could make or break us. The level of precision required for us to manage effectively was extraordinary.

The meetings in which we reviewed our businesses were highly detailed and often contentious. Some people found them exhausting. But everyone agreed that they were invaluable. After a few sessions of working the numbers with me, most of the managers who reported to me developed an intuitive understanding of the analytic methods I used—and soon they became adept at using them on their own. Leaders who once dreaded sitting down with me to be "grilled" about the fine details of their departmental results even began looking forward to the sessions, having become fact-finding masters in their own right.

Jerald "Jerry" Gooden, a gifted manager who held numerous leadership roles during his thirty-one-year career at Aetna, got to know me and my methods well during the two years he spent as my chief of staff. He contrasts the management culture within Aetna before and after my arrival in this way:

> Before Ron, it was understood among managers at Aetna that "close is good enough." Ron quickly showed us that that was *not* his approach. He wanted us to know *exactly*

what was happening in the businesses that we ran. Because, after all, unless we knew exactly what was going on—where we were making money, where we were losing it, and why— how could we know exactly what adjustments we might need to make? You might say that, before Ron, Aetna managers were generalists. Understanding the business at a generalist level was what was previously expected of them. Ron turned us into specialists. We needed specific, precise knowledge of our businesses—as well as a broad understanding of the larger context in which we operated.

During my tenure at Aetna, we took steps to institutionalize fact-based problem-solving across the organization, along with developing a deep understanding of what our data was telling us. Aetna had huge databases available but wasn't always using the data in meaningful ways. To remedy this, we put in place a new corporate division dedicated to *health analytics*. Its purpose: to study Aetna's medical costs according to all the relevant variables—service type, geography, patient demographics, provider category, and many others—all of them in constant, largely unpredictable flux. We aggregated the data and built algorithms—formulas—that we could use to analyze the data. Then I mandated monthly meetings with our divisional managers to examine the data in search of hidden problems and opportunities.

The questions we tackled were numerous and wide-ranging: How and where have our costs increased beyond expectations? Are there adjustments we can make to get our results back on track? Are particular health-care providers being used to a much greater extent than anticipated? If so, why? Are lab costs out of whack? What new clinical protocols, procedures, and medications are about to be introduced, and how will they affect medical expenses? Has a certain drug price escalated beyond what we expected? If so, can we renegotiate a contract or two to reduce expenses without unduly limiting service?

We also tried to anticipate trends: Does the evidence suggest that next year's accident rate is likely to rise or fall? Will this winter's flu epidemic be on the mild side, or will it be particularly severe? Which hospitals are likely to experience particularly heavy usage? How do we need to work with doctors and hospitals to make sure their practices are being adjusted to deal with these changes effectively?

Focusing intensely on data-driven questions like these, and developing systems to improve the company's decisions around them, helped us turn around Aetna's business, enabling the company to move from massive losses to significant profits even as we dramatically improved our rates of patient care and stakeholder satisfaction.

In the years since, "big data" has become a popular buzzword in businesses of almost every kind. Thousands of companies are now learning what Aetna figured out a long time ago—that the data you collect and the algorithms you use to analyze it can be a fount of invaluable insight.

Beyond the Numbers: Listening to What People Tell You

Mastering the numbers is hugely important. But some of the most important things a leader needs to know aren't quantitative but qualitative. You learn them not by crunching numbers but by *listening* to what people tell you.

One of the ways I worked hard to stay in touch with the small, crucial details that determined the daily health of Aetna was by applying a practice I'd first adopted as an executive at WellPoint. The company had some two thousand customer service representatives fielding phone calls and emails from many kinds of customers—health-care recipients, doctors and other providers, employers. Those reps were our most important, most direct link with the many people who relied on coverage from WellPoint; the quality of their work had a huge impact on customer satisfaction and our reputation among all our stakeholders.

I wanted to keep track of what those customer service reps were doing. Numbers did offer a part of the story. So I arranged to have a two-by-three-foot electronic monitor installed on a wall in my office. It showed a continually changing readout of customer service metrics, including the volume and nature of calls, the average speed of answer (call wait time), the average length of call, and the first-call resolution percentage. These numbers were similar to the vital signs of a hospital patient—a simple set of figures that gave me a quick but mostly accurate picture of the overall health of our customer service system.

I knew, however, that I also wanted to delve beyond the numbers into the nuts-and-bolts realities that our customer service reps had to grapple with. I had a device called an automatic call distributor set up in the adjacent conference room. This was essentially a big phone that could connect to all the lines used by the customer service reps. I used this three or four times a day, for four or five minutes at a time, to listen in on customer calls to learn what the issues were. (Of course, both the service reps and the customers themselves were informed that their conversations might be overheard for this purpose.)

These listening sessions gave me a real sense of the impediments that our service staff faced in trying to provide customers with the best possible service. In some cases, our service reps lacked access to the data they needed to answer customer questions accurately and quickly. In other cases, our systems didn't even contain the basic information needed to pay claims accurately—for example, the agreed physician pay rate for a particular service. In still other cases, there was a conflict between the insurance contract and the plan documents delivered to customers, making disappointment and anger practically unavoidable. Every time we identified a problem like one of these, we took steps to alleviate or eliminate it. With the input of our frontline staff, we created an entirely new service system that put the right information at our employees' fingertips, which significantly increased their ability to solve customer and member problems.

At Aetna, I continued many of the same practices I'd developed at WellPoint, including listening in on selected customer service calls. In addition, with the help of my chief of staff and my executive assistant, I arranged and undertook monthly site visits to the various locations where Aetna employees were based. Naturally, I took time to visit with the managers. But more important were the face-to-face meetings with rank-and-file employees (conducted *without* their bosses in the room to ensure honest and uninhibited sharing). I wanted to hear the realities of their work at Aetna. I asked questions like these: What is your job like these days? What are the customers saying? and, perhaps most significant, What could we be doing to make your work easier and better? I often used what you might call the "King or Queen for a Day" gambit: If you had the power, what would you fix around here to enable us to serve our customers better? Some powerful ideas for process improvements emerged from those conversations.

It's startling how often the biggest barrier to people doing their jobs is their own organization! If you're an organizational leader, it's essential that you develop a good grasp of the facts on the ground—not the way you assume things are, or the way you might wish them to be, but the way they truly are. Once you have the facts, you can discover when you are inadvertently blocking your own path to success and take steps to do something about it.

I first met Pam Kehaly when we were both team members at WellPoint. Later, she worked with me at Aetna for several years, serving as our president for national accounts. Today she is CEO and president of Blue Cross Blue Shield of Arizona. One of the ways Kehaly practices fact-based problem-solving is by dedicating one day a week to visiting with a customer or a care provider. She almost always learns something of value—and sometimes comes away with a simple insight that leads to a significant business improvement. Kehaly shared one such example:

> I recently visited with a team of people from one of our bigger customers—the city of Chandler, whose employee health benefits we administer. During our conversation, one of the benefits administrators offered an observation about a challenge they face in taking care of city employees: "When someone is hit with a health catastrophe, affecting themselves or a family member, they don't know what to do. In fact, they're often so emotionally distressed, they can't even think what questions to ask. The result is that the decisions they make about medical care often aren't the best for them. It's a real dilemma."
>
> We discussed this painful problem for a while. At Blue Cross Blue Shield, we have care managers who are well equipped to help members deal with issues like this. But members rarely call on them for help when they need it most. It seems that few people think about their insurance company as a source of helpful advice and guidance.

So we've come up with a plan that we hope will help. We're creating a new team of employer service representatives dedicated to providing just this kind of help. They'll be available to the benefits managers we serve through a special phone line. Now, when they get a call from a distraught employee saying, "I just received a cancer diagnosis. What should I do first?" they can immediately bring the Blue Cross Blue Shield expert on the line. |Our service rep| will thoughtfully, compassionately guide the member through the most urgent decisions, outlining a plan to help the member get started on accessing the highest quality care, and suggesting the best available sources of additional help and support.

We hope to have this new service up and running within a few months for our largest customers. If it works as planned, we'll expand it thereafter. It all came about through a routine conversation designed to help me stay in touch with the needs and concerns of our customers.

FINDING THE DETAILS THAT MATTER

Fact-based problem-solving can be enormously powerful. But it takes sensitivity and emotional intelligence to lead your team members through the process. You'll find that everyone varies in their ability to tolerate uncertainty. Experience makes a difference. A newer manager who may be overseeing a division budget for the first time may feel the world is coming to an end if asked to cut spending by ten percent. In the same situation, a more experienced manager can separate what's crucial from what isn't and can figure out how to reallocate limited funds in a sensible and effective way. When you are working on a problem with your team, knowing the decision-making maturity of the others in the room is important. You can better gauge when to gently push for a decision and when to hold back and allow a little more time for reflection.

One of the most useful decision-making techniques that I learned came from my executive partner at Aetna, the physician Jack Rowe who served as CEO during my first years there. Drawing on his clinical background, Rowe pointed out to me that the human body can yield hundreds of metrics, but in most circumstances, a physician needs to consider only twelve or fifteen—and in an emergency, only three or four are usually essential. In a similar way, the business decision maker should constantly strive to identify the few key data points in any situation rather than being overwhelmed and confused by a vast array of secondary information.

When I joined Aetna, the company was embroiled in litigation that had been brought against us by no fewer than twenty-six medical associations across the country. We weren't the only insurance company in that situation. With the health-care system in our country in disarray, and with patients and providers alike struggling to deal with changes they found confusing and sometimes troubling, many competing insurers were also being sued. Unhappy with the way health-care coverage was evolving, physicians and hospitals were demanding changes to health insurers' business practices, including notifying providers prior to any change in coverage. The instinctive reaction from Aetna's previous leadership team had been to simply resist and ignore key stakeholders. Hence the lawsuits we now faced.

Our lawyers walked us through the details of the litigation and spelled out various scenarios with differing odds of victory, and the whole executive team debated the potential financial impact of our alternative strategies.

Jack Rowe cut through the complexities of the debate by focusing on the single most important issue. "This is all about Aetna's reputation," he insisted. "We can't do anything without the support and confidence of physicians. Yes, we could prolong this legal battle against them. Maybe we could even win. But in the process, we'd do more damage to the relationship between us. We'd end up losing much more than we'd gain."

Rowe was right. Aetna became the first major insurance company to move quickly to negotiate a reasonable settlement with the health-care providers. This was a huge step in the process of repairing our damaged reputation and a milestone on the road that ultimately led to Aetna becoming the most respected company in the industry. It came about because Rowe helped us sort out what was insignificant from what was material—a crucial skill for every decision maker to master.

I tried to pass that skill on to the people who worked for me during our regular business review meetings. When a manager's report or presentation contained excessive or irrelevant detail that obscured rather than clarified the issues, I would ask, "Can you please make this accessible to me? A one- or two-page explanation will work better for me than this twenty-page document." I think people appreciated my wording it that way; asking them to make their knowledge "accessible" didn't imply a rebuke, but simply suggested that I needed their help so I could focus my attention on the essentials. I believe that, in many cases, the exercise of translating the twenty-page report into a two-page précis probably forced them to figure out for the first time what the real heart of the message should be—a classic case of "less is more."

PULLING THE TRIGGER: WHEN DO YOU HAVE *ENOUGH* FACTS?

Of course, simply "getting the facts" is not by itself an adequate guideline for making smart decisions in the face of massive uncertainty. Some organizations succumb to "paralysis by analysis," in which they delay crucial decisions in an interminable search for yet more information, as if hoping to eliminate all uncertainty and therefore all risk. It's ultimately a futile endeavor.

I have certain rules of thumb that I think are helpful in recognizing whether you have the data needed to make a good-enough decision under real-world conditions of uncertainty and risk:

Listen to many voices. Before pulling the trigger on a decision, always ask to hear competing arguments. Make sure you've given a fair hearing to multiple points of view, from varied levels and organizational functions, rather than relying on a single, potentially biased perspective, or being swayed by a presentation that is glib or emphatic.

Create a clear, simple decision framework. Define the key issues: What are the pros? What are the cons? What are the implications of a decision either way? Use this framework to clear away the clutter and focus the many-voiced discussion that may be complicating the process.

Gauge the importance of any missing data. As you analyze your options in light of the facts before you, compare what you know with what you might *like* to know. Then ask yourself and your team: What kinds of information are we now lacking? How difficult and time-consuming would it be to gather that information? Is any data missing due to tactical efforts by people who might want to manipulate the decision? (You might be surprised to discover how often this happens, even in well-run organizations.) If we *could* gather the missing data, how material is it likely to be—that is, how likely is it to change our ultimate decision? The answers to questions like these will help you decide whether you've devoted sufficient time and energy to the fact-finding process.

Avoid recency bias. This is the human tendency to be overly swayed by the most recent piece of data you've received or by the last argument that has been presented to you. After weighing all the information, allow a little time to elapse before you make a final decision, so all the data and arguments can settle into their proper perspective.

Protect your future flexibility. When deciding whether you are ready to pull the trigger, ask yourself: How difficult will it be to modify or reverse the decision once it's made? Can we tweak the details over time? (It's one thing to pour three cubic feet of concrete that will harden in three hours; it's another to launch the first tentative steps in a process that will allow learning, change, and adjustments over time.) The more your choice is "carved in stone," the greater your need for informational certainty. Whenever possible, acting now while protecting your ability to learn and shift course in the future is the most prudent option.

Take levels of risk into account. Some decisions are relatively low risk. For example, if a CEO faces pressure to reduce costs dramatically because of big financial losses (as I did when I joined Aetna), selling off a fleet of company cars or planes is not a highly risky option; when circumstances permit, buying new vehicles will be easy and fast. By contrast, firing a large number of frontline customer-facing workers to save money may be very risky, since it could force service reductions and thereby drive away customers, making the financial losses even worse. When considering an option that is low risk, don't be afraid to act. But when considering one that could have dire consequences, insist on weighing *all* the important facts before pulling the trigger.

Don't dither needlessly. Once you've gathered the necessary information and analyzed it to the point where a reasonable decision is possible, don't temporize or delay unless you have a good reason to do so. Avoiding a decision rarely improves the ultimate outcome of the problem. Remember that refusing to decide is, in fact, a decision—in effect, a decision to stay on whatever course you are currently taking, whether it is good or bad. So you might as well buckle down and make a choice rather than go on dithering.

Disagree but commit. When eliciting opinions from the people around you, help them understand that they do not have to agree with every decision—but that once a decision is made, they will be expected to commit to it and implement it as if they fully agree with it.

Heed your inner voice. Before making a final commitment, ask yourself whether you have heard your inner voice—the voice that tells you when you are comfortable with your chosen course of action. If not, try to determine why. Is something in the situation striking you as odd or incomplete, even if you can't articulate it? Is there an underlying assumption that needs to be questioned and possibly modified before a decision can be reached? If so, take time to fully process the information you've gathered. Sleep on it overnight and review the problem in the morning. You may find that your unconscious mind has come to grips with the problem while you slept, and that your inner voice is ready to speak with clarity.

I have a reputation among the folks I've worked with for being detail oriented. It's a slight misinterpretation of my decision-making philosophy. I do indeed believe in the importance of critical details; after all, I've seen too many instances in which carelessness about details has caused significant, avoidable problems. But I've seen other instances in which flawed decisions were made because of broad, macro-level assumptions that were never examined—for example, assumptions about the persistence of current social attitudes or economic trends that were due to shift.

Therefore, I don't recommend obsessing over minor details for their own sake. Instead, figure out which details are the *important* ones—and then do whatever you need to do to make sure you've got those details right.

Follow that rule, and most of the tough decisions you make are likely to work out fine.

TAKEAWAYS FROM CHAPTER 6

- Many of the controversies that arise inside business organizations can be traced to a paucity of hard facts. When in doubt, stop arguing and find the underlying facts!

- If you're an organizational leader, make data discovery and analysis a regular routine among the members of your team. Periodic meetings to review and discuss current information can help focus people on this process.

continued

- Spending time talking with and listening to organizational team members on the front lines—those working with customers, for example—can be a powerful method for staying in touch with what is really happening at your company.

- An overwhelming array of data points can be as bad as too little information. Work to separate the facts that matter from those that don't.

- Develop a reasonable process for determining when you have enough data to make an informed decision. Don't rush to judgment—but don't dither needlessly, waiting for perfect information.

- Avoid recency bias—the tendency to attach special significance to the last piece of information you happen to receive.

- When you're faced with an important decision and you've uncovered all the relevant data you can find, check that your inner voice confirms your choice. When that happens, you can pull the trigger with confidence, knowing you've made the best decision possible under the circumstances.

- Be sure your team members understand the importance of the "disagree but commit" principle: Once a decision is made, everyone must commit to it and implement it wholeheartedly.

7

Changing the Problem
Changes the Solution:
Reframing for Business Leaders

*In addition to opening up personal opportunities, reframing
can also help business leaders discover unexpected solutions
to knotty strategic problems. Here are some examples that
illustrate how the process works.*

IN A PREVIOUS CHAPTER, I discussed how reframing can help
you discover new career possibilities for yourself. In other cases,
reframing is about changing the way you look at a business problem.

When I joined Aetna, it was attempting to transform itself from
a traditional insurance company into a managed care company. This
was a new model of health-care provision, one that required new
skills and expertise as well as substantial local market scale to be economically viable. In comparison with its main competitors, Aetna

lagged in adopting this new model. Like many legacy companies, Aetna had been built to do yesterday's work and was ill-equipped for tomorrow's—the creation of a new generation of managed care products and services.

To catch up, Aetna had embarked on an aggressive acquisition strategy to gain scale and the new competencies it needed to migrate to the new business model. By the time I came on the scene, the company was awash in red ink. This was in part because Aetna's previous leaders had assumed that *size* was the key to profitability and success in the health insurance business.

The notion wasn't completely unfounded. Experts on business strategy have long recognized the ability of size to boost the profit potential of companies. Bigger organizations can benefit from economies of scale (which reduce the unit costs of the goods and services you produce), market power (since a bigger company has the ability to reach more customers), and lower expenditures on marketing and advertising as a percentage of sales. So, all things being equal, a bigger company has definite competitive advantages when compared with smaller rivals in the same industry.

Of course, all things may *not* be equal. In Aetna's case, the company's leaders had applied the concept of growing your way to success a bit too literally. The acquisitions and growth had been undertaken without due regard for the people, processes, and technologies needed to make the transition smoothly. They'd also ignored issues of corporate culture, which made integrating the acquired businesses into Aetna's existing operations particularly difficult.

In business and in life, the questions you ask invariably determine the value of the answers you get. Aetna executives had gotten into the habit of asking themselves, "How much have we grown this year?" Since the answer was always "a lot," they assumed that the company's overall state was healthy. Even when profit margins shrank and then disappeared, management explained away the problems as a result of "growing pains" that would go away as soon as the process of absorbing the new acquisitions had been completed. Then the magical economies of scale would kick in and profits would soar.

Beyond the "how much have we grown" question, Aetna's leaders should have also been asking, "Do we have a sustainable business model that is adapting to changes in the economic environment? Do we have the information, people, processes, and technologies needed to integrate the companies we've acquired? Are we maintaining good relations with our key stakeholders, and are we making sure that our company's reputation for integrity and service is being protected?"

Because of the failure to ask this broader array of important questions, the magic that Aetna's leaders were counting on failed to materialize. Financial losses continued to mount. Making matters worse, Aetna's failure to successfully integrate and operate the acquired companies led to a crisis of stakeholder relations. It culminated in a wrongful death suit based on the tragic death of an Aetna subscriber in California, which led to a $120.5 million judgment against the company.

These cascading problems forced the Aetna board to act. Board member Bill Donaldson assumed the role of chairman and CEO, and the board then recruited Jack Rowe to begin the process of healing Aetna.

One thing Rowe did *not* have was traditional management training, financial expertise, or experience in running a big for-profit company. But in a way, that worked in his favor. Never having earned an MBA or studied the theory of corporate strategy, Rowe wasn't wedded to the concept of economies of scale and had no preconceived opinion about the power of acquisitions to drive enhanced profitability. So he was well positioned to help Aetna reframe the financial problems that its out-of-control growth had caused, simply by applying some common-sense thinking. As a newcomer to the world of corporate management, Rowe was well aware that he needed to work with a partner who had deeper knowledge of the operating requirements of a complex business. That's why he brought me in to manage the job of fixing Aetna.

Working with Jack Rowe, I helped Aetna's managers to begin focusing on the right questions—about the business model, information, people, and technology. We developed a new strategy and a new operating model focused on general managers being responsible for the profits and losses incurred by their departments. In operating reviews, we started asking our executives, "How much money has this division made this year? And this one—and this one—and this one?" The answers would help the company determine which businesses to keep and grow, and which to sell off.

Of course, the process of deciding which operations were money losers with little or no hope of being salvaged, and then finding appropriate ways to sell those businesses or spin them off, was not a quick or simple one. Rowe and I worked closely with the experts on our teams to examine the strategic circumstances of each troubled division. One by one, we identified the businesses that made no sense for Aetna to retain. As Rowe recalls, "We found we were running companies whose competitive position was just terrible. When you're operating the fifth-biggest insurance business in a modest-sized market like Wichita or Toledo, your chances of growing enough to make any money are slim. Redoubling your sales efforts so you can sign up a few thousand more customers isn't really going to make much difference. The only sensible thing to do is to get out of that market and leave the business to other, better-positioned companies."

The philosophy Aetna applied in making these winnowing decisions recalls a famous dictum of General Electric's legendary longtime CEO Jack Welch—"If you're not number one or number two in a particular market, get out." It worked for GE, and it worked for Aetna, too. Over time, the company gradually divested businesses with a total of some eight million customers. Those customers didn't join the ranks of the uninsured; their policies were taken over by competing insurers in their specific markets. And dropping those unprofitable businesses also allowed Aetna to reduce its workforce. We laid off around fifteen thousand employees, although we did this as humanely as possible, providing them with appropriate severance packages, benefits extensions, job transition counseling, and other services.

These job cuts were painful. They disappointed many longtime Aetna employees and members of the communities where company facilities were housed, who noted that Aetna had never before undertaken layoffs on such a big scale. But like emergency surgery on a badly injured limb, the layoffs helped save the patient. Aetna stopped losing money and regained its financial stability, in part thanks to our willingness to reframe Aetna's strategic focus from growth to profitability. Once the latter had been achieved, the company was poised to grow again—and this time to do so profitably.

Other forms of reframing were equally important in driving the Aetna turnaround.

Aetna was also plagued by the fact that it had become widely disliked by physicians. Because doctors are important stakeholders in the world of health insurance, this was a major challenge that we needed to tackle. As a respected physician and medical researcher, Jack Rowe had the trust of most members of this crucial stakeholder group. So Rowe devoted much of his energy during his first year on the job to communicating with doctors, nurses, hospital administrators, and other health-care providers about Aetna's determination to partner with them productively to improve patient outcomes, enhance efficiencies in care, make information flows more transparent, and encourage reform of the entire health-care system. Rowe's speeches and meetings with members of the provider community played an important role in turning around the negative perceptions about Aetna.

While Rowe worked to build communication bridges with Aetna's stakeholders, I set out to address one of the most urgent operational problems we faced—complaints about slow and inaccurate responses by Aetna's customer service representatives—the frontline employees who were charged with solving problems and answering questions for physicians and other health-care providers as well as for our other customers.

The obvious solution—one applied by many insurance companies—would be to retrain our customer service reps and increase the pressure on them to respond to questions more quickly. That might have improved things a bit. Maybe we could have shaved response times by a few seconds; maybe we could have gotten our reps to do a slightly better job of identifying the right information from one of our databases to answer physicians' questions more accurately. Measures like these are important; as I explained in a previous chapter, I care about them so deeply that I installed a tracking system in my office to help me monitor them continually. But I also knew that simply pressuring employees to do better without fundamentally improving the process can easily backfire. Morale suffers, and sometimes service personnel get so focused on sheer speed that they stop hearing what customers truly need.

Instead, I asked my team to reframe the issue. Rather than asking what we could do to induce our service reps to respond more quickly to questions, we asked, What kinds of questions are doctors asking us? What kind of information is needed to respond to those questions? What can we do to provide that information more quickly and accurately?

This reframing of the problem led us in a new, more fruitful direction. The managers in charge of customer service spent some time talking with their frontline employees to discover the roadblocks that were making it hard for them to help doctors with their concerns. They discovered that the real problem was not the training, talent, or motivation of the service reps—it was a structural problem.

Aetna's service teams were organized around employers and their insurance policies, which made sense from an internal perspective; it meant that a given service rep could concentrate on mastering the details of the insurance coverage we provided to the thousands of employees working for Corporation A, University B, or State Agency C.

But this structure made little intuitive sense to the doctors and other health-care providers who called us with questions. After all, when ophthalmologist Dr. Jones calls with a question about his patient Nancy Smith, he isn't thinking about the company Nancy works for—he may not even know its name. Instead, he is thinking about Nancy's cataracts and about the coverage Aetna will provide for her upcoming surgery. Having our service reps organized by employer often meant that providers like Dr. Jones would be shunted around from one rep to another before finding one who could help with a simple question. And when a physician's office called with questions about several patients, the calls would get even more convoluted and time consuming.

Reframing the problem of response time by considering it from the external perspective of the care provider rather than from the internal perspective of our service team helped us recognize that our organizational structure was backward. We decided to reorganize part of our service system into physician-centered teams. We created groups of reps who worked consistently with specific care providers and were equipped to answer their questions no matter which patient, employer, or insurance policy was involved. Now Dr. Jones could call Aetna and expect to speak with a familiar representative who knew him, his specialty, and his practice, and was prepared to answer his most likely questions with speed and accuracy.

Redesigning our service system and retraining our reps was a complex and costly undertaking—but it improved Aetna's relationships with doctors in a way that simply cracking the whip on our employees could never have done. It would never have happened without our initial reframing of the problem.

REFRAMING AS A SOURCE OF NEW OPPORTUNITIES

In addition to helping you solve thorny problems, reframing can also help you look at areas of your business that are working fine and see opportunities you never noticed before.

Elease Wright served as the head of human resources at Aetna for fifteen years, including several years while I was CEO. She's a talented executive who quickly won my respect and admiration, and I like to think that we learned a lot from one another during our time as colleagues. I know I certainly learned a great deal from her.

One of the cultural shifts Wright and I worked on together at Aetna was trying to encourage leaders in every department to move from being internally focused to being customer focused. As with how we reorganized our customer service structure to focus on the needs of our health-care providers, we tried to make similar shifts throughout Aetna, even in departments that people might not ordinarily think of as having "customers"—one of which was Wright's own department.

A company's HR department, of course, doesn't sell goods and services to external customers the way, for example, the sales and marketing people do. But it still has customers—internal customers who are served by the processes, information, support, and systems that HR provides. These customers Include employees (who are provided by HR with information about company policies, vacation time, taxes, and other personnel matters) and departmental managers (who get help from HR with the processes of employee recruitment, hiring, training, evaluation, promotion, and separation). When an HR department strives to become more customer focused, it makes a deliberate effort to identify the needs of these customers, to develop working methods designed to meet those needs more effectively, and to measure its success through objective tests of customer satisfaction—employee surveys, for example.

In the case of a health insurance company, the HR department has the potential to be customer focused in an even more interesting way. Most company HR departments are in charge of managing employee benefits—including, of course, health insurance. Aetna's HR department was mandated to provide our employees with the same "product" we sold to outside customers. Discussing this fact, Wright and I realized that we had an opportunity to make Aetna's HR department into a laboratory for designing and experimenting with new kinds of health benefits services. With more than one hundred thousand employees of our own, we'd have people to test our ideas on and provide us with feedback. If the new products or services we developed proved valuable, we could make them available to Aetna's external customers for use with their employees.

In effect, we reframed Aetna's HR department as a research and development (R&D) unit for innovative health benefits programs, and it worked remarkably well.

Aetna developed, tested, and refined several health-enhancing projects for employees, including programs designed to encourage exercise, quitting smoking, and other beneficial lifestyle changes. For example, we created Get Active Aetna, a six-week program that engaged employees to form competitive exercise teams, keep track of their daily diet choices, and take small but meaningful steps to burn up more energy in the course of a day—like taking the stairs rather than riding the elevator. We hoped for twenty percent participation, but instead almost fifty percent of employees signed up. Stories began to circulate around the company concerning all the personal health improvements people were enjoying, further stimulating employee enthusiasm. We used our company intranet to share these stories and spur conversations on health and wellness, creating even greater interest in the program.

Later, we packaged a version of Get Active Aetna for sale to our client companies. The leaders of those companies loved it because a healthy workforce is more productive and generates lower healthcare costs; the employees loved it because they felt better, enjoyed life more, and became more happily engaged at work.

Our reframing of Aetna's HR department produced yet another ancillary benefit. Elease Wright herself derived tremendous satisfaction from the program. She developed a whole new side of her career, becoming a pioneer of creative ways to build happier, healthier workplaces. She began giving talks to executives and HR organizations around the country and became a well-known expert in the field.

Reframing is all about uncovering new and exciting possibilities you never imagined before—and that can include personal possibilities as well as new directions for your organization.

TAKEAWAYS FROM CHAPTER 7

- When an organization is struggling, an underlying cause may be misguided assumptions about the nature of the business. The first step toward solving the problem may be reframing it by challenging the false assumption.

- Reframing can suggest an innovative solution to a familiar challenge. Aetna dramatically improved its customer service capabilities by reframing the problem, leading to a new and much more effective solution.

- Reframing can illuminate unexpected opportunities for experimentation and growth by shining a fresh light on neglected resources. Aetna reframed its HR department as an R&D division, turning it into a source of new ways to improve employee benefits programs.

- Whenever your organization is stalled or failing to take full advantage of its potential, ask yourself whether reframing the challenges you face may suggest a solution.

8

The Search for Truth:
Asking Questions That Open Minds

We sometimes assume that the leader in a group is the person who knows the most. It's not always true! Sometimes the most effective leader is one who knows what he doesn't know—and uses well-crafted questions to uncover hidden realities that make innovations possible.

THE ARRIVAL OF A new leadership team, with Bill Donaldson as chairman and Jack Rowe as CEO, did not immediately stem the tide of Aetna's financial and operational troubles. Within months of Rowe's arrival, ten of their top thirteen direct reports left the company. At least one major investor sold his shares, having lost faith in Aetna's ability to recover from its troubles.

Aetna needed to refocus on the basics—to ask everyone in the organization the fundamental, "obvious" questions that the entire leadership team badly needed to reconsider.

A conversation at a meeting of top executives early in my tenure at Aetna captures the dynamic. We asked those gathered around the table to answer a seemingly simple question: Who is our customer?

The first executive replied, "Our customer is the employer who hires us to provide a group insurance policy to his workers. After all, the employer is the one who pays us—so he has to be our customer."

The second disagreed. "Employers pay our premiums, but so do their employees—in fact, the percentage of health insurance costs covered by workers' salaries has been increasing at most companies. So employees who help foot the bill for their own coverage have to be considered Aetna customers."

The third executive offered another response. "Physicians and other health-care providers are our main customers. Without them, there would be no health care, and Aetna wouldn't have any reason to exist. And if doctors and hospitals don't sign up to be members of our networks, our product disappears. So they are important customers for us, no question."

The fourth executive suggested yet another answer. "We're answerable to government regulators, mainly at the state level. Insurance commissioners have to approve everything we do, from the coverages provided by our policies to the rates we charge. Since we have to continually 'sell' our work to the regulators, I think they're our chief customers."

Others around the table chimed in with even more ideas, such as hospital administrators, pharmaceutical companies, medical device manufacturers, and health maintenance organizations.

This cacophony of responses was a testament to the complexity of the health insurance industry. It is indeed a complicated business with many varied stakeholders whose mutual relationships are tangled and sometimes conflicting. But the diversity of answers to our seemingly simple question also helped to explain the business troubles Aetna was experiencing. Given the fact that there was no single clear answer to the question "Who is our customer?" it's not surprising that different people and groups within Aetna were operating at cross-purposes, pursuing goals and serving agendas that produced a confused mishmash of results.

As the conversation continued, the members of Donaldson and Rowe's leadership team gradually realized the nature of the dilemma they faced. Without intending to, they'd allowed Aetna to drift into a situation in which the company lacked a clear, over-arching strategy that united all its varied activities behind a single fundamental purpose.

But we didn't leave the problem there. We cleared away the clutter by asking a second, different question, one designed to drill down to an even more basic level. "It's clear that there's a lot of uncertainty as to who our customer is, but one thing we do agree on is the fact that we're a health insurance company. Is that right?" There were nods around the table.

"So *whose* health are we talking about?"

"The patient's health!" someone blurted out, as if that was obvious—which, of course, it was. And again, everyone nodded.

Here was the solution to our dilemma. We could all agree that our number one customer was the person whose health we were supposed to support—the patient. With "patient health" now understood as the central goal of everything Aetna did, every activity by every division and department could be guided and measured against that goal.

For example, in negotiating over policy details with state regulators, Aetna's compliance managers could shape their goals, priorities, and tactics by the overarching objective of maximizing patient health. In the same way, Aetna managers charged with working with physicians and other health-care providers could focus their efforts on discovering and promoting practices and principles that demonstrably improved patient outcomes.

Suddenly the babel of competing interests could be reduced to relative simplicity, creating the possibility of developing a coherent strategy for the entire organization. It was one of several important first steps in launching the Aetna turnaround—made possible by asking a fundamental question that helped us get back to basics.

Over time, we evolved a more sophisticated view based on the concept that the customer was the center of everything we did. The customer, we decided, could be anyone we served: a patient, a plan sponsor, a benefit broker, a consultant, another Aetna employee. By considering each link in the chain a customer, we were positioned to give everyone in the organization a line of sight to the ultimate customer—the patient. As I'll explain in a later chapter, this became a core element of the company's value statement, the Aetna Way.

By the way, if the major investor who bailed out of Aetna during our darkest days had maintained his holdings, he would have made a billion dollars over the next few years.

FIVE KINDS OF QUESTIONS THAT CAN HELP YOU CHANGE YOUR ORGANIZATION'S REALITY

In crafting an inspiring vision of change, a leader is likely to encounter barriers of many kinds—in particular, mental barriers—those unquestioned assumptions, unexplored options, or unchallenged rules of thumb that keep people stuck at a low level of achievement. Thus, an essential skill for anyone who wants to do the impossible is the ability to ask questions that expose and remove those mental obstacles. The challenge is to frame questions that can provoke people into thinking about the problems they face in a new way—questions that guide people toward recognizing and reexamining the mental barriers that are holding them back—and to ask these questions in a style that doesn't elicit defensiveness, resistance, or fear.

Depending on the context, several kinds of questions can serve this mind-opening function.

Questions that highlight key problems. You may want to use questions that focus the conversation on the existing roadblocks to achievement—for example:

- What are the barriers that are stopping us from achieving our goals?

- Can you help me understand the difficulties that are in our way?

- What methods have we already tried to alleviate the problem, and what specifically happened that caused those efforts to fail?

As you may recall, I used this technique in helping my team at Aetna to understand and overcome the challenges we faced in designing and implementing our new executive management information system—a task that seemed impossible at first but that became manageable through our thoughtful analysis of the problems it posed and through creative questioning of the assumptions that were holding us back.

Questions that clarify the facts. When there is significant uncertainty over the nature of the problems you face, confusion over the facts, or disagreement as to the cause-and-effect processes that are creating your current difficulties, questions that probe the reliability of information can be important—for example:

- This report describes our company's competitive situation—can you explain how it was developed?

- You've indicated that X is the biggest challenge we currently face—can you describe how you reached that conclusion?

- We've been discussing the main kinds of customer complaints we are dealing with—what is the source of the data on which that list of complaints was based?

Questions that probe an underlying story. Asking questions designed to elicit explanatory narratives can illuminate how the current problems of your organization came to be, which can be crucial to understanding their cultural, social, organizational, and psychological roots—for example:

- How was the current system designed?

- What's the story behind this issue?

- Tell me about the decision-making process that was followed when our current strategic plan was developed.

Questions that suggest alternatives. When your team members' thinking seems to have gotten stuck in a rut, questions that raise alternative possibilities can be quite powerful—for example:

- What might be another way of achieving the same goals?

- Can you think of other organizations that have faced similar issues and used different approaches to address them?

- What do you think might happen if we tried X as a first step toward tackling our current problem?

Questions that drill down to basics. When your organization is grappling with problems that go to the heart of its purpose—that is, when you suspect the organization may have fundamentally lost its way—then questions designed to raise basic, existential issues may be in order—for example:

- What is the central goal of our organization?

- What business are we in?

- What is the single most important purpose that we exist to serve?

Chances are good that most of your team members rarely think about these questions, because they're immersed in the everyday activities and challenges that every business faces.

Taking a big step back to gain a fresh perspective can shed a powerful light on what you *should* be doing every day—and asking fundamental questions can be a good way to start the process. We used this technique at Aetna to help refocus the leadership team on the basic nature of our health insurance business—which made possible the strategic reset that the company so desperately needed.

THE POWER OF NOT KNOWING IT ALL

American humorist Will Rogers is supposed to have said, "It isn't what we don't know that gives us trouble, it's what we know that ain't so."

I can vouch for the accuracy of Rogers's observation. In my career, I've rarely experienced any difficulties—or seen others suffer from them—simply because of gaps in knowledge. But you must be willing to acknowledge that those gaps exist and be ready to do what it takes to fill them. If you approach life and work in a spirit of continual questioning and learning, you can eventually find out practically everything you need to know to make the right decisions.

On the other hand, I've seen plenty of situations in which people and organizations got hurt because they believed untruths—and, worse, were so wedded to those illusions that they ignored the evidence that should have alerted and enlightened them.

This illustrates a counterintuitive truth I've mentioned before in this book—the fact that people who don't "fit in" to organizational norms can often enjoy significant advantages as managers, leaders, and strategic thinkers. The team member or manager whose personal or professional story is very different from that of their colleagues can be a source of unusual—and powerful—insights that emerge simply from questioning the assumptions and practices that everyone else takes for granted. The story of Jack Rowe's early days at Aetna offers a great example.

However, you don't have to be a newcomer or an outsider to use the technique of asking offbeat questions to encourage out-of-the-box thinking. Even the leader with significant experience and seniority in an organization can employ it. No one can be equally expert in every area of an organization's work. If you launched your career in the information technology department, you may not be an expert in finance or marketing; if you come out of manufacturing, then human resources or strategic planning may be foreign to you. When you have occasion to connect with colleagues whose specialization differs from your own, take advantage of your relative lack of knowledge to ask questions that an expert might never think to ask: "Forgive my ignorance, but what's the reason you use process X? What would happen if you tried something else? Has anyone ever suggested doing Y or Z instead?" Probing questions like these are sure to increase your understanding of a different aspect of business—and occasionally they may even lead to new insights that both of you can benefit from.

My friend Pat Russo, whose story I've shared in this book, likes to say that one of the secrets to her success in steering Lucent Technologies through some of the toughest business conditions in recent memory is that she gave herself permission to keep learning. "I don't know everything," she says, "and I made sure that the members of my leadership team understood that. So rather than set myself up as the expert with all the answers, I worked on figuring out the right questions to ask. That way, we could take advantage of the knowledge and intelligence of many minds—not just one."

THE ART OF ASKING: SMART WAYS TO LEVERAGE THE POWER OF QUESTIONS

When using questions as an effective leadership tool, it's important to ask them in a way that elicits information, ideas, and shared exploration, rather than defensiveness, resistance, or fear. We've all had the experience of being questioned, particularly by a person higher in the corporate pecking order, in a fashion that feels more like a hostile cross-examination or a third-degree grilling than a friendly exchange of ideas. Some leaders may think that asking questions in this way shows toughness and authority. But I've found it's a sure way to get people to clam up and withdraw their cooperation—which makes it that much tougher to solve the problems your organization may be facing.

Here are some suggestions for positive, constructive questioning that you may find effective.

Avoid starting questions with the word "why." It's often important to get at the underlying reasons for people's behavior. Yet somehow that innocent word *why* has a way of sounding like an accusation. The question "Why did you do X?" seems to inevitably convey the implication that X was a stupid thing to do. I've found that I can elicit a less defensive, more forthcoming response to the same fundamental question by using a phrase like "what is the reason"—for example, "What is the reason you tackled the problem that way?" This wording assumes that there *was* a reason for the person's behavior and encourages them to share freely . . . and that's far more likely to enable you both to get to the heart of the problem more quickly.

Avoid yes-or-no questions. These often evoke one-word responses, especially when you're talking to someone who is nervous or intimidated (which is often the case when you happen to be the boss). Instead, try to phrase your questions so that they are open-ended and therefore more likely to elicit substantial information. Instead of asking, "Did you know the client had threatened to sue us when you turned down his request?" you might say, "What did you know about the client's attitude at the time you turned down his request?" or even, "Tell me what was happening when you turned down the client's request." These broadly worded questions give you a good chance of getting the whole story rather than just one or two details—or, even worse, a mere confirmation of what you already believe.

Don't ask questions for which you think you already know the answer. The goal of asking questions is to garner information and to inspire creative thinking—not to quiz people, put them on the spot, or trap them. If your team members stop believing that your inquiries are an honest attempt to learn more, they will soon find ways to avoid participating.

Actively listen to the answers people give you. Don't be dismissive or scornful of the answers, even if you consider them misguided. Even answers that are factually incorrect are valuable in that they give you greater insight into the way a team member thinks and feels—and if one person thinks and feels that way, the chances are good that others do too. Use "wrong" answers as an opportunity to introduce alternative ideas: "I understand what you're saying. Here's another way of thinking about it that I've found helpful . . . What do you think about this concept?"

Ask follow-up questions. In many cases, the answer to one question merely points in the direction of the truth without delving deeply into it. One, two, or several follow-up questions may be needed to elicit a full picture of what is happening, and to open up the possibility of change.

Sakichi Toyoda, the Japanese inventor and founder of Toyota Industries, championed the use of follow-up questions as the basis of a management technique he called the Five Whys. The idea is to ask *why* repeatedly when seeking the cause of a problem. The answer to each question leads to another *why*, until the ultimate root cause is uncovered and can be acted on. (The *why* wording can work well in organizations where people have been explicitly trained in so-called lean management methods, which often use *why* questions. In other cases, as I noted previously, I prefer to rephrase these questions using words other than *why*.)

Encourage others to ask questions, including ones that are "stupid" or "naïve." As the old saying has it, the only stupid question is one you don't ask—and quite often the question whose answer seems obvious or not worth discussing opens up a topic that has been ignored or taken for granted but deserves exploration. So treat every question directed to you with respect and patience, even if you are unsure why it's being asked.

Use questions to ensure that your team members are all on the same page. I developed the habit of concluding every meeting with a few minutes dedicated to asking questions with this purpose. I would ask each attendee, "Do we all know what we're supposed to do next to keep this project moving forward and to tackle the problems we face? Is there any detail that anyone is unclear about? Are there any questions we need to ask that we've forgotten to raise? And is there any resource or support you need from one of your colleagues?" Questions like these help the group to anticipate any significant roadblocks to progress that they're likely to encounter in the weeks to come—and reduce the likelihood that, at the next meeting, someone will say, "I know I agreed to work on that task, but I couldn't do it because I didn't have access to the right data" (or "the team from marketing" or "the software support").

Not everyone will use the opportunity you provide to ask questions; some will fear that doing so will make them look foolish or uninformed. So be careful how you respond to the questions *you do* get. If you take every question seriously and respond to it thoughtfully, over time, more people will be willing to take advantage of the chance to reveal their problems and concerns, making long-term success for the whole team far more likely.

When problems arise, question the issue, not the person. This is a mantra I introduced at Aetna as a way of encouraging everyone to focus on the right things during strategy or problem-solving sessions. Leadership is about helping people achieve great things together—and we can't make that happen if we expend energy on tearing one another down. When you are tempted to personalize a discussion by making a teammate, colleagues, or competitor the focus, rethink your approach. Focus on the issue at hand so everyone can contribute to fixing it.

Yes, this means that you will often have to stop and think hard before blurting out a comment during a meeting. When the remarks (and the accusations) are flying fast and furious, it can be hard to remember to do this. But it's an important practice for anyone who aspires to true leadership.

When you are considering saying something like, "The problem is that Gary hasn't trained the new people in the customer service department in how to use the database correctly!" stop and reframe your comment to focus on the issue instead, saying something like, "It seems that when calls are fielded by the newest members of the customer service department, the necessary information from the database isn't being used—is that right?" Posing the observation this way makes it much easier for Gary to respond honestly, and it reduces the likelihood that the meeting will devolve into verbal warfare, with the group dividing into pro-Gary and anti-Gary teams. Instead, everyone can work cooperatively to define the problem accurately and develop a practical solution—which may indeed require Gary to improve his training techniques.

When tough questions are needed, use them with care. I don't mean to imply that tough questioning is always out of bounds.

Sometimes it's essential—particularly when self-interest or bias may be distorting people's perceptions.

Along with other leaders in the world of health care, Aetna has been trying to advance the cause of evidence-based medicine in its work with care providers. That means insisting on facts to back up assertions regarding the best ways to treat patients. Jack Rowe offers this example of the kinds of pointed questions that Aetna claims experts sometimes have to employ with physicians: "You've said that this patient needs an MRI"—an expensive imaging test—"at least once every three weeks to track the progress of his condition. Can you explain your evidence for the value of this procedure? Do you have any data to back up your belief, or is it simply your medical judgment?"

Questions like these may make some doctors uncomfortable. But they are necessary as tools in the battle to reduce needless health-care procedures and excessive costs—especially, I might note, when some doctors share in the ownership of the imaging centers that administer the MRI tests—and in their profits. These kinds of questions, however, should be couched as efforts to clarify the underlying issues, not as personal attacks. And, of course, if the evidence tells us that an MRI every three weeks is medically necessary and leads to better outcomes, then it should be covered under the patient's insurance plan.

In the hands of a skilled leader, questions can be remarkably powerful tools for stimulating insight, understanding, and creativity. Just be sure to wield them carefully so they remain useful tools rather than turning into needlessly aggressive weapons. Asking the tough questions in the *right* way can help to ensure that the facts are revealed, making it possible for the appropriate decision to be reached.

TAKEAWAYS FROM CHAPTER 8

- When a company is troubled, one great way to tackle the problem is to ask questions that force people to get back to basics. Asking the question, "Who is our customer?" was a turning point in refocusing Aetna on the core of its insurance business.

- Five kinds of questions can help unlock frozen thinking: *questions that highlight key problems, questions that clarify the facts, questions that probe an underlying story, questions that suggest alternatives,* and *questions that drill down to basics.*

- Practice the art of asking good questions. Master strategies such as avoiding the word *why,* which often makes people feel defensive; avoiding yes-or-no questions, which tend to short-circuit discussions; asking follow-up questions to delve more deeply into core realities; encouraging your team members to ask questions; and using questions after a plan has been formulated to ensure that everyone is on the same page.

- When problems arise, question the issue, not the person. This minimizes the emotional impact of the question and encourages everyone to contribute to discovering a solution.

9

Define What's Really Important—
Then Make It Happen

We all fall into the trap of spending time, energy, and other resources on activities that don't really matter, while neglecting the things that do. Here's a system for figuring out what's truly important for your organization (rather than what's merely urgent), then making sure it gets taken care of—on time and within budget.

IN TODAY'S BUSINESS WORLD, internal and external pressures often seem unrelenting and ever increasing. We're all being asked to do more every year—often with fewer resources. In this kind of environment, one of the most crucial tasks of the leader is to help her team members set priorities and stay focused on the tasks that are most important.

It sounds simple—but, in practice, it's quite difficult to do.

The anxiety and fear that accompany life in a struggling organization make it harder for leaders to define what's most important in a way that is both accurate and effective. When you are receiving a steady bombardment of bad news—negative financial reports, customer or client complaints, key employee defections—it's easy to start responding in knee-jerk fashion to the latest bulletin rather than taking the time to sort out what's truly important from the merely urgent.

In many cases, the truly important—the issue or problem that will have the greatest long-term impact on your organization—arrives unaccompanied by any obvious warning signals. For example, a gradual deterioration in the quality of your customer service or the arrival of new competitors with products that outperform yours may register as merely a subtle blip on your data screen. By the time these problems are serious enough to produce a noticeable impact on your revenues or profits, it may be almost too late to solve them.

DEFINING IMPORTANCE: HOW TO FIGURE OUT WHAT *REALLY* MATTERS

It's not easy for a leader to figure out, on a daily basis, how to separate the challenges that are important from those that are merely urgent. Here are some questions you can ask that can help you determine whether an issue is truly important or simply eye-catching:

- **Financial impact:** If this issue were left unaddressed, how could it affect the finances of our organization over the next week? Over the next month? Over the next six months? Over the next five years?

- **Stakeholder impact:** How directly and significantly is this issue likely to affect our organization's key stakeholders, including customers, employees, investors, suppliers, business partners, and community members?

- **Future scope:** How probable is it that this issue will become more serious or widespread? How quickly is this likely to happen?

- **Reputational impact:** What is the likely impact of this issue on the reputation of our organization?

- **Underlying cause:** How likely is it that this issue is caused by underlying problems that are not yet presenting themselves directly? Is addressing this issue likely to help us uncover and begin to deal with those underlying problems?

- **Degree of uncertainty:** What is the degree of uncertainty regarding our knowledge of this issue? How confident are we that we understand the nature and the scope of the issue?

The answers to these questions can help you gauge the real importance of the issue before you.

Note that even though an issue may not be considered "truly important" as defined here, that doesn't mean you can necessarily ignore it. Every organization has challenges that *must* be addressed for various reasons, even if, in the grand scheme of things, they are fundamentally minor. When you are dealing with such a problem, your goal should be to handle it as quickly and efficiently as possible while investing the smallest amount of resources.

For example, an embarrassing incident involving a single customer—even if it sheds a negative light on your organization—is likely to register fairly low on the importance scale. But you still need to address it. This kind of "merely urgent" problem should be dealt with as swiftly and efficiently as possible. Depending on the nature of the incident, you might want to assign one competent customer service expert to handle it, giving them carte blanche to take any reasonable steps to satisfy the customer and defuse the potential embarrassment.

On the other hand, the discovery of a product defect that seems to have resulted from a flawed process in your manufacturing facility might affect thousands or millions of customers—perhaps with a devastating impact on your company's reputation and on its bottom line. This issue would qualify as important by any standard. It may take significant resources to determine the nature and scope of the problem and implement a solution. Team members from several departments, such as production, customer service, public relations, and legal service, may need to be involved.

When an organization is fundamentally well run, serious unexpected problems shouldn't keep arising. Instead, the most important issues you face should be ones that are somewhat predictable—for example, the need to continually rethink your strategy in light of evolving market conditions or the need to adjust your recruitment and training strategies based on changing workforce demographics.

If serious emergencies requiring "all hands on deck" seem to crop up every few days, this is probably a sign of important underlying leadership problems that you need to address. Take the time to figure out how and why you are missing the early warning signals that ought to alert you to systemic weaknesses, and make whatever changes are necessary to remedy the problem.

THE NEGLECTED ART OF SMART PROJECT PLANNING

A common mistake that we make is to equate importance with the need to engage in what I call "unnatural acts." Some leaders routinely respond to important problems by asking team members to perform heroic feats of exhausting, frantic work.

Occasionally, there's no way to avoid such drastic measures. But they can exact a high price in terms of focus and morale—particularly when they are made necessary by mismanagement or poor planning, or when they become habitual rather than rare. It's far better if you can avoid crisis mode through smart, deliberate planning. The existence of important problems shouldn't force your team to conduct fire drills. Instead, it should spur them to thoughtfully determine the minimum amount of time and resources necessary to complete the job, analyzing what the work *really* requires, and assigning the appropriate amount of time and resources to accomplishing it—no more, no less.

Smart planning requires paying attention to the process rather than rushing through it. When scheduling a complex project, you should start by breaking it down into its component parts. List them in the order in which they need to be done. The parts of the project now become steps in a process that you and your colleagues will be carrying out.

You then should list the resources your team needs to perform each step. Be sure to note which resources will require help from other people or organizations—for example, step three may not be possible until you get data from the production team in your company's overseas manufacturing plant. In other cases, you may require support from IT, marketing, or finance, which means these departments also have to allocate resources and plan to support you. Requirements like these can cause delays; anticipating them makes it easier to prevent them from becoming bottlenecks (for example, by sending a request for the data a week or two earlier than it's needed).

For each step, you should estimate the time required, taking into account other demands on the people involved. If several steps appear to be especially lengthy, look for ways to streamline them. Can additional people be brought in to help speed up those steps? Can any part of the work be outsourced? Can similar work done for a different project be adopted to this purpose?

Finally, you should define the results to be achieved in each step as clearly and specifically as possible, along with communication methods to be used to keep the whole team informed about what is happening. Your plan should make it abundantly clear when Step 5 will be finished, thereby triggering work on Step 6 without needless delay.

Instead of following this methodical approach, many organizations treat planning as a rote, unreflective process. Ask someone how long they will need to produce a report on Project X, and the chances are good they'll take only a few seconds to reply, "Oh, two weeks should do it." The reality is that the report might truly be a one-week project or a three-week project.

Making matters worse, many people follow the rule of thumb, "When in doubt about how long something will take, always err on the side of longer." Their goal is to create a buffer and place less performance pressure on themselves. This approach is also, in part, an outgrowth of the well-intentioned principle of customer service, "Always under promise and over deliver." The idea is that, if you promise the job in two weeks and then deliver it in ten days, you'll look like a hero—whereas if you promise the job in one week and deliver it in ten days, you'll look like a failure.

The result is the common phenomenon of *schedule bloat*—a multipart project that should take three months turns into a six- or eight-month job simply because a series of individual contributors have each overestimated the time needed to complete their portion of the work. And since human nature dictates that at least some of those contributors will turn in their work late, the *actual* working time is likely to end up being closer to a year. By the time the job is done, any sense of its importance will have long since dissipated; in many cases, the project's usefulness may have even disappeared.

The habit of overestimating the time needed for a task consumes organizational resources and blocks other activities that could be done, because, if everything is over-budgeted by a hundred percent, you reduce the capacity of the system by fifty percent. The only solution is to teach your team to take the planning process seriously, which means that the actual steps required to complete a task are thought through, defined, and assigned a realistic time frame in a purposeful, planned way.

Smart planning is easier said than done. In some organizations, people are so constantly buffeted with interruptions that the temptation to overestimate the time required for a task becomes even greater. A friend of mine recalls working for a company like this:

> Suppose I had a plan to get Project A done this week. More often than not, my boss would call me up on Wednesday morning and say, "Drop whatever you're doing. I need a report on Project B by tomorrow morning." Suddenly my best-laid plans would be out the window. When that happens repeatedly, you get into a mode where you schedule tasks defensively. Presented with a one-week task, you say, "Well, it's going to take two weeks or even three weeks, because I know I'm going to be interrupted six times."

The problem is a genuine one—another reflection of the common confusion between urgency and importance. The solution requires increased transparency and communication. The boss who has cavalierly ordered an employee to drop his work on Project A needs to be brought into the loop. What's the completion date for Project A and how was it determined? What's a higher priority for the organization as a whole—Project A or the report on Project B that your boss is requesting? When something has to give, as is so often the case, the sequencing needs to be determined based on the needs of the company rather than the arbitrary preference of one manager. This kind of problem is especially prevalent in large corporations that use the so-called "matrix management" system, in which one person may have two or more bosses.

In addition, it's important to be clear about your own intentions and purpose. Why do you need the report on Project B? Has your boss requested a brief update on the project for an upcoming meeting? If so, a fifteen-page report requiring a day's work is probably unnecessary; perhaps a two-paragraph summary that takes fifteen minutes to write would suffice. Anyone who has worked in corporate America will agree that misunderstandings like this occur surprisingly often, simply because people don't take the time to ask appropriately probing questions.

Finally, when there is a genuine conflict between two or more scheduled tasks, a conversation about priorities may be needed. The *materiality* of a given project may be quite different from what surface appearances suggest. In other words, what strikes one person as crucial may, with a bit of broader perspective, be fairly unimportant and therefore can be handled with scheduling flexibility.

I learned this lesson while attending an audit committee meeting with one of our executives at Aetna. While reviewing a problem that had arisen, maybe due to an accounting error or a mistake by a manager, one of the committee members asked the executive, "Is this problem material?"

The executive replied, "I should say so—the mistake cost us two million dollars!"

The committee members exchanged glances, and then the chair responded, "Actually, that's not what we consider material. We're running a thirty-five-billion-dollar company here. So two million dollars is less than one hundredth of one percent."

You can see the source of the misunderstanding: Two million dollars was material to that executive—it would certainly be a lot of money out of anyone's pocket, and it probably made a noticeable dent in his department's budget. But while it was a reasonable cause for concern, it wasn't material to the enterprise as a whole.

The lesson is clear: Defining the importance of any issue includes understanding the whole context in which you're operating. If you're a midlevel manager, make sure you are setting priorities in a way that makes sense for the whole organization, not only for your little corner of it. If you do this, you will be able to organize your own work plans and those of your team in such a way that the truly important projects—those that will have the greatest impact on the success of your entire company—will get the attention and resources they deserve.

DEFENDING THE PLAN: THE ACTION-FORCING EVENT

Once you've developed a realistic plan that is driven by your organization's true priorities, you face the challenge of getting people to stick to the schedule. Somehow you need to ensure that the sense of importance that guided the conversation when you were planning the project remains in place during the days, weeks, or months it takes for the project to come to fruition.

One powerful tool for defending the plan is the *action-forcing event*. I've used this concept to help hundreds of projects with multiple participants stay on track and on time. The action-forcing event is a bit like a deadline. The major difference is that an action-forcing event involves a deliverable outcome—a concrete, specifically defined work product—whose timing is carefully and thoughtfully planned based on an analysis of the prior step. By contrast, most deadlines are set arbitrarily and with minimal thought, which is why they tend to be missed.

Suppose one of the action-forcing events in your project plan is the completion of an employee survey to determine the three most important functions that a proposed new internal company website should carry out. You could establish a date for this event by just plucking it from the air—but that's a recipe for disappointment and delay. Instead, you need to work with the people who will be performing the required tasks to define *precisely* what needs to happen and how long each step will realistically take. In this case, the necessary steps might include the following:

- **Step 1:** Drafting the survey questions—3 working days

- **Step 2:** Having the survey content and format vetted and revised by experts in the HR department—3 days

- **Step 3:** Making a list of employees and departments to be included in the survey and having the list okayed by the project director—3 days (simultaneous with Step 2)

- **Step 4:** Disseminating the survey to employees via email—1 day

- **Step 5:** Allowing time for employees to respond to survey; gathering and tabulating results—5 days

- **Step 6:** Analyzing the results and writing a two-page report summarizing the key findings—3 days

The action-forcing event can only occur after all six steps have been completed. Since the time required for the steps totals fifteen working days, you can safely schedule the action-forcing event for three weeks from the starting date (assuming a standard work week of five days).

The number and kind of action-forcing events you should build into your project plan depend on the nature and complexity of the project. A huge project involving contributions from dozens or scores of people over six months or more may require ten to twenty action-forcing events, each carefully defined and assigned a particular target date. A smaller, simpler project may require only two or three action-forcing events. In both cases, the action-forcing events serve as milestones, driving the work schedule and triggering alarm bells whenever one or more events are missed.

As you can see, action-forcing events not only help to alert you when the project plan may be slipping, but they also focus the attention of everyone participating in the project, since a looming action-forcing event (together with the agreed-on list of preliminary steps needed to make the event possible) creates a real-time milestone that the entire project team should be watching.

If you do it correctly, defining one or more action-forcing events for any important project and using them to keep track of your progress is a simple yet startlingly effective way to help your team members make commitments they can really honor, which in turn can enable them to consistently achieve the key milestones that define success.

WHEN LIFE HAPPENS: GETTING BACK ON THE GLIDE PATH

There's an old saying, attributed to a variety of sources as far back as the 1950s, that says, "Life is what happens to you while you're busy making other plans." We all know that in life—and in business—unexpected events inevitably arise that can make it challenging to stick to a schedule, no matter how thoughtfully designed and well monitored it may be.

Sometimes, encounters with the unexpected can reveal opportunities. Members of your team may discover that a seven-step process you've carefully designed to complete a particular part of the project may be more complicated than needed. Maybe circumstances have changed so that three of the steps are now redundant or unnecessary. If so, that's great! Make sure everyone on your team understands that the process is there to serve them—not the other way around. If there's an opportunity to change the process so that it saves people time, energy, and other resources, they should speak up so the change gets made, rather than simply accepting the process as if it's carved in stone.

In most cases, however, a deviation from the plan usually reflects not an opportunity but a problem—a deadline missed, a task forgotten, a message unsent. Having a defined sequence of action-forcing events can make it easier for the team to quickly get back on the glide path to success when the project gets derailed by an unexpected occurrence. In fact, the whole point of building a detailed project plan is precisely because you *know* it's unlikely that the future will unfold precisely the way you've planned it. Having a plan enables you to (a) recognize when events differ from the plan, (b) measure the direction and the magnitude of the variance, and (c) plan and carry out corrective actions.

During the weeks or months the project is unfolding, the steering team should be meeting regularly, in person or electronically, to review the plan and to compare it to what is really happening. Each meeting should revolve around the same set of crucial questions:

- Are we on track to deliver the work product in accordance with the plan?

- Will we be on schedule when the next action-forcing event occurs?

- If the answer to either of these questions is no, what are the barriers and issues that we've run into?

- What do we need to do to get back on the glide path? How can we make up any time lost so that we will be on schedule when the subsequent action-forcing event occurs?

People in organizations tend to be impatient. Everyone is busy, everyone has too much to do, and everyone is eager to "finish up this meeting so we can get back to doing our *real* work!" But for leaders, working the process to refine and improve the plan *is* in fact our real work—or at least a crucial piece of it. So resist the temptation to make your steering committee meetings short and superficial. Ensure you hear from the people who are actually working on the next steps in the project. Get concrete information from them as to their progress and any issues they are facing. Yes, it will take time; yes, it may get complicated. But unless you get down into the weeds and analyze what is truly happening, you are likely to be blindsided at some point by a serious problem that may derail the project completely.

I've found that, in most organizations, the biggest challenge of project management is getting people to communicate openly about problems—to share bad news quickly, honestly, and early. It helps enormously if you consciously foster a culture in which blaming is discouraged, and in which the focus is always on the goal and what it will take to achieve it.

Once problems are revealed, you will need to work to solve them. As we saw in an earlier chapter, open discussion and probing questions will be your most vital tools. If you've found that Step 3 in your process isn't possible as originally defined, start asking questions: What's the obstacle to completing the step? Can the obstacle be removed? Is it possible to work around the obstacle in some way? What would happen if we omitted Step 3? Can we still achieve the next action-forcing event without it? Is there a compromise step we can devise to accomplish most of what we need? What would be the implications of such a compromise?

Don't ignore deviations from your plan or silently accept delays as an inevitable aspect of business life. Force issues to the forefront of your steering meetings, and don't settle for half answers. You and your team should make a commitment *not* to leave the meeting until you've answered these questions and developed a plan for getting back on the glide path.

Defining what's truly important, thoughtfully calculating the time and resources needed to complete essential tasks, establishing a schedule of action-forcing events to keep a project on track, and using frequent meetings to monitor the project and get back on the glide path as needed—this process is no simple matter. But mastering the process and imparting it to your team members is crucial to the success of any leader—particularly in today's high-pressure business world, in which virtually every important goal needs to be completed "yesterday, if not sooner."

COMMUNICATING SERIOUSNESS IN TIMES OF CRISIS: FAREWELL TO "AETNA NICE"

When circumstances are dire, the importance of clear and constant communication is greater than ever. A leader who sends daily messages about what is happening and what needs to be done reinforces the feeling of seriousness and commitment throughout the organization.

I've already described several high intensity programs that we launched after my arrival at Aetna to begin turning around the company's dire financial situation. When a company's entire top leadership team is gathering for intensive work sessions with the CEO or president in "the Bunker" every Saturday (as well as most Sundays!), that makes it difficult for other employees to ignore the fact that the business is facing some serious problems.

And the message *must* begin with the leadership team. If they don't behave as if the boat is on fire, no one else will believe it. Fortunately for me, and for Aetna, my team members got it—and their response helped send a clear signal to everyone else in the company. That's a big part of how our turnaround happened.

Smaller symbolic gestures can also be important, right down to the language you use and the tone of your conversations. One of our problems was the phenomenon of "Aetna nice"—a culture of polite conflict-avoidance and problem burying that had built up at the company over many decades. Being nice can be pleasant, but in times of crisis, it can also be deadly, because it means that honest discussion of problems and what it will take to fix them never happens.

One of the things I did during my early months at Aetna was to deliberately challenge the culture of Aetna nice. During meetings, I had my antenna up for symptoms of Aetna nice. These included behaviors like quietly ignoring factual errors or omissions in reports; changing the subject when conflicts arose that didn't lead to quick, painless resolutions; refusing to probe the reasons behind internal failures such as missed deadlines or flawed procedures; and being unwilling to address or even acknowledge conflicts between groups or departments, even when these conflicts led to systemic breakdowns.

When one of these symptoms appeared, I didn't raise my voice, bang on the table, or level any accusations. But I did make a point of intervening in the conversation and forcing the crucial, hidden issue into the light of day. I might say something like, "I think we're ignoring an important problem here," or "It looks as though we have a discrepancy here that we'd better tackle rather than leaving it for another day."

If I received pushback—and in the early days, it happened more than once—I might have to get a little more forceful: "You know, we're facing a financial crisis here. We don't have a lot of time to skirt or ignore important issues. We need to fix this company, and we need to fix it *now*. So let's get started. Okay?"

I didn't have to make statements like that very often before the word got around: *The days of Aetna nice are over. It's time to get down to business.* And soon, everybody did.

Over time, I developed other ways of using language to challenge the culture of nice and send signals that we had a serious need to up our level of performance. For example, in a meeting, after hearing a manager's report that fell short of what we needed—it was vague and incomplete, and failed to address a key problem—I broke the company habit of offering an empty compliment or a meaningless line like "thanks for the effort." Instead, I came up with a shorthand phrase that conveyed the right message very clearly: "That report is a very good *down payment*, John." Translation: "You've given us half of what we need. Now go back to your desk and get us the other half—because we can't move forward until the whole payment is provided." And I would generally include the question, "What help do you need from others to deliver the balance of your commitment?"

Don't get me wrong, I don't have anything against people being nice, but companies don't run on nice. I'm proud of the fact that many of the folks I worked with at Aetna came to me after a few months or years and said "You know, Ron, I like the way we've changed our culture. Aetna has gone from being a nice place to work to being a *great* place to work!"

That's what instilling an appropriate sense of commitment can do for an organization.

GETTING DOWN IN THE TRENCHES

Another way a leader can convey an issue's importance is by their presence and involvement in particular projects or problems. There's nothing like "rolling up your sleeves" and getting hands-on to tell the people on your team that "this is a big deal—and we're going to do it now and do it right."

Of course, to make this strategy work, you need to be very good at what you do. The legendary David Ogilvy, who founded the great advertising agency Ogilvy & Mather back in the *Mad Men* era of the 1960s, said that he learned about leadership from Monsieur Pitard, the head chef at the Hotel Majestic in Paris, where Ogilvy worked as a young man. Pitard used the hands-on technique to elicit the greatest effort from his team members. Ogilvy recalls:

> To begin with, he was the best cook in the whole brigade, and we knew it. He had to spend most of his time at his desk, planning menus, scrutinizing bills, and ordering supplies, but

once a week he would emerge from his glass-walled office in the middle of the kitchen and actually *cook* something. A crowd of us always gathered around to watch, spellbound by his virtuosity. It was inspiring to work for a supreme master.[1]

I would never claim to be "a supreme master" of anything. But I think I am a pretty good hands-on systems analyst and problem-solver. I've used that talent periodically as a way of signaling to my team members when an issue needs to be dealt with in a more serious, high-intensity fashion. Joe Zubretsky, a senior executive who worked with me at Aetna and today is the CEO and president of Molina Healthcare, has referred to me as a "player-coach"—someone who can offer advice and guidance from the sidelines but who is capable of jumping into the game when necessary. If a high-priority project wasn't coming together quickly enough, I might visit the manager in charge, call his team together, and spend a couple of hours in the trenches with them, asking questions and forcing the action: "What seems to be blocking your progress? Have you done an analysis of the underlying problem? Have you asked your colleagues in the next department for assistance? Have you looked at how other companies have tackled the same issue?"

In many cases, a session like that has been enough to break the logjam and get the process moving forward once again. If nothing else, the presence of "the big boss" in the department, taking a personal interest in the project, sends a strong signal to everyone involved that this is an *important* job that we'd better get done right—and soon.

---

1   David Ogilvy, *Confessions of an Advertising Man*, rev.ed. (New York: Atheneum, 1988), 7.

Zubretsky divulged another reason this hands-on leadership technique is so effective. As a leader, it can be unnerving when "the big boss" appears in your shop. No leader likes to be upstaged in front of their own people! As Zubretsky confessed, "Whenever you used to pull that one on me, Ron, I always said to myself, 'If I want to get Ron Williams out of my hair, I'd better figure this problem out myself, and do it quickly!'"

That's exactly the response I was aiming for.

TAKEAWAYS FROM CHAPTER 9

- To help determine which problems are truly important (rather than merely urgent), use this checklist of six issues: financial impact, stakeholder impact, future scope, reputational impact, underlying cause, and degree of uncertainty.

- Once you've determined that a particular issue is important, develop a plan for addressing it. Make the plan as detailed as necessary to ensure each step is completed accurately and on time.

- To keep your project plan on track, identify several action-forcing events—deliverable outcomes, precisely timed, that will trigger the next steps in the plan.

- When an important project is underway, schedule regular meetings to monitor progress, to ensure that action-forcing events are taking place, and if slippage occurs, to quickly identify the steps needed to get the project back on its glide path to completion.

continued

- As a team leader, learn to use all of your abilities—including your communication skills and the power of personal example—to instill and foster the sense of commitment your team members need to make timely achievements possible.

10

Winning the Talent Hunt:
How to Build Your Team

One way to define leadership is the art of achieving things through other people. To make that possible, you have to learn how to recruit, train, and motivate the most talented working team possible. Here are some ideas about how to make it happen.

ONE OF THE MOST crucial challenges you'll face as a leader is the development of an empowered, highly motivated team—a team that is capable of achieving extraordinary things even in the most challenging circumstances. To create such a team, the leader must always remember that the people he works with are *even more important* than the job or the organization and its problems, and behave accordingly.

Several basic skills are involved in building your team of miracle workers. These include learning how to set expectations rather than simply issuing demands, being able to accurately read and describe reality rather than being imprisoned by false assumptions, and putting people first rather than killing their zeal through indifference, as many would-be leaders do. These fundamental leadership techniques add up to what I call *people-centered leadership.* Applying them can help to transform a seemingly modest collection of talent into a team of world beaters.

Of course, a fundamental element in building your team is recruiting and hiring the right people in the first place. Doing that isn't quite as simple as many leaders appear to assume.

THE VALUE OF INCLUSION: IT'S NOT JUST ABOUT DEMOGRAPHICS

A leader should recruit a team that complements the leader's own strengths—and compensates for any weaknesses—rather than simply mirroring the leader's personality. Especially in times of stress and turmoil, the smart leader recognizes the power of attracting team members whose unique perspectives may offer fresh problem-solving approaches that the organization desperately needs.

For this reason, some of the most common ways of thinking about the recruiting and hiring process are dangerous, even potentially fatal, to the effort to build a powerful team.

For example, many hiring managers and human resources professionals talk about "cultural fit" as an important element in selecting new employees. In one sense, this is correct: You want to have a clear sense of the values that your organization seeks to embody, and you want to attract people who generally share those values and will be proud to help you uphold them. Thus, at Aetna, we tried to hire people who truly cared about the health-care needs of ordinary individuals and would always aspire to making sure that our customers and clients would be treated with respect and consideration.

But all too often, leaders use the word "fit" to describe people who are culturally and personally similar to an organization's current employees—the kinds of people they are accustomed to working with and whom they might enjoy hanging out with in the company cafeteria or on off-site retreats. This in turn tends to morph into a search for people who come from the same background as the leaders—who grew up in the same kind of neighborhood, went to the same kind of college, studied the same kinds of subjects, and have the same kinds of personal tastes and interests. When they find a job candidate who gives them this kind of warm-and-fuzzy feeling, they say, "He really looks as though he'll fit in here!" or "I can definitely see her becoming a part of our team!"

Conversely, people involved in the hiring process often use vague observations like "I'm not sure he fits in to this department" or "I don't think she's ready for the assignment" as a way of vetoing a particular candidate. I don't believe in blocking an opportunity for an otherwise well-qualified candidate based on such data-free comments. I think a leader should challenge remarks of this sort by asking probing questions: What *exactly* do you mean? In what specific way is he unready? What particular skills do you think are missing? Can you give me an example of what you are saying? These sorts of questions gently force people to "get real" about the hiring process rather than falling back on empty assertions about "fit" that often amount to nothing more than "I kinda like her! Let's hire her."

More important, the search for "fit" can hurt your quest to build the most powerful, effective team. In practice, it often means avoiding people with new perspectives, ideas, approaches, and personal styles—which can be a big mistake. Hiring people who are in the same mold as everyone else in the organization strongly reduces the odds of getting the kind of innovative, out-of-the-box thinking that makes reframing possible. In an age when change and adaptation are among the chief imperatives for every organization, choosing people in a way that reinforces the path of least resistance is a recipe for long-term decline.

Instead, I suggest you make a deliberate effort to choose people who are *different* from those you already employ. This is about much more than just demographic diversity. Yes, it's valuable to build a workforce that includes people of differing ethnic, racial, religious, and class backgrounds, as well as people of different genders and of varying sexual orientations. The best way to understand the needs and values of customers from every background is to have employees from every background who speak their language and understand their experiences. But the deepest value of diversity is derived from cultural and intellectual inclusion, not just demographic variation. When employees with a wide range of different sensibilities offer fresh perspectives on the organization and its mission, it helps you tap new sources of knowledge and creativity that will enable your organization to thrive and grow.

When you approach the recruiting challenge with this in mind, you avoid the trap of hiring too many people in your own image. Instead, you open your doors to the broadest possible candidate pool, and you develop the ability to recognize and appreciate talent no matter where you find it or what it may look like on the surface.

In many cases, the most effective leadership teams involve "odd couple" combinations of individuals who seem, at first glance, wildly different, even incompatible—but who have complementary skills that, taken together, provide exactly what the organization needs to succeed.

At Aetna, Jack Rowe and I formed such a team. When the head-hunter for Aetna originally called Rowe to ask if he would be interested in joining the company, he was incredulous. "Are you kidding? I'm *suing* Aetna!" he replied. That was more or less true. One symptom of the problems Aetna was having with its physician stakeholders was several lawsuits against the company, one of which had been brought by Mount Sinai, where Rowe was president. Recognizing the seriousness of this issue, Aetna was determined to fix it, which was why they were recruiting their "enemy," not only to join but to lead the Aetna team.

Rowe knew the world of medicine inside and out. But he knew little about insurance and had never studied management, although his role with Mount Sinai called for considerable leadership and organizational skills. When he agreed to take on the chairmanship of Aetna, Rowe knew he needed to complement his own talents with a second-in-command whose aptitudes and knowledge were drastically different from his own. Rowe recalls:

> I needed someone who understood everything about the nuts and bolts of health insurance—someone capable of taking the engine apart, spreading out all 250 parts on the floor of the garage, and putting it back together better than before. And then, when the key was inserted and turned, we needed to be sure the engine would start! So we started searching for that kind of guy—a person who understood the atomic structure of insurance right down to individual products and the markets they served. I could help formulate a top-down vision for our industry. But I couldn't make it real without the help of a bottom-up guy.

Rowe and I became a highly effective team. I could take the broad ideas we developed, translate them into practical, concrete steps, and then show people how to implement them. I had the patience and fortitude needed to stick with the task until all the thousands of tiny administrative, organizational, and systemic pieces were fitting together and operating smoothly. Our complementary strengths and our mutual respect enabled us to effectively guide the company's turnaround.

Working with Rowe reinforced my appreciation for pursuing inclusion in hiring—not by checking off demographic traits on a list, but by recruiting people who differ from you rather than people you are "comfortable with." When you cast a wider talent net, you're likely to hire people with a less traditional image—in terms of gender, race, ethnicity, age, and other characteristics—but more important, they will bring varied backgrounds, perspectives, insights, and gifts to the challenges you face. The result: fresher ideas, greater creativity, and a higher rate of successful innovation.

With this kind of inclusion in mind, as president and CEO of Aetna, I consciously recruited and promoted team members who were nontraditional. Even before I joined Aetna, the company had many successful female managers, and I maintained and expanded this emphasis. I also looked for smart, talented people with unusual business backgrounds and then tried slotting them into assignments that would give them a chance to grow in new ways. For example, I took Kim Keck out of Aetna's finance department and gave her the job as my chief of staff. She had to take a crash course in the entire structure of our corporation, which she knew little about before. But working with me, she quickly got up to speed and used her people skills, her communication talents, and her leadership instincts to become an amazingly effective right-hand person for me. As I've mentioned, Keck has since gone on to become a CEO in her own right.

DEMOGRAPHIC INCLUSION: IT STILL MATTERS

I've been emphasizing the importance of intellectual and cultural diversity when building your organization's team. But demographic inclusion based on concrete traits like race, ethnicity, religion, gender, and disability is also important.

Surveys show that many Americans—especially white Americans—assume that racial prejudice is a matter of ancient history, that programs of affirmative action have long since equalized the opportunities available to people of all races, and that therefore deliberate efforts to encourage racial inclusion in US businesses are, at best, unnecessary, and, at worst, divisive and harmful.

These assumptions ignore the reality that people of color are still quite rare in American boardrooms and executive suites. They ignore, too, the fact that efforts to integrate US society began only recently in historical terms. I mentioned earlier that landmark laws and court rulings eliminating legal segregation occurred during my own lifetime (and in fact have yet to be fully implemented in practice). I am a member of the first generation of black Americans to enter historically white institutions—colleges, universities, social organizations, and businesses—in significant numbers. Like practically all other black Americans, I'm familiar with the experience of being the only person of color in a conference room or lecture hall filled with white people. I'm profoundly aware of how awkward and disconcerting it can be to feel culturally isolated from those around you; to encounter no natural role models or mentors when entering a new environment; to be the subject of embarrassing questions, comments, looks, and assumptions; and to be accepted, if at all, merely as a token representative of "my people" who is supposed to speak for an entire race rather than simply myself.

At the time I started my business career, few black Americans held leadership positions. Those who'd managed to climb a few rungs up the corporate ladder were often confined to a handful of specialized departments—human resources, community relations, "special markets" (a term often used as a euphemism for "black customers"). These were mostly staff jobs rather than line jobs, which meant they were viewed as cost centers rather than profit centers. Those who held these positions had extremely limited growth opportunities and were highly vulnerable to layoffs in times of financial stress, since they weren't believed to be generating profits for the corporation. The real power centers in most companies were off-limits to blacks, so virtually no CEOs, chief financial officers, chief marketing officers, divisional vice presidents, or factory managers were black.

The reality is that, had I been born just five or ten years earlier, none of the opportunities that I've experienced would have been available. I've mentioned the chance I had to go to a better public school outside of Chicago because of my grades. During and after college, I was able to get jobs at the Federal Reserve and in the Illinois governor's office. These were all opportunities that simply hadn't existed for black Americans of previous generations. I have a tremendous amount of appreciation for those people who dedicated their lives to creating the social changes that opened those doors.

Yet today, fifty years after the heyday of the civil rights movement, the process of creating a society in which all Americans have equal opportunities has barely begun. Black executives lead only a handful of major US corporations—for example, three in the Fortune 500. (For the record, they are Merck, headed by Kenneth Frazier; TIAA, headed by Roger Ferguson Jr.; and Lowe's, headed by Marvin Ellison.) Until the retirement in May 2017 of my friend Ursula Burns, Xerox was also on this list. Importantly, Burns was also the first black *woman* to serve as a Fortune 500 CEO.

The United States has done much to break down institutional barriers between races in recent decades. But the work of creating true diversity, and of taking full advantage of the rich variation in perspectives and life experiences that Americans of all backgrounds offer, is far from complete.

For these reasons, as Aetna's CEO, I put my weight behind the traditional kinds of demographically oriented diversity programs, which helped to bring fresh talent and new thinking to the company. I chaired Aetna's corporate diversity council, an unusual step for a CEO, and made sure it included many of the company's most important executives—the directors of purchasing and marketing and the chief IT officer, for example. We urged Aetna's vendors—outside companies that provided us with services such as advertising, media, printing, accounting, investment banking, consulting, and legal advice—to create inclusive client services teams so people from many backgrounds could learn about our business and provide us with their unique insights.

Also, within Aetna, we created affinity groups to address the needs of specific sectors of our workforce and to represent their interests in the company's councils. We had affinity groups for black Americans, working parents, LGBT employees, and veterans, among others. Encouraging and supporting these groups, listening carefully to their concerns, and helping to address their problems made it easier for Aetna to draw on the talents of a wide array of people—all of whom had something important to contribute to our long-term mission as a company.

I also pushed the envelope on racial awareness through an occasional personal gesture. For example, I made a point of inviting several top Aetna executives to the annual Golf & Tennis Challenge, a networking event hosted by *Black Enterprise* magazine. I suspected these colleagues of mine—who happened to be white—might find it interesting and eye-opening to spend a weekend as members of a racial minority group (since the vast majority of attendees at the Golf & Tennis Challenge are black). They did. A number commented about the awkwardness they felt, the difficulty in launching conversations, and the anxiety about saying and doing "the right thing" in an unfamiliar cultural setting. Several later thanked me, commenting on the greater sense of empathy they now felt for people of color.

When you have the opportunity to help select new people to join your organization, I urge you to consider inclusion of all kinds as part of the recruitment and hiring process. We live in a world where people from every background are important—as customers, suppliers, investors, and fellow citizens. So organizations need input and contributions from people of all kinds—and the most successful businesses are likely to be those that draw on the widest possible pool of talent.

If Silicon Valley wants to make significant progress on this front, companies like Apple, Alphabet, Amazon, and Facebook need to make inclusion a high priority. Rather than delegating the job, their CEOs should devote some portion of their own time and energy to leading the charge. They need to insist on considering diverse slates of candidates for every important position before hiring the best person. When a CEO fails to personally emphasize and invest time in this effort, it sends a signal that the issue isn't really important.

Demographic diversity often pays immediate, short-term benefits. I've seen it happen many times. Here's an example. When I was at Blue Cross of California, we were once in competition with another health-care company for a major contract with a large corporate client. After both potential suppliers had provided written proposals with contract terms, costs, and other details, the day came for an extensive presentation before a group of executives who would make the final decision.

I arrived at the client's offices with my team from Blue Cross. It included our network manager, who was a Hispanic man; our chief actuary, an Asian-American woman; our general manager of geography, another woman; and me, a black man. In the waiting area outside the boardroom where the big presentation would take place, we met our counterparts from the rival supplier. Every member of their team was a blond, blue-eyed male between six feet and six feet three inches tall. We shook hands and wished one another well—and of course we couldn't help noticing the surface differences between the two teams.

Our team from Blue Cross made the second presentation that morning. When we walked into the room, we saw that the members of the client's team were as diverse as we were—there were men and women of various ages, colors, and ethnic backgrounds waiting to hear our presentation. The team was a cross-section of the company's working population—and, like our team, it was also a cross-section of twenty-first-century America. We immediately felt confident that we could "speak the language" of everyone in that room.

Blue Cross won the contract.

CREATING A HIGH-PERFORMANCE CULTURE: THE LEADER SETS THE PACE

Building your team isn't only about choosing the right people. It's also about creating an organizational culture that enables your team members to give the best of themselves to the organization. And here again, I return to the theme of self-leadership. Unless you learn to manage your own time, energy, and focus so that you are giving one hundred percent to the organization—or even a bit more than that—you will never be able to get one hundred percent from your team members.

I'm generally recognized as a hard worker. It's a habit I developed long ago, going back to when I worked alongside my dad in the car wash. I maintained that self-discipline during my years in high school, college, and graduate school, as well as throughout my working career. The habit was facilitated by the fact that I *liked* my work. When you are fascinated by the challenges and problems that crop up every day on the job, then you don't mind devoting countless hours to them, even on evenings and weekends—just as an avid painter, surfer, rock climber, or dancer never gets tired of the long hours they dedicate to mastering the activity they love.

I didn't necessarily expect the people who worked for me to put in the same kinds of hours I did. But I did expect them to devote the time and energy needed to attain the results that the organization needed and expected. If they couldn't or wouldn't, then they needed to find another job that suited them better, and I needed to replace them with someone who could pull their weight as a member of our team.

Over the years, I had to learn the right ways to communicate my work expectations to my team members. I think people sometimes felt intimidated when they saw how many hours I put in. I guess it can be a bit daunting when your boss is at his desk before you arrive in the morning, is still there when you leave in the evening, and sends you work-related emails throughout the weekend—maybe even in the wee hours of Sunday night. But my intention wasn't to impress people or to extract the same level of dedication from them. If a team member could accomplish everything that was required at a high level of excellence within the hours of nine and five, more power to them! I became concerned only when people let the clock dictate the amount of work they put in rather than obeying the genuine demands of the job.

I've been told that my style of relating to my team members was also a bit intimidating. I've never been one for small talk. The typical watercooler chitchat is mostly uninteresting to me. So I tended not to participate in the usual conversations about movies, family outings, or the performance of the local sports teams. As a result, people would get the idea that I was all work and no play—and that I expected the same from my colleagues. Some even assumed that I was unconcerned about them as people—that I viewed them simply as cogs in the corporate machine, and that all I cared about was their productivity.

That's certainly not the message I was trying to convey. Reflecting on this issue, I came to realize that my level of focus on the tasks we needed to accomplish was so high that I needed to raise my level of focus on the people I worked with as well. When I didn't do this, the disproportion felt jarring to those around me. So over the years, I learned to adjust my communication style to express more accurately my concerns about the people I worked with. I developed the habit of checking in with people about their family lives and their personal interests—to ask how an elderly mother was doing or how a teenaged daughter's latest track meet went. I even learned to show a little interest in how the New York Giants football game turned out on Sunday! (Although if the sports talk dominated the office for more than a few minutes on Monday morning, I was known to remind my team members that there was work to be done.)

Setting appropriate expectations for your team members involves understanding their individual capacities. The metaphor of the

Navy SEAL that I explained in an earlier chapter can be helpful here. SEALs and regular Navy sailors are two different kinds of people with different roles. You bring in your SEALs for crucial, time-sensitive tasks that require maximum sustained effort for a specific period of time. Your sailors may be equally talented, but they are steadier and more capable of working on the same task over a long period of time. To get the most satisfactory results for the company as well as for the individuals involved, make sure that both you and your team members recognize the difference and know which group they fit into best.

Sometimes, setting the right tone is a matter of clearing up misunderstandings. When I would ask to review my team members' vacation schedules, they occasionally thought I was trying to keep tabs on them, or even hinting that a week in the Caribbean might be excessive. That wasn't my purpose at all. Actually, I just wanted to be sure I could anticipate issues that might arise during their absence so I could avoid interrupting their vacations with emails or phone calls. Once I realized the confusion I was causing, I found that explaining my real intention made a big difference in people's reactions.

Still, there were times when I drove people hard—especially during my early years at Aetna, when the company was in crisis and we were devising and implementing emergency measures. Evening and weekend meetings fueled by pizza and cartons of Chinese take-out were common. For many on my top leadership team, family lives were disrupted, vacations were short and infrequent, and thoughts about work and the problems we faced were constant. I know that the stress this caused on people's personal lives was real and sometimes quite painful.

I hope and believe that I never exerted more pressure on my team members than was absolutely necessary to meet the genuine needs of the organization. And I hope, too, that the rewards we shared over time—both financially and in other, less tangible forms—made the sacrifices worthwhile. The fact that so many of the people I worked with during those tough times at Aetna have remained colleagues and treasured friends of mine suggests that's the case.

In my latter years as Aetna CEO, people sometimes told me that I seemed to be "mellowing" as a leader—that I wasn't quite as demanding and single-minded as when I first joined the firm. Maybe there's a bit of truth to that. But more important is the fact that all the hard work we put in enabled Aetna to get out of crisis mode. Once the company was on an even keel, there was less need for evening and weekend sessions and emergency meetings to put out the latest fires. What's more, as the pressure lessened, the leaders around me were able to devote more of their time to developing the people who worked for them. As my team members built teams of their own that could keep the business running smoothly in their absence, it became easier for people to take weekends off and vacations.

A well-run company doesn't require routine superhuman feats of effort to remain successful. An organization that accomplishes great things without outrageous work schedules is one of the rewards you get for building a smart system and staffing it with talented people in the first place.

THE REALITIES OF WORK-LIFE BALANCE

Having said all this, let me be clear: Even when the business is running smoothly, being the leader of a large, complex organization is *never* less than extremely demanding. If you aspire to leadership, don't imagine it will ever be easy. It will be engrossing, challenging, fascinating, and at times exhilarating—but easy? Never.

Earlier in this book, I described how my friend Ursula Burns learned so much about the life of a top corporate leader when she served as the executive assistant to Wayland Hicks at Xerox. She traveled with him, organized and attended his meetings, and managed his contacts with hundreds of colleagues inside and outside the company. In Burns's words, Hicks was "all in, all the time"—engaged at the highest possible level every moment of the day. For example, she recalls seeing Hicks fly coach from the United States to Japan—working most of the way—check in to a Tokyo hotel on arrival, take a quick shower, and immediately head out to a round of business meetings. This was a typical performance, not an extraordinary one. Burns remembers telling her boyfriend (now her husband), "If this is what it takes to be a top executive, I never want to do it!"

But Burns changed her mind when she went to work as the executive assistant to Paul Allaire, then chairman and CEO of Xerox. Allaire was every bit as engaged, energetic, and dedicated as Hicks. But he had a wider array of outside interests that fascinated and revitalized him, and he'd managed to develop ways to integrate them into his schedule without sacrificing his productivity and focus. Allaire was an avid biker and motorcyclist, and he made the time to take cross-country trips; he was also a ballet aficionado and occasionally arranged his schedule so he could leave the office early to attend a special performance. Watching Allaire in action made Burns realize that it might be possible to be a super-effective corporate leader while also enjoying a semblance of normal life. In her later roles—first as Xerox's vice president for global manufacturing and eventually as the company's chairperson and CEO—she consciously modeled her work style on Allaire's.

Make no mistake, Burns works extremely hard. "I'm a natural loner, an introvert," she says:

There's nothing I like better than taking a solitary run in the park or curling up with a great book on my sofa at home. But as a leader, I don't usually have options like that. I'm responsible for tens of thousands of people! They rely on me to keep them going, to help make them successful, to keep our company afloat. So I have to be thinking about those responsibilities constantly. Instead of enjoying a quiet meal with a friend, I'm more likely to be attending a big dinner with dozens of people from one of our facilities, so I can hear about their plans for a big new project or a factory expansion. It's interesting and important, but it's also time-intensive and very demanding. At times, I get cranky! But it comes with the territory.

Like most successful executives, especially women, Burns is constantly asked by aspiring leaders how she balances her work and her personal life. She explains that, for anyone in the highest ranks of leadership, the idea of work-life balance is often misunderstood. "You have to bring *your entire self* to the leadership role," Burns says. As a result, having work and life in balanced portions at any given moment in your career is almost impossible. "You can have work-life balance over a lifetime," she has concluded, "but not necessarily all the time."

Burns learned some valuable lessons about how to enjoy a happy and successful family life from her mother, who worked as a maid and house cleaner. "My mom worked very hard—she had to," Burns explains. "So I learned from her that being with your kids every minute of the day is *not* what good parenting is all about. I learned to be a tactical parent—to pick and choose the most important moments when I needed to be there for my kids, and to make the most of those."

Burns was fortunate to have a supportive husband on whom she could lean for help with family responsibilities. She missed a lot of her kids' basketball games and music recitals, but when she did, her husband was usually there. And Burns figured out where to draw the line between life and work so that she could fulfill her most important family obligations. "Even when my kids were young, I had to travel constantly," she says. "But I made a rule that, with almost no exceptions, I would be home with them for the weekend—and believe me, I did some crazy things to live up to that rule, even if it meant taking three flights to arrive at my doorstep at midnight on Friday!"

Burns's experiences resonate with me. When you're a leader—whether in business or in any other arena, from the nonprofit world to government to academia—you need to be prepared to sacrifice personal needs and interests for the good of the organization. There are people relying on you, and you can never forget that.

Of course, your family and others in your personal life rely on you, too. So while it may be impossible to achieve work-life balance in any neat, convenient way, you owe it to yourself and to those who love you to draw lines to protect some sacred personal space. Burns did it with her home-for-the-weekend rule. I did it by having crucial family events built into my schedule by the same assistant who managed my company travels, my board meetings, my facilities tours, and all my other work activities. It was her job to figure out on a weekly basis how to fit someone's request for an urgent project review in between my 2:00 p.m. television interview with a stock market reporter and a 4:00 p.m. soccer game at my kid's school. Having the soccer game on the same calendar with the TV interview and an employee roundtable helped me keep some family time "untouchable" and as important on that day as anything else.

Of course, once the soccer game ended, I'd likely be heading back to the office for a couple of hours of additional meetings and preparation for the next day's gauntlet of events. But that's the life of a leader.

For many of us, the quest for work-life balance is a continuing journey. Kay Mooney, who served as my capable and dedicated chief of staff for three years during my tenure at Aetna, recalls how challenging it was to adjust to the realities of working for a constantly-in-demand CEO:

> I started working in Ron's office in April. A month later, I planned to take a day off on the Friday before Memorial Day. Ron and I were at the office until 9:00 p.m. on Thursday. Before I left, I put my "out of office" message on my email, indicating I would be out of the office until Tuesday.
>
> When I got home forty-five minutes later, I checked my email and found two new emails from Ron. The first was about a business issue he needed me to address. The second read, "You don't need to use that 'out of the office' message on your email, because as my chief of staff, you're *never* really out of the office."
>
> Of course, Ron didn't mean it literally—he was fine with me taking some time away from the office. But his point was that I could never be out of touch or unavailable, because the CEO can never simply ignore the problems of the organization, no matter when they arise—and as the CEO's chief of staff, I couldn't ignore them either.

Mooney's conclusion: "Work-life balance has to be defined by every individual based on what is right for you at a particular moment in your career." She goes on to say:

As Ron's chief of staff, the proportion between work and life for me was around ninety-two percent to eight percent. Later, when I was asked to build Aetna's public exchange business in the wake of the Affordable Care Act, I still worked very long hours, but the pressure and the demands were considerably less on a relative basis. As the work changes and as your role evolves, so does the balance you strike. All you can do is strive for a balance that works for you at a given time—and adjust it as your needs and tolerance demand.

Like Kay Mooney, I had to wrestle with issues of work-life balance. I was lucky: I could never have accomplished what I did in my business career without the support of a committed, generous, and understanding spouse. When tough decisions had to be made—for example, moves that would uproot us from one city to another—Cynthia recognized the trade-offs required and discussed them frankly with me so we could make the best decisions for our family.

My advice to would-be leaders: Understand the difficult demands that are inherent in the leadership role. If you're involved in a serious relationship, talk with your partner about the challenges ahead as honestly as you can. Don't make promises you may not be able to keep.

And when your significant other says, "Please call me when you're on your way home," don't dial the phone until you're actually out of the office and in your car or on the bus or train. I've learned from painful experience that if you call any sooner than that, you're sure to be hijacked by a colleague on your way out the office door—leaving you with an embarrassing half-hour delay to explain to your loved one.

TREATING YOUR PEOPLE AS IF THEY REALLY MATTER

People-centered leadership can unleash amazing levels of energy and creativity—provided everyone retains a shared focus on the needs of the organization.

In my pursuit of the goal of people-centered leadership, I tried hard to keep my finger on the pulse of my team members. Simply paying close attention to what was going on around me was an essential element of this process. There's no substitute for being a good listener. That's not a passive skill. It includes *actively probing* for the underlying emotions, fears, dreams, aspirations, and worries that people may be expressing indirectly when they talk with you about the issues they're facing in life and work.

Remember that, in most organizations, there's a subtle but real dividing wall between rank-and-file team members and the boss who leads them. It's true at every level of the organization, whether you're considering the relationship between a factory foreman and the assembly-line workers who report to him or the relationship between a CEO and the members of his executive team. Team members are typically reluctant to "bother" the boss unless they have something important to share, and in one-on-one meetings they usually communicate using language they've carefully planned in advance.

As the leader, you should consider *every* conversation with a team member as potentially sensitive and important. The people who work for you care a lot about everything you say—or don't say. They want badly to earn your approval, your support, and your understanding. Learn to listen carefully to the unspoken concerns that resonate through every conversation, and try to respond not only to the literal words you hear but also to the emotional currents that underlie and motivate them.

In addition to being a good listener on an everyday basis, you should purposefully make time for one-on-one meetings with those who rely on your leadership. As CEO, I met regularly with each of the ten people who reported directly to me and also with their key direct reports—about twenty-five people in all. These meetings weren't usually lengthy—half an hour or so was typical—but they included time for a brief recap of how the team member's most important projects were unfolding, a conversation about the biggest challenges or obstacles they were wrestling with, and a look at the biggest goals they'd set for the months ahead. Most important, I tried to come away with a sense of how my team member's personal aspirations were meshing with those of the organization and if there was anything I could do to help ensure that the fit was as strong and mutually nurturing as possible.

Making sure these brief but meaningful conversations were sacred on my schedule, and not postponed or canceled for other activities, was an important part of my leadership style. When you blow off a meeting like this, you're indirectly communicating to your team member that they are not *really* important to you. That's a sure way to alienate them and, eventually, lose at least a portion of what they have to offer. As my chief of staff Kay Mooney used to say, "You've always got to show your people the love!" Just being there, to talk with them and to listen deeply, is an essential first step.

TAKEAWAYS FROM CHAPTER 10

- One key to success in today's business world is creating a diverse team of employees from varying backgrounds. This will maximize your organization's ability to understand and address the problems and needs of widely differing customers.

- Demographic diversity (in terms of race, gender, religion, and other basic characteristics) is desirable and important. But even more important is diversity of work background, experience, values, attitudes, and knowledge.

- Don't fall into the trap of seeking employees who fit a predetermined cultural or personal mold. Instead, look for people who will bring fresh ideas and new personality traits to your organization.

- As the team leader, you set the work pace for your team. If you model dedication to the organization in your daily behavior, the members of your team will usually follow suit.

- Work-life balance is often misunderstood. At any given moment, a worker must determine their own appropriate relationship between personal time and work time—and that relationship is ever-changing and only occasionally comfortably balanced.

- The lives of your team members are vitally important, and as the team leader you must never forget that. Your team members want to align their life goals with those of the organization, and helping them achieve that will elicit their dedication and their best efforts.

11

Master the Art of Mind Reading:
The Two-Up/Two-Down System

*In any large organization, the existence of hierarchical levels
can make clear communication difficult. Those on the front
lines are often at a loss as to what those in the executive
suite have in mind . . . and those on top often have no idea
what their frontline employees are thinking. The two-up/
two-down system offers a way to bridge such gaps.*

ANY EXPERIENCED LEADER KNOWS that countless well-intentioned team-building efforts have been derailed through needless misunderstandings. Every day, such failures lead to internal conflict, frustration, anger, low morale, and burnout.

Sometimes these communication failures stem from sheer inattention: the email unsent, the phone call unmade, the meeting not held. But more often they arise from misunderstandings—well-intentioned communication efforts that somehow go awry. The memo is written, but the key information it contains gets overlooked or misinterpreted. The manager leads a team meeting to address a thorny problem that is hampering the group's efforts, but those who attend leave the conversation feeling more confused than before. When missteps like this occur repeatedly—as they do in too many organizations—you start hearing comments like:

"People here just don't seem to *get* it!"

"Why can't we all get on the same page?"

"We just can't seem to get our ducks in a row!"

Why does this happen so often? My years in leadership have convinced me that the main problem isn't lack of goodwill. Almost everyone *wants* to do the right thing for their organizations, and they try their level best to do it. Nor is it lack of intelligence. The real problem, I've found, is that most people at every level simply don't devote enough time, thought, and energy to the two big challenges involved in clear communication—the challenge of conveying your messages clearly and the challenge of understanding and absorbing the messages sent by others.

UNDERSTANDING YOUR BOSS'S BOSS: MANAGING TWO UP

Paying close attention to the ideas, information, and concerns of the people around you—especially those operating from a different perspective or from a different location in the organizational hierarchy—is a key to leadership success. It's particularly crucial to devote time and energy to accurately interpreting the motivations of your team members, colleagues, and superiors. Learning to correctly grasp what I call the *strategic intent* of those in important positions above you and below you in the organizational hierarchy is a vital leadership practice, one that you should try to make into a daily habit. I call this practice the *two-up/two-down system.*

Here's how this system works in relation to a typical business challenge. Imagine that you've been hired to work for a manager we'll call Joe, and Joe reports to a company vice president named Nancy. Nancy is in the two-up position—which means she occupies a crucial strategic role in relation to you.

After several months, you discover that you and the rest of Joe's team have few resources. Funds for new product development and marketing support are scarce; even the office equipment is dated. Through a few discreet inquiries, you learn that Nancy is channeling most of her budget to a different department headed by Gary, leaving Joe and his team, including you, feeling short-changed and frustrated.

It's a common situation, and many people would respond by getting angry or succumbing to despair. But a practitioner of two-up/two-down thinking takes the time to study Nancy's strategic intent—asking questions and scrutinizing corporate statements and executive pronouncements for clues. You may discover that Gary's department has been targeted by the corporation for rapid growth in the next two years—while Joe's department is expected to decline and ultimately fold. Recognizing this enables you to get past resentment and begin developing a realistic plan for the future—for example, by studying the strategic problems that are hobbling Joe's department and looking for a new product, service, or market opportunity that may restart its growth. Sharing what you learn with Joe *and* Nancy may mark you as a "big picture" thinker with something valuable to contribute, no matter which department you might later join.

A key to understanding the strategic intent of people higher than you in the corporate ladder is learning to listen perceptively—developing the ability to hear more than the words that your boss says. Seize every opportunity to hear from your company's top leaders. When a "town hall" meeting is announced, come early, sit in the front row, and be prepared with a question or two related to your work.

Even more important than the words your boss utters is the *purpose* behind those words. Don't simply ask yourself, "What is my boss saying?" but also ask, "Why are they saying it? What is their purpose? What goal are they pursuing? And what role can I play in helping them achieve that goal?"

MAKING IT EASY FOR YOUR BOSS TO BACK YOU

Of course, "managing up" effectively isn't an easy task. Having to answer to a boss can sometimes be frustrating. There are times when you simply *know* you're right about a strategy, a project, or a plan, but your boss disagrees, preventing you from doing what you want. When that happens, it's fun to fantasize about the day when you won't face that kind of obstacle—about the day when, as the king of the corporate hill, you'll be able to make all of the decisions without having to convince anyone else.

Unfortunately, that day will probably never come! As you may have already realized, there is actually no one in the world of business who doesn't report to someone else (with the possible exception of the owner and CEO of a small private company—in which case the sphere of control is relatively modest). Even a corporate CEO reports to a boss—or, more accurately, a whole collection of bosses. They're known as the board of directors, and they have the power to thwart a CEO's plans and even, ultimately, to fire and replace him.

The challenge of "managing up" is truly ubiquitous in business, and it doesn't disappear no matter how high up the corporate ladder you rise.

Fortunately, you can learn a lot about managing up the hierarchy by watching some of the most effective CEOs. The techniques they use to communicate and work with their boards of directors can be adapted by leaders at every level of the organization. You can use these methods to make it easier for your boss, or your boss's boss, to agree with you, to support your ideas, and to provide you with the resources you need to succeed.

My friend JD Hoye has had a successful career in government and the nonprofit arena. She is president of NAF (formerly the National Academy Foundation), which runs a network of career academics located in public high schools that prepare young people for future careers through industry-focused curricula and work experiences. While NAF is a nonprofit organization, Hoye can tell you that the challenges she faces in working with her board of directors are comparable to those faced by the CEO of a for-profit company. Nurturing her relationship with board members is an essential aspect of her work as an effective organizational head, since without the board's support, it's unlikely that Hoye would be able to accomplish the daily work of the organization or pursue any of its long-term goals.

Here are some techniques Hoye uses to keep her board members informed, happy, and supportive.

Frequent personal communication. Hoye personally sends a letter to each board member monthly, relating current news about the organization, its short-term plans, and any current challenges.

Rich flow of information. Hoye makes sure the members of her management team gather detailed information about the organization's activities, organize the data in a clear and understandable format, and share it on a timely basis with board members.

Careful planning for board meetings. The quarterly board meetings are thoroughly planned to be as engaging, informative, and interesting as possible. Advance information on topics to be discussed is provided in a bound book of materials, and time is scheduled for open-ended discussions and question-and-answer periods.

Availability as needed between meetings. When a board member calls with a question or concern, Hoye responds promptly or connects the member with a staff member who has special expertise in the subject area.

Above all, Hoye tries to consider the role of the board member from that person's perspective:

> Our board members are very busy people with lots of other responsibilities. Many of them are running companies or other organizations of their own. They are traveling constantly and have schedules that are crowded and unpredictable. They focus on NAF with just a fraction of their time and energy—and we are lucky to have it! So we do everything we can to make working with us a "light lift." We pay attention to their individual needs and interests, we provide them with all the tools they need to understand what we are trying to do, and we listen carefully whenever they communicate with us. Our goal is to make them feel that they are getting as much from the relationship as they are giving—or even more, if possible.

Maybe you can see how Hoye's approach to managing her board can be applied to managing your boss, or your boss's boss. Try to see your department and your role in it from the two-up perspective. Ask yourself questions like these:

- What do I contribute to the overall success of the organization?

- What do I think my boss's boss would like to see me accomplish?

- How can I make their life easier, more satisfying, more productive?

- What kinds of information do they need to understand what my team is doing?

- How can I convey that information in a way they will find relevant, compelling, and easy to understand?

- What do they need to know—about me, my team, my strategies, my customers, my goals—to provide me with the support I'd like to have from the organization?

By asking such questions—and developing accurate answers—you can determine what you need to do to make yourself a "light lift" rather than a heavy burden for your boss's boss.

Hoye summarizes her strategy as a leader with the words "Everything is built on relationships." Remember that the people you report to are just that—people—and treat them that way, as human beings with interests, priorities, needs, problems, and goals that are important to them. Help them achieve their long-term objectives, and you will become a valued member of their team—with significant long-term benefits to you and your career.

REPORTING TO MORE THAN ONE MANAGER

Learning to read the minds of the people who are above you on the corporate ladder is always challenging. But reporting to *multiple* bosses can be particularly tricky. In an entry-level job, for example, you might be an administrative assistant working for two or more managers. Later in your career, you might be a manager in charge of a function that serves two or more departments in the organization—for example, you might be running a service team that handles customer complaints, questions, and problems related to two different product lines, which means that you are answerable to the heads of two different company divisions. Or you might be directly supervised by one person but have a "dotted-line" relationship with one or two other supervisors—an indirect connection that sometimes feels like a reporting role. Each of these situations can create ambiguities and tensions that you may find tough to navigate.

There are several strategies you'll want to consider if you find yourself in the position of having more than one boss.

Master the differing communication and management styles of each boss. Reporting to two or more people is like being bilingual: You need to understand their differing languages, vocabulary, and communication styles, so you can interpret their instructions and requests accurately. This takes time, careful listening, and maybe even some deliberate note-taking. Eventually, you'll realize that when Boss A says, "This report is very important," she means "I need it as quickly as possible so we can review and revise it together," while when Boss B says the same thing, he means "I need you to research it intensely so the first draft you hand me is flawless."

Be as open and up front as possible. The best way to avoid confusion and conflict is to speak up. If Boss A hands you an assignment with a schedule that butts up against a different project you've already started for Boss B, you need to discuss the situation, preferably with both managers. Enlist their help to sort out the priorities and to help you figure out how to meet both sets of needs.

Help your bosses lead you better. If you develop a working system or process with one boss that is particularly productive or efficient, try tactfully and positively suggesting it to the other: "When I have to conduct a survey for Barbara, I usually use this software, and it works very well. Would you like me to try the same for you?" If you have a personal working preference that affects your productivity, share it with your bosses: "I find I get the most complicated jobs done best early in the morning. Would it be possible for you to give me tough assignments like this one during the afternoon, so I can clear my desk to work on them first thing the following day?"

Don't take sides or get caught in the middle. If your bosses are in conflict with one another, avoid becoming an ally with either one. Your loyalty is to the organization as a whole, and as long as both managers are part of the team, your job is to try to serve both as best you can. Above all, don't criticize either boss to the other. Bad-mouthing a colleague behind their back can only earn you a reputation as untrustworthy, which will never serve you well. If the conflict leads to the departure or demotion of one of them, you don't want to be stuck as an ally of the "loser"—whose identity may be difficult to predict in advance.

Learn from both bosses. Serving two masters can be complicated, but it's also a great way to expand your insights into the organization and the industry. The differing ideas, work styles, priorities, networks, and strategies of your two bosses can each provide you with knowledge that would be much harder to gain from just a single boss.

It so happens that JD Hoye is a master of the two-boss challenge. At more than one stage in her career—when she ran the Oregon Private Industry Council, a nonprofit organization focused on statewide education reform, and then later, when she launched and ran the Office of School-to-Work at the US Department of Education under President Bill Clinton—Hoye has had jobs where she reported to more than one boss. She has always viewed those positions as great learning experiences, and she likes to tell young people about the *advantages* of having multiple bosses:

> Reporting to two or more bosses prevents you from falling into the trap of trying to emulate the style of one leader—especially someone who may have unique personal qualities that are very different from your own. When I reported to three people back in Oregon, it gave me the opportunity to pick the most effective leadership techniques of each one and incorporate all of them into my own style of management.
>
> The key to serving multiple bosses is to strive for transparency and accountability. Let everyone know what you are working on, what your priorities are, and what resources you need to accomplish the mission. When you run up against an unexpected problem, speak up right away and ask for the advice or help you need.
>
> And don't worry too much if two of your bosses have slightly different values or working styles. That's almost

inevitable. And it doesn't have to be a problem, as long as the differences don't rise to the level of absolute incompatibility. It can actually be more interesting—even exciting—when one of your challenges is to figure out how to find common ground among different people who are pushing you in different directions. Just remember to keep the overall mission of the organization at the forefront, and you can't go too far wrong.

EMPOWERING YOUR PEOPLE TO SPEAK THE TRUTH

Managing down the hierarchical ladder is just as important as managing up. In fact, understanding and respecting the goals and values of the people below you in the organization is crucial to your effectiveness in motivating and leading them. Your subordinates are not cattle to be herded or a problem to be solved; they are smart, caring people who want to contribute to a worthy cause, and they deserve to be treated that way. Sadly, many leaders never make this mental adjustment. Once you do, previously impossible accomplishments suddenly become possible.

One fundamental truth about communication in a corporate context is that the freedom to speak up is largely about *power*. People will share information and ideas only to the extent that they feel empowered to do so. If the organization's culture discourages honest communication—or if the leader of a particular team sends signals that honesty may not be welcome—employees will clam up. When that happens, you can forget about being fully informed about what is happening in your organization—which means unpleasant surprises and avoidable disasters are almost sure to follow.

Early in my time as CEO at Aetna, I had an experience that

taught me the importance of empowering people to speak up. Our executive committee planned a session with a highly rated outside expert chosen by our innovation group, who was supposed to lead us through a ninety-minute presentation about quality improvement in the insurance industry. At the appointed time, we gathered in the boardroom and the guest speaker began his talk, illustrated with the typical array of PowerPoint slides and handouts.

Everyone in the room, I'm sure, was hoping for a highly enlightening, inspiring presentation. But within a few minutes, I began to sense that the speaker knew very little about Aetna or about the insurance industry in general. Everything he said was a vague generality with little value or relevance to us. I gave him the benefit of the doubt, thinking maybe he simply needed a little time to warm up. After twenty minutes, all doubt was gone. Whoever had selected this speaker had made a huge mistake—and our high-priced executive committee members were embarked on a time-wasting exercise that would cost Aetna the equivalent of thousands of dollars.

However, I said nothing. Why? Because I was wondering which member of my executive committee would speak up first. I noticed them exchanging glances. A few were even rolling their eyes. It was clear that everyone in the room felt exactly the same as I did. Which leader would have the courage and honesty to call a halt to the charade?

The clock kept ticking. The deadly presentation droned on. Bottoms wriggled uncomfortably in chairs. But still, no one said a word.

Finally, when an hour had passed, I broke the silence. "I'm sorry to interrupt," I said to the speaker. "But I think you've delivered all the insights and information we can get from you. Thanks very much for your time." He packed up his slides and disappeared.

As soon as the door shut behind him, the room exploded with complaints: *What a fiasco that was! I didn't learn a single thing. I don't think that guy ever set foot in an insurance company before. Thank goodness that's over with! My ten-year-old could have given a better presentation.*

I waited for the comments to die down. Then I quietly said, "You all knew I didn't sponsor this speaker. Any one of you could have spoken up. You could have politely tried to focus him on useful topics, or asked for a break so we could devise an exit strategy. Why wait for me to take charge?"

A long, embarrassed silence filled the room as everyone absorbed the message. The fiasco had turned into a teaching moment. I'd made it quite clear that I expected everyone who reported to me to be honest and unafraid about communicating what they saw happening around them—even if that meant sharing bad news.

From that point on, my team members understood that they were empowered to speak the truth under all circumstances—and that's exactly what they did.

COMMUNICATING WITH THOSE ON THE FRONT LINES: MANAGING TWO DOWN

It's one thing to teach the people who report directly to you to communicate honestly with you. It can be an even greater challenge to open up lines of communication with people two or more levels below you. But doing so is tremendously important—because unless you know what is *really* happening on the front lines of your organization, you're likely to be blindsided by serious problems affecting customer service, product quality, and other issues crucial to your success.

Communicating appropriately and effectively with those two levels below you can be tricky. For most routine messages, it's best to work through the hierarchical pipeline—to let supervisors communicate directly with those who report to them. This practice strengthens the bonds between people who work together daily and allows team leaders to confirm that they and their immediate followers are on the same page about the tasks they're tackling. It also ensures that managers are fully informed about details pertaining to the operation of their units. A leader needs to know what's on the minds of the people who work for them. When staff members get into the habit of communicating directly with a boss higher on the totem pole—especially when their direct supervisor is left out of the message chain—it can create a dysfunctional atmosphere in which members of the organization use roundabout channels to complain about things rather than going openly to those they work with.

Nonetheless, when you've risen a few notches in the corporate chain of command, you'll find there are times and circumstances when it's healthy, even necessary, to connect with the people who report directly to someone you supervise. Insisting on rigid adherence to a "chain of command" that precludes conversations among people at widely varying levels can produce narrowness of vision and loss of perspective. For example, a factory manager who never talks to the frontline employees on the assembly line and instead relies solely on reports from shift managers or department foremen often ends up being the last person to hear about emerging problems on the factory floor.

There are effective ways to maintain your connections with the people two down on the chart—ways that will help you stay fully informed without making your direct reports feel undermined or excluded from the conversation. Here are some tips on how to make it work.

Make communication across hierarchical lines part of your leadership routine. Daily work pressures are likely to create a situation in which you talk mostly with the people who report to you (and those to whom you report). Make a point of breaking this pattern by scheduling get-togethers with the two-down folks you might not normally see. For example, you might arrange monthly lunches with a rotating collection of employees with varying job functions and experiences who can share with you whatever is on their minds—problems, opportunities, ideas. You may also want to make a habit of "managing by walking around"—strolling through the locations where frontline employees work to watch how things are going, fielding spur-of-the-moment questions, and getting a feeling for the issues that people are confronting.

Invite open-ended feedback about the organization and its workings. When meeting with team members from various levels, I like to use my "Queen for a Day" or "King for a Day" questions: "If you were in charge of your department for a day, what would you change? What could you do to make things run more smoothly, to serve customers better, to save money, or to make your work more satisfying?" Some great ideas for operational improvements have emerged from responses to these questions.

Be open about the fact that you are in touch with people at various levels of the organization. When you connect with people two down in the chain—or further—let their bosses know that it's happening. Don't let the people who report to you directly feel blindsided or as if anyone is "going behind their back" in an effort to weaken their authority or get them in trouble.

Be available to hear people's problems or complaints—but always close the loop by keeping the relevant manager involved. Sometimes one or more of the two-down folks in your department may want to speak with you about an issue they find difficult to share with their immediate supervisor. Perhaps it's a problem with the supervisor—some perceived unfairness, for example. Or perhaps they've been told, explicitly or implicitly, that you are the only person with the authority and resources to address their complaint. It's usually appropriate for you to listen to the message—in fact, this can be a crucial leadership role for you to play. But as soon as possible, close the communications loop by bringing the relevant supervisor back into the conversation. If the problem involves a conflict between a manager and their direct reports, you may need to have your human resources department play a mediating role. Use this kind of conflict as an opportunity to help the manager improve her communication and management skills. Don't get caught up in taking sides—you'll find every issue has several sides, each with some claim to truth!

Don't give work direction to those you don't personally supervise. It's fine and often important to gather detailed information about conditions, processes, and problems from people at various levels of the organization. But keep the lines of responsibility and control crystal clear by allowing managers to do their jobs. Don't get between a team member and their supervisor by giving substantive orders to people who aren't your direct reports. Instead, make a note of the issue and discuss it later with the manager involved, who can deal with it as appropriate.

Don't shoot the messenger. When a team member has the courage to bring you bad news—a product delay, a revenue shortfall, a logistical snafu—you may feel upset about the problem. But don't take out your feelings on the messenger. If you do that, you are signaling, "The boss doesn't like to hear bad news." That's a good way to guarantee that, next time, you won't hear the news at all—or not until it's too late to do much about it.

Let everyone know that they're responsible for keeping the lines of communication open and clear. As CEO, I always emphasized to every manager that an important part of their job was to pass along key information and messages from me to their staff. For example, when a new strategic initiative was launched or a policy change was announced, I would naturally play a personal role in communicating the news throughout the organization through speeches, presentations, newsletters, and other means. But I also expected the managers who worked for me to reinforce the same news when communicating with their people—discussing it at staff meetings, responding to employee questions, and so on. Then, before visiting with frontline staff, I would be sure to tell their supervisors, "By the way, I'm going to ask your people how—and whether— you've been communicating with them about the latest corporate strategies. I hope to find they've been getting the message loud and clear."

As you might imagine, this was a surefire way of ensuring that the folks two levels down from me—or more—were kept fully informed of the latest company news and objectives. If everyone in your organization isn't on the same page, the chances of achieving your long-range goals will be severely diminished.

SPREADING THE TWO-UP/TWO-DOWN SYSTEM

In an earlier chapter, I spoke about the value of creating a personal board of advisors—a group of acquaintances with experience and expertise who can provide you with advice and guidance when you face career challenges or difficult choices. One or more of these informal advisors could even become a full-fledged mentor, advocating for you and opening career doors for you. As I explained, a mentorship relationship can't be planned, much less forced; it grows naturally from a two-sided connection in which both parties are benefiting.

As you rise in your career, one strongly positive impact you can have on your organization is to look for opportunities to nourish two-up/two-down communications among the people you work with. When you find yourself being sought out for advice or information by people who are junior to you, do your best to make time for them. Encourage your colleagues to do the same. Include "development of junior team members" as one of the job responsibilities of managers and professional staff members in your organization. And when appropriate, devise ways to make connections between individuals working at different levels of your company or your industry.

For example, you might invite some less-experienced team members to take part in conferences, conventions, or meetings from which they might normally be excluded, or suggest they "audit" planning or strategy sessions involving higher-level managers as a way of enhancing their understanding of your business. Even hosting occasional breakfasts or lunches at which groups of newer team members get a chance to ask questions of company veterans can be a great way of breaking the ice between the generations and ensuring that young and old have opportunities to learn from one another.

Consistently practicing the two-up/two-down system can make you one of the few indispensable people in your organization, no matter what rung of the corporate ladder you currently occupy. More important, it can help ensure that everyone in your organization has a shared understanding about your strategic goals and the principles and values you will apply in pursuing those goals. As a result, your chances of achieving the successes you seek will be dramatically enhanced.

TAKEAWAYS FROM CHAPTER 11

- As a team leader in an organization, one of your key roles is to facilitate communication up and down the business hierarchy. The two-up/two-down system can help you achieve this, serving as a tool for spreading knowledge and developing the skills of newer team members.

- Two-up communication is about understanding the ideas and needs of the leader two levels above you—your boss's boss. Practice seizing opportunities to talk and listen to the person two levels above you, and use what you learn to inform the daily decisions you make about goals, priorities, and methods.

- Two-down communication is about understanding the people who work two levels below you and communicating clearly with them. Make time to talk with them, understand their perspectives, and learn what is happening on the front lines of your business.

- Communicating up the ladder can be complicated at times—for example, if you report to more than one boss. To minimize problems, be up front about potential conflicts, and always seek ways to put the organization's interests ahead of any individual's goals.

- Communicating down the ladder also has its challenges. Strive to empower truth telling among those who report to you rather than discouraging the delivery of bad news. Encourage open conversations across hierarchical boundaries—but respect the prerogatives of team leaders who may report to you, and avoid injecting yourself into conflicts.

12

Find the Magic Words:
Discovering Your Authentic Leadership Voice

Leadership requires the ability to communicate effectively with people—a talent that comes naturally to very few people. Here are some suggestions about ways you can hone your public speaking ability in the service of more effective leadership.

MAYBE THE SINGLE MOST important skill any leader must develop is the ability to communicate—to share ideas clearly, engagingly, persuasively. If people inside and outside your organization don't understand your message or find it unappealing, they won't follow you—and your ideas, no matter how brilliant, will go to waste.

You can communicate your message in many ways—through public speaking, writing, video and audio presentations, talks accompanied by visual aids, and online tools like blogging, social media, and podcasts. Today's leader needs to be familiar with all these communication methods and at least passably effective in using each one. "Finding your voice" means learning how to present yourself and your ideas in a way that audiences find authentic, understandable, and persuasive no matter what communication medium you use.

EVERYBODY'S NIGHTMARE: SPEAKING IN PUBLIC

Virtually everyone, it seems, finds speaking in public terrifying. When surveyed, people routinely name "giving a speech" as their number one fear—one spot above "death"!

Fortunately, you don't have to be naturally eloquent or charismatic to be an effective communicator. I'm proof of that. Most people describe me using words like "low-key," "quiet," "soft-spoken," and "understated." I tend to listen and reflect more than I talk. That hasn't stopped me from becoming a successful leader or from conveying my thoughts clearly to an audience.

Complicating the challenge, my public speaking ability has been affected by a problem most would-be leaders don't have to grapple with—a tendency to stutter. It has been a problem since boyhood, though not consistently. Rather, I found myself stuttering particularly in times of stress—when asked by a teacher to recite before the entire class, for example. I also noticed that certain sounds were problematic for me to pronounce. The letter *s* was a difficult one, which means that a word like "suppose" would tend to trip me up.

Stuttering was most stressful for me early in my career, when I had much less experience at communicating to a large audience. Even seemingly simple tasks like introducing myself or telling a quick story to illustrate an idea took significant concentration and effort. Later, I still worried about my stutter in challenging situations like making a business presentation in front of an auditorium full of employees or being interviewed on radio or TV.

Over the years, I honed my public speaking abilities through thoughtful self study and constant practice. I picked up hints from others who stuttered and discovered useful techniques through sheer experimentation. I learned to slow down, to rephrase tricky sentences so they are easier to pronounce, and to avoid sound combinations (like repeated *s*'s) that give me trouble.

Most important, I found that speaking *spontaneously* from a simple outline works far better for me than reading a prepared script. I have tried a couple of times to read a speech drafted for me by a talented writer. You might think that having all the words predetermined would simplify the speaking process and make it more effective. But I found the opposite to be true. I focused on reading the speech and delivering the words accurately, one phrase at a time. As a result, I ended up using vocal tones and hand gestures disconnected from my meaning. I came across as inauthentic, and audiences were distracted by my delivery rather than persuaded by my message.

Over time, I developed a method for preparing a speech that has worked well for me. Perhaps you'll find it helpful, too. The basic approach is straightforward:

Simplify your message to a handful of key points—no more than four or five concepts for a fifteen- to twenty-minute speech. (No leader should ever give a speech that lasts longer than twenty minutes. Forty minutes should be legally banned as cruel and unusual punishment!)

Fight the temptation to include more information. Be ruthless about cutting less-important details so the truly crucial ideas can emerge with the clarity and emphasis they deserve. Keeping your talk brief also leaves ample time for questions, which many audience members consider the most important and valuable part of the presentation.

Start your preparation process well in advance of your scheduled talk—two or three weeks ahead, if possible. This means you have time to learn your key ideas so well you can explain them in your sleep. Spend a few minutes every day reviewing your key ideas and explaining them. Work at it until you know the material so well that you find it utterly boring. (Education experts call this *overlearning*, and it has been shown to be crucial to outstanding performance.)

Add a touch of humor in the first few minutes of your speech, and be sure to let your enthusiasm and passion for the topic shine through.

If you follow these guidelines, when D-Day arrives, you'll be able to deliver a clear, crisp fifteen- or twenty-minute talk that will capture any audience's interest and embed itself in their memories.

I've found that many of the best business communicators share my preference for spontaneous speaking over a scripted speech. My friend JD Hoye discovered this about herself years ago when she was a high school student in California. She participated in a program called "Girls State" that gave her the opportunity to run a mock political campaign as a candidate for the US Senate. The event climaxed with an outdoor speech to be delivered standing on a forty-foot stage in front of a large crowd.

Despite having taken a public speaking course and having thoroughly prepared her speech using neatly printed three-by-five-inch index cards, Hoye was pretty nervous. She swallowed hard and began reading aloud, when a sudden gust of wind scattered the index cards in all directions. The crowd gasped, and for a moment Hoye was nonplussed. But then she began delivering her message from memory—and from the heart. The rest of her speech was far more passionate and engaging than the opening had been, and she won an ovation from the crowd.

Ever since, Hoye has stuck to speaking from a handful of notes rather than a detailed script—even when public relations "handlers" have tried to intervene with a more thoroughly programmed presentation. Spontaneity works for her.

"OUR GOAL IS SURVIVAL": HOW PAT RUSSO TRANSMITTED URGENCY AT LUCENT

In earlier chapters, I've shared portions of my friend Pat Russo's story. She is one of the most remarkable turnaround leaders in the history of high-tech management.

Russo has built a career through her willingness to tackle a series of tough business challenges. The first such challenge came her way in 1992, when she accepted the job of running AT&T's troubled Business Communications Systems division. This division sold and serviced private branch exchange networks that operated within large enterprises. It was a big business and one that AT&T dominated, but because it was a shrinking segment within a rapidly evolving telecommunications industry, it got short shrift from the technology experts and salespeople at AT&T.

As the division's revenues stalled and profits shrank, Russo was asked to take on the role of president. She was forced to lay off thousands of workers, many of them longtime AT&T employees with nowhere else to go. Russo's office mail included pencil-scrawled letters from children begging, "Please don't fire my daddy." Seeing Russo agonize over every layoff, her husband asked her, "Why do you take these decisions so personally?" Russo replied, "Because the letters are addressed to me." As division president, Russo knew the buck stopped with her, and she found the burden a painful one to bear.

For a time, Russo struggled with the emotional challenges of leadership. The higher she rose in the company, the brighter the glare of the public spotlight, and she found that every decision she made was second-guessed by someone—often on network television or on the business page of a national newspaper. She hated being a lightning rod for controversy. Russo finally managed to shift her attitude on election night in 1993, when she and her husband watched on television as another strong woman leader—New Jersey's Christine Todd Whitman—won the gubernatorial election with just forty percent of the vote. As Whitman gave her victory speech that night, Russo's husband turned to Pat and said, "Maybe you need to take a page from Christie Whitman's book."

"How do you mean?" Russo asked.

"Maybe you need to get used to having half of the people mad at you, the way politicians do."

The advice hit home. Russo accepted the reality that no leader can ever find a way to please everyone. Sometimes, a plurality of support is all you can hope for—and if you're convinced you're doing the right thing, that can be enough.

Armed with this new philosophy, Russo learned to live with the burden of tough choices. Her shepherding of the Business Communications Systems division through its tough times, though painful, ultimately was successful, allowing the company to remain in business and saving the jobs of thousands of employees. That became the first turnaround in Russo's career, and a major milestone on her path to becoming one of the first female CEOs of a giant technology company.

In 1995 AT&T underwent one of the most dramatic pieces of corporate surgery in business history. The giant company was split into three businesses—one focusing on computers, one on telecommunications networks, and one on equipment and services. Russo's Business Communications Systems division became part of the third company, which was named Lucent Technologies. By this time, the division turnaround that Russo had directed was complete, and Lucent's initial stock offering was one of the biggest and most successful in history. For a time, Lucent became a darling of Wall Street, and Russo was named its executive vice president of corporate operations.

Russo was named CEO of Lucent in 2002; the next few years were a critical time, as the industry was experiencing unprecedented turmoil. Her successful guidance of the company through that maelstrom is, among other things, a case study in effective communication by a business leader.

Lucent's struggles in the early twenty-first century had several causes, but chief among them was the so-called dot-com crash—the collapse of the wildly overinflated high-tech industry sector. As Wall Street recognized the unrealistic expectations that had built up around the growth of Internet-related companies, one business after another shut its doors, and those that survived were forced to drastically cut back their expansion plans. The impact on companies like Lucent that made their money as suppliers to other businesses was dramatic. Huge orders for telecom networks and other equipment were canceled; Lucent's revenues cratered, causing the company's stock price to plummet. That in turn hurt the pension plans that cared for Lucent's large retiree base (tens of thousands of people who had once worked for the AT&T monopoly), driving up the company's costs for health care. Anxious, angry shareholders mounted lawsuits against the company, draining time and energy that the leadership team needed to focus on keeping the business afloat.

Russo had to lead the company through a painful turnaround, much as she had done years earlier at AT&T, though on a much larger scale. Once again, she had to make painful decisions about cost cutting, including layoffs of longtime employees. Every possible way to save money was exploited: Russo ordered the maintenance crews at headquarters to stop washing the windows and mowing the lawns, and every third light bulb in the hallways was unscrewed to trim energy costs.

When a company's problems are this serious, the top leader's communication style is critically important. "Everything matters," Russo says. "What you do, what you say, and who you are—all are essential. When people are worried about their future and about the future of the company, they watch everything you do. They pay attention to your facial expressions and your body language. And they listen carefully to every word you say. You've got to come across as realistic but confident. It's a tough line to walk."

Russo's focus on communication started at the top. During the most critical twelve-month period, she held no fewer than forty-eight meetings with her board of directors, some in person, some by conference call. Some observers wondered whether this was overkill. "People would say to me, 'Getting input from your advisors is good, but maybe you get *too much* input!'" Russo recalls. But she knew that, in this time of crisis, keeping her board members fully informed—and maintaining their unified support for the turnaround efforts she was developing—was essential.

Furthermore, she recognized that her chance of making the right calls on each of the urgent, rapid-fire decisions she was being forced to address would be greatly increased by having a steady stream of ideas and feedback from the most knowledgeable sources. "I don't have all the answers," Russo says. "And as a leader, I reserve the right to learn."

At the same time, Russo pushed her leadership team to rapidly develop and implement plans for getting Lucent back to break-even. "Our goal is survival," she declared. With the company on the brink, Russo emphasized that "good-enough" strategies that could be put in place within days were far more valuable than perfect strategies that would require months to execute.

Finally, Russo made sure that the seriousness of the crisis was conveyed throughout the organization. She used every communication method available to her, up to and including quarterly broadcasts to the entire base of sixty-five thousand Lucent employees. For these critical presentations, every word was carefully planned and vetted, ensuring that the sense of concern Russo wanted to convey never shaded into uncertainty, anxiety, or fear. For example, in sentences describing the company's plans, she crossed out the words "we hope" wherever they appeared and replaced them with "we will."

In combination, all these actions orchestrated by Russo—the series of immediate, visible cost-cutting measures; the continual consultations with the board and other top leaders; the focus on quickly putting "good-enough" strategies in place; and the carefully crafted communications to employees—sent a powerful message throughout Lucent. The next three years were difficult, but under Russo's leadership, the company returned to profitability and then resumed its growth. By 2007, Lucent was ready to lead the next phase in its industry's evolution by merging with Alcatel, pioneering a period of consolidation that continues today.

You may never be faced with the task of leading a multibillion-dollar corporation through a period of crisis. But to be an effective leader, you should learn how to instill an appropriate sense of the seriousness of problems throughout your team. The communication tools described and illustrated in this chapter should help.

TAKEAWAYS FROM CHAPTER 12

- A leader doesn't need to be a spellbinding orator—but they do need to be able to use the power of words to connect clearly, authentically, and passionately with team members.

- One key to improving your speaking ability is sheer practice. The more often you speak before groups—whether leading a team meeting in your office or giving a formal address before a sales conference or convention—the greater your comfort level will become.

- You should experiment to develop a system of preparing for a speech that works for you. Many people find that working from a simple outline (listing five to ten bullet points) rather than a written script yields the best results—a speech that sounds and feels spontaneous rather than labored.

- No matter the purpose or the precise format, keep your talk short and simple. Audiences will appreciate and remember the contents of a ten- to fifteen-minute speech far better than they will one of thirty minutes or more.

- When practicing for a presentation, strive to overlearn the material—that is, study it repeatedly until you know it by heart and can even modify the presentation on the spot if needed.

- Remember, as an organizational leader—no matter your level in the company hierarchy—your words and behaviors will be closely scrutinized. Think carefully about the messages you send, deliberately or inadvertently, and be sure those messages match your intentions.

PART

3

LEADING AN
ORGANIZATION

13

What Only the CEO Can Do:
Creating a Positive Company Culture

Leading an organization brings with it a new set of challenges. One of these is the job of defining and nurturing a positive company culture—a set of values, behaviors, and expectations that help make the organization a satisfying and successful place to work. Here are some observations about what it takes to make such a culture a reality.

ONCE YOU HAVE DEVELOPED and practiced the skills of leading others, and established a track record of strong results—improved financial performance, high-quality productivity, positive employee morale—you may be fortunate enough to ascend to the highest levels of an organization. You may be invited to join a company's leadership team and receive a title like executive vice president, chief marketing officer, or head of operations. You may be asked to serve on a corporation's board of directors. Or you may be selected as company president or CEO and assume the ultimate responsibility for both the day-to-day activities of the firm and its long-term strategic direction. Any of these scenarios is a high honor, one that relatively few people ever achieve.

In some ways, leading or helping to lead an organization is much like leading a small team, only writ large. It takes many of the same skills, such as:

- the ability to reframe problems to open up solutions to dilemmas that seem impossible to solve;

- the ability to discover the facts behind a challenge, which makes effective problem-solving possible;

- the ability to pose probing questions that challenge assumptions and open people's minds;

- the ability to define what's truly important and develop plans for achieving it;

- the ability to recruit a talented team of employees and elicit their best work;

- the ability to develop winning and innovative strategies, products, and services;

- the ability to communicate clearly with those two up and two down in the company hierarchy; and

- the ability to speak powerfully in a clear, distinctive voice.

If you've risen to the ranks of organizational leaders, it's probably because you've exhibited these skills in your previous jobs. You'll now be called on to use them on behalf of an entire company.

However, you'll find that leading an organization also imposes some new demands. There are things that only the CEO or the members of the CEO's leadership team can do. Being an effective organizational leader requires that you step up to this new level of accomplishment and tackle tasks you've probably never given much thought to in the past.

Corporate work that only the CEO can perform includes the following:

- shaping, nurturing, and enforcing a corporate culture that makes high performance possible;

- defining and sharing values that will guide the organization's activities;

- developing an inspiring vision for the organization's future and communicating that vision persuasively;

- guiding the creation of an innovative competitive strategy for feedback and approval by the board of directors;

- assembling the human capital needed to accomplish the strategy;

- guiding the allocation of financial capital and other resources;

- leading the organization through times of crisis, challenge, and change;

- ensuring that employees share in the benefits derived from the organization's success;

- representing the organization in the outside world and taking responsibility for its reputation; and

- helping to create a succession plan that will foster the long-term success of the organization.

It's not feasible to provide a complete how-to manual for this entire list of CEO challenges. The only way to truly master some of them is by doing them. But in this portion of the book, I'll share with you some of my experiences, observations, and advice from my years as a corporate leader, including my roles as a CEO, a board member, and a board chairman at seven publicly owned and four privately owned companies. I think my insights are interesting in themselves. But more important, they will help you tackle any leadership task you undertake, at any level, in an organization of any size. Think of it as the ultimate example of the two-up system: Getting a glimpse of the issues confronting the CEO and their executive team can make it easier for you to understand how you can provide them with the most useful support. Of course, in the process, you'll also be preparing yourself to answer the call to shoulder a top leadership job . . . and increasing the chances that the call may come someday.

The great general Napoleon said, "Every French soldier carries a marshal's baton in his knapsack." He meant that, in his ideal army, even the lowliest recruit should be prepared to lead if necessary. I think the same applies in business. The better you understand the challenges of leading the organization you work for, the better you can serve in any capacity—and the more you can achieve, for your own benefit and the benefit of everyone around you.

CREATING A POSITIVE, HIGH-PERFORMANCE CULTURE

Lack of engagement on the part of team members is one of the biggest barriers that corporate leaders must overcome. Sad to say, many organizations do a poor job of giving their workers a purpose that makes them feel engaged and energized. This is why creating a *high-performance culture* is such an important challenge for the CEO to address.

More than one kind of corporate culture can generate high performance among employees—at least in the short run. My friend Ian Davis saw this truth play out firsthand during his thirty-one years at the global consulting firm of McKinsey & Company, including seven years as the firm's chairman and managing director. Davis's work gave him a perspective on the inner workings of every conceivable kind of company in virtually every industry, and he says that he has seen high-performance cultures of many varieties. Some drive high performance through intimidation and fear; some through financial incentives; others through a sense of teamwork, camaraderie, and *esprit de corps*; and still others through idealistic motivations like a commitment to the company mission or a desire to make the world a better place.

"There are successful companies that rely on all of these forms of motivation," Davis says. "So one of the key challenges that the leader faces is to choose among them. The choice depends, in part, on the leader's own values. What do you believe in? What are your views of human nature? What sort of organization are you seeking to build? What kind of atmosphere do you personally want to work in? The answers to questions like these will help to determine the kind of high-performance culture you choose to nurture.

"At the same time," Davis continues, "the business and social context in which you are operating is crucially important." Davis explains that his leadership style was effective at McKinsey in large part because his personality fit the corporate culture—that of a people-intensive, knowledge-intensive business—and the context of the firm at that time. "There are other industries, and other contexts, in which my style of leadership would not have worked," he says. "I believe that all leaders are defined by the context in which they are leading."

Davis adds that the same divergence can be seen at work in every leadership arena, pointing to Winston Churchill's leadership in Britain during the Second World War as an example. Churchill's orotund rhetorical style provided the inspiration necessary to fight the war against fascism. "But after the war ended, Churchill was no longer the right man in the right place at the right time," Davis says. "The British people turned elsewhere for leadership."

As I've mentioned, my own experience in the corporate world suggests that the best way to inspire high performance for most people is through positive goals that transcend the immediate, short-term objectives of the company or the individual worker. Let's face it—few employees feel excited about coming to work every morning solely to earn a paycheck. Even fewer are galvanized by typical corporate goals like "increasing profits" or "improving shareholder value." Instead, most people need a bigger, more inspiring goal to elicit their greatest creative efforts. They want to believe that the work they're doing is benefiting themselves and their families while also helping, at least in a small way, to make the world a better place.

In my view, the leader's goal in most industries should be to build a culture that insists on dedication to excellence—but that does so by appealing to the best in people rather than attempting to motivate through intimidation, criticism, or fear, as so many organizations do. I believe the evidence shows that, over time, a *positive,* high-performance culture will consistently outperform a negative one—because a culture driven by punishment, demands, and fear tends to lead, in the long run, to burnout, alienation, and failure.

The need for positive motivation is especially true in times of adversity, when lagging company performance, scanty resources, and intense time pressures can create an atmosphere of anxiety and despair. In such times, the leader who hopes to achieve the impossible must find ways to connect the organization's goals to the highest personal aspirations of team members. This leader needs to formulate a dream that team members will find inspiring and that they are happy to share and identify with. Then the leader must work with their team to define the dream in concrete terms and to map out a journey that will make it real.

DEFINING THE VALUES THAT SHAPE YOUR DREAM

The first step toward defining an exciting, inspiring dream often requires clearing away the negativity and cynicism that, over time, come to pervade too many organizations. When I joined Aetna, one of my most important tasks was to help reposition the company from being viewed as "one of those self-serving, greedy health insurance companies" into one that insiders and outsiders alike could regard as a progressive organization helping to lead America toward a more humane, efficient, and inclusive health-care system.

Embracing this aspirational goal wasn't an empty "feel-good" gesture designed for public relations consumption. I was serious about putting it into practice as a guiding principle behind our daily business decisions. At the same time, it didn't mean weakening our dedication to traditional business goals like profitability. Just the opposite, in fact. Although it might seem paradoxical, aligning the organization around that seemingly idealistic goal also helped us make Aetna into one of the most productive and profitable companies in the industry. It illustrates how effective leadership can make it possible to achieve two essential objectives that might seem, at first glance, to be diametrically opposed.

Before I joined Aetna, company leadership had tried a very different approach to employee motivation, one that on the surface might appear more realistic and tough-minded. Kathy Mentus, who then ran executive communications at Aetna, recalls the Aetna culture of the 1990s. "We had big posters on display around the building spelling out the key ideas of our company mission statement," she says.

The first line of the mission statement was something like "We will deliver a financial return of X percent to our shareholders." Of course, shareholders are important and so are financial returns. But this was the wrong message to send to employees. Highlighting financial results in the first line of the mission statement said to everyone at Aetna, "It's *all* about the shareholders." It implicitly put everyone else—clients, customers, health-care providers, patients, even employees themselves—on a lower level. The mission statement did mention those other stakeholders, but they didn't appear until much later in the document.

The symbolism of that mission statement helps to explain the poor state of employee morale at Aetna during that period. It also explains some of the strategic mistakes the company was making at the time. For example, when Aetna went on its acquisition binge, buying smaller insurance companies without thinking about how they would fit into the business or how they could be integrated culturally, it was being driven above all by the need to produce a high financial return for the shareholders. Achieving that goal year in and year out meant the company *had* to keep growing, no matter what.

So it behaved accordingly. Aetna's leadership made strategic decisions that reflected the fact that growth was more important than delivering service to customers—and even more important than building a healthy, sustainable business.

Everyone knows that a strong organization must be aligned around a well-defined purpose. Aetna was aligned around a purpose, all right. But it was the wrong one. And that made all the difference in the world.

Jack Rowe recalls that, when he joined Aetna, many of his new colleagues confessed that they'd lost much of the pride they'd formerly felt about being Aetna employees. Rowe says, "When Aetna people were asked at cocktail parties, 'So, what do you do?' they'd respond by mumbling, as if they were embarrassed to mention the company name." Internally, the integration of newly acquired businesses had gone so badly that many employees still identified with their original company, not with Aetna.

I was determined to change all that. I started by taking steps to figure out the underlying causes of the problem. Simply talking to as many Aetna team members as we could—for example, through the listening tour that I described in a previous chapter—was part of the process, as were more rigorous efforts to take the pulse of the Aetna community. The company's previous leaders had been well aware that worker morale was a problem, and they'd tried hard to study the problem, in part through a continual barrage of surveys asking employees their opinions about everything from human resources policies to customer service issues. In fact, the surveys had become so frequent and numerous (at last count there were fifty-two surveys being conducted every year) that people stopped taking them seriously. We fixed this by conducting a single annual survey that was thoughtfully designed and administered to yield meaningful results.

More important, the surveys had never seemed to result in any visible or substantive changes. We realized we had to figure out how to transform employee surveys into a truly useful leadership tool.

One crucial requirement was that the survey responses be anonymous. Only in that way would employees feel comfortable being truly honest about their feelings and the problems they'd experienced at the company.

Company leaders also needed to take the survey responses seriously, which included responding in an honest, timely fashion to any comments and questions that employees submitted with their surveys. Since the surveys were anonymous, that meant assembling a list of the most frequently raised issues and finding opportunities to address them publicly. We used employee town halls and other gatherings as venues to discuss some of the questions, complaints, and comments we encountered during the survey process. Our team members appreciated the fact that we cared enough about their concerns to respond to them personally.

We weren't surprised by many of the issues that surfaced in our employee surveys. The company's financial troubles had done a lot to damage morale. After decades as a rock-solid economic presence, Aetna had become a shaky, money-losing business, causing many employees to worry about their own future prospects. The rash of ill-considered company acquisitions had hurt, too. Many employees felt that Aetna's traditional conservative culture had been cast aside, with nothing to replace it; the giant new company bearing the Aetna name seemed to many a mere grab-bag of businesses with no defining identity, strategy, or purpose.

Perhaps most serious, we discovered that some Aetna employees had begun to question the ethical underpinnings of our business. That shouldn't have been surprising in an era when the rising costs of health care had become a national issue and when many in politics and the media had begun to scapegoat insurance companies as a major cause of the problem. We'd always claimed that our business decisions were rooted in "doing the right things for the right reasons." But some employees in our service centers were wondering whether those ethical claims were valid. When they had to turn down an insurance claim for a medical procedure not covered by an individual's policy, was it really "the right thing for the right reason"? Or was it simply a hard-nosed business decision forced by the commitment to keep shareholder returns as high as possible?

DISTILLING THE AETNA WAY

We took our employees' concerns seriously. We started by addressing the financial and strategic issues that had led many workers to question the soundness of the company's management and the strength of its culture. On the ethical front, we responded by meeting with the people who were concerned and addressing their questions directly. We visited Aetna service centers in places like Bismarck, North Dakota, to talk with the employees about client claims and how they were being handled. We conducted educational programs to make sure that everyone on the team understood how the insurance business really worked, the principles behind our underwriting decisions, and the financial realities that dictated specific coverage rules.

In a few cases, we discovered that policy claims were being denied unfairly. We promptly changed our rules and made sure the new guidelines were understood and followed. In other cases, the denials of coverage were appropriate, but our service people hadn't been taught the solid reasons why that was the case. So we began doing a better job of communicating the reasons for our policies to our people and training them in explaining the same principles to the customers.

We realized that, at times, addressing the challenge of "doing the right things for the right reasons" required a degree of courage. At Aetna—as at other well-managed health insurance companies—we empowered the chief medical officer in each business division to make the toughest calls regarding coverage of particular services and procedures. These decisions could have significant financial impact, both individually (since some medical procedures involve costs running into the hundreds of thousands of dollars) and cumulatively (when multiplied by thousands of patients). We were honest with our team members about these realities. But we made it clear that the medical officers had final say when it came to clinical decisions. Our business managers were not empowered to override them, regardless of the financial pressures they might be feeling at the time. That's simply the way it has to be when you are in a business like Aetna's, which profoundly affects people's lives.

The collaborative process of exploring, defining, and implementing a set of ethical standards and values for Aetna eventually became codified in the "Aetna Way." This was a written document that spelled out the guiding principles behind our company's strategies and the decisions we made on a daily basis. It identified four core values that we strove to embody in all our actions:

- Integrity

- Quality service and value

- Excellence and accountability

- Engaged employees

The Aetna Way proved to be a powerful tool for leading the company toward a values-driven future. I made a point of discussing it explicitly at the start of every speech or presentation I made. I felt it was important to signal to employees that the Aetna Way was not just a source of inspiration, but also a guide to daily decision making—a tool that could tell them when it was time to pull the handle to stop the bus if they sensed we were veering off course. To emphasize this, we sought concrete examples that illustrated how to apply the principles of the Aetna Way on the job.

One story I found inspiring and often shared with my colleagues was the experience of an Aetna customer service representative who took a call one day from a health insurance customer. She quickly realized the call wasn't simply a routine request for information about a claim; instead, the customer was a deeply suicidal person on the verge of killing himself and desperately reaching out for some reason to stay alive.

Our service rep rose to the challenge. Channeling the Aetna Way, she threw out all the rules that ordinarily governed service calls and decided to do whatever it took to meet that customer's needs. She spent two hours on the line with him, listening, encouraging, and supporting him—literally saving his life (and incidentally earning an Aetna Excellence Award in the process).

I used her story many times as a vivid illustration of my vision of a values-driven Aetna. It was a tale that any employee could quickly understand, identify with, and use as a guide to personal practice and as an inspiring reminder of what our company stood for.

In time, as our business prospects improved and as word about our commitment to the Aetna Way began to spread, employee pride returned to its once-high levels—then soared even higher. (Early in the Aetna turnaround, the "proud of where I work" rating among our employees was thirty percent. Over time, we raised it to eighty-five percent.) Gradually, the dream of making Aetna a corporate leader with the mission of making America's health-care system fairer, more efficient, and more inclusive began to seem believable to our team members. With belief came commitment . . . and with commitment, the hard work that leads to change and achievement.

SHARING THE DREAM—THE IMPORTANCE OF BEING THERE

Another step that Jack Rowe and I took early in our joint tenure at Aetna was holding an employee meeting at the office we then owned in Middletown, Connecticut. Why was that significant? Because Middletown had formerly been the home office of our health insurance business, our biggest and most important line of work. But during our acquisition frenzy, much of the corporation's management energy had shifted to Blue Bell, Pennsylvania, the home of one of our biggest merger partners. Middletown had become, in the words of Elease Wright, "almost a leper colony" as far as the company's top leaders were concerned. Suddenly, all the key decisions were being made at Blue Bell, with the folks at Middletown simply being informed after the fact.

When Jack and I traveled to Middletown and met with all the people there—using a satellite hookup to broadcast the conversation to every Aetna facility—we were sending a clear symbolic message: "Middletown matters again." We went on to send the same message to many other Aetna outposts that had felt neglected or ignored for too long. During my years as CEO, I set myself the goal of visiting every single Aetna facility. I wanted everyone who worked for the company to have a chance to see me and talk to me face-to-face about their work and about what Aetna meant to them. And before my time at the helm was completed, I managed to do just that.

When you are a leader, simply showing up—being personally present among the people you are relying on to make your dream a reality—carries enormous symbolic weight.

FIXING A BROKEN CULTURE: GETTING BEYOND FINGER-POINTING

Sometimes, creating a positive culture requires fixing a dysfunctional culture that makes effective fact-finding, open dialogue, and logical problem-solving difficult.

As I've noted, when I joined Jack Rowe at the helm at Aetna, the company was losing almost a million dollars a day. Investors, Wall Street analysts, and Aetna's own people were frustrated, angry, and scared. Many expected and demanded immediate, sweeping action to stop the bleeding—for example, deep, across-the-board cost cuts like those seen at many troubled businesses.

The previous management team had risen to the top in the wake of a series of acquisitions. They embodied a mixture of corporate culture and decision-making styles inherited from fundamentally different organizations that had been yoked together by mergers. The members of this leadership team were smart and well intentioned, but as a group, they appeared to subscribe to what I call the Attila the Hun school of management: They encouraged ruthless competition and conflict among divisional and departmental managers, perhaps believing that this would drive people to work harder in an effort to outdo one another.

This trial-by-combat philosophy made an awkward overlay for

the traditional "Aetna nice" culture, which encouraged people to suppress their differences and gloss over the organization's problems. Making matters worse, some of Aetna's best people had begun to depart for competing companies. These defections left us with a cultural void in many departments. Those left behind lacked a deep memory of the company's history and its values; many wondered what Aetna really stood for. We also suffered serious gaps in crucial leadership skills. In one department, the entire long-term supervisory level had practically vanished, while in another the members of the regional sales leadership team had all departed.

As the company faced the worst crisis of its history, these dysfunctional circumstances gave rise to a passive-aggressive style of conflict that got in the way of open communication and rational problem-solving. Soon after my arrival, departmental and divisional leaders began lining up outside my office to offer their differing diagnoses of the company's problems, often blaming other units for the losses and lobbying to protect their own budgets. The sales representatives would complain, "We can't sell these insurance policies because the pricing is all wrong!" The underwriters who managed the pricing, in turn, would blame the people in charge of negotiating contracts with health-care providers: "If only we got better deals from the hospitals and the doctors, then we could price the contracts better!" Meanwhile, the contracting teams laid their problems at the feet of our information technology services, saying, "If we want better deals, we need to have more accurate and timely information about our claims experience!"

As the finger-pointing escalated, the real underlying facts inevitably became lost or seriously distorted. As a newcomer to Aetna, I found it impossible to figure out what was actually going on at the company and why we were suffering such a serious misalignment between our pricing decisions and our cost experiences, producing those million-dollar-a-day losses.

I realized that making any hasty decisions would be a serious mistake given the circumstances. I knew I had to apply rule number one of systems thinking: *Never take anything apart that you don't fully understand.* Any car mechanic will tell you that sometimes a vehicle needs to have major repairs—but you'd better not start cutting wires inside the engine without knowing whether they lead to the brakes or the steering wheel.

So, despite the fact that we were hemorrhaging money, I resisted the panicked demands from the Wall Street analysts to make drastic, immediate cost reductions. Instead, I took the counterintuitive step of delaying most cost reductions for more than eight months after my arrival at Aetna. "After all," I explained, "we can't make cuts until we have a strategy—because how will we know what to cut?" While it was obvious that we needed to reduce costs and boost revenues, making those adjustments in the context of a smart, customer-focused strategy was essential.

To devise that strategy, we would have to gather leaders from every company unit into a single room so we could unearth and then jointly analyze the hard data about Aetna's performance—its strengths and weaknesses, its systemic problems, our competitive position, and the specific business segments that needed retooling. Above all, I wanted to avoid being stampeded into making a decision based on one point of view. When a company is tackling complicated, interlocking problems, getting everyone in the same room and laying the hard data on the table enables you to sort out what is really happening, where the systemic problems are, and what a real solution requires. I strongly suspected this process of discovery would reveal that there were elements of *every* department that were flawed.

To make our problem-solving sessions effective, I also had to create a culture of honesty and transparency. As a leader, I generally avoid playing the role of dictator, seeking to operate by consensus as much as possible. But establishing and enforcing clear standards of communication and cooperation is one essential team-building task that only the leader can do.

In this case, I had to get tough. The dysfunctional styles of communication and conflict that Aetna had fallen into had to be eliminated. I laid out some basic ground rules that I called "expectations of leaders." They were simple principles designed to help us work together more effectively—ones like "Assume positive intent," "Attack the problem, not the person," "When you have bad news, deliver it early and in person," and "Remember that leading an organization is a marathon, not a sprint."

I shared these expectations with our leadership team, answered their questions, and made a few modifications to the list based on feedback. Then I said, "*This* is how I expect you to behave if you want to be part of the recovery team at Aetna. If you don't want to follow these guidelines, please let me know. If that's the case, I will help you leave."

We went around the table so that each member of the team could affirm their acceptance of the guidelines. When their turns came, a couple of people merely nodded; with a smile, I told them, "I can't hear the sound of your head moving. Please respond in words." I wanted it clearly understood that we were all making a firm personal commitment—not simply acquiescing without true agreement.

Everyone joined the pact. In truth, I think most of my team members felt relieved. They were happy to finally have a leader who wanted to focus the organization solely on identifying and fixing

EXPECTATIONS OF LEADERS

Integrity	Employee Engagement	Excellence & Accountability	Quality Service & Value
1. Live the company values	1. Assume positive intent	1. Disciplined performance management process	1. Lead customer-focused change
2. Be a leader, not an administrator	2. Communicate Communicate Communicate	2. Awesome execution	2. Head in the clouds, feet on the ground. Know when to be where
3. Model and instill a sense of urgency	- Make what you know accessible to others	3. Deliver bad news early and personally	3. Imagination: have it or hire it
4. Understand the issues and take action	3. Challenge the "idea," not the person	4. Proactively manage variances to achieve the plan	4. It's about the "and," not the "or"
- What, so what, now what?	4. Consideration for the person should be higher than consideration for the work	5. Be expert on what is critical to success	5. Delight and surprise our customers positively:
5. Demonstrate courage in the moment	5. Maintain balance	6. Make your team flexible and better	- members
6. Disagree but commit to ultimate decision	- It's a marathon, not a sprint	7. Be at least 15% better every year	- plan sponsors
	6. Assure proper fit		- providers
	- "sailor or SEAL"—okay to be either		- brokers/ consultants
	7. Develop, retain, and share diverse top talent		- regulators

what had gotten broken rather than tolerating endless rounds of backbiting and political gamesmanship.

RULES OF THE SANDBOX: THE LEADER ENFORCES NORMS

I'm a believer in the value of constructive tension within an organization. But the line separating it from dysfunctional conflict can shift and be hard to define. The leader must manage the personal tensions that may arise among team members and make sure the focus on organizational needs remains clear.

As you might imagine, this can be a sticky task. The higher echelons of many businesses are populated by people with strong egos—unsurprisingly, since it takes a lot of self-belief to achieve that level of power in an organization. As a result, personality conflicts and battles over control and influence are not unusual.

Sometimes, an organization gets unduly "squeaky"—plagued by tensions and discomforts due to persistent conflicts and unresolved frictions. In circumstances like these, the leader plays an important role by assuming positive intent and doing so in a rather obvious, explicit fashion. This educates people about the right way to deal with disagreement and models the kind of team-building culture you want to create.

During my first months at Aetna, managers besieged me to complain about teammates sabotaging their efforts. The company's willy-nilly growth by acquisitions, combined with the passive-aggressive "Aetna nice" culture, had created serious management dysfunctions that people felt unable to discuss openly. I defused the hostilities by gathering the relevant people together and putting the issues openly on the table. Then I urged my colleagues to sheath their swords and talk through their problems with candor and mutual respect. My mantra was "Challenge the issue, not the person."

When office politics threatens to stall your organization's progress, assuming positive intent will help your team focus on the *real* problems rather than getting bogged down in needless personal battles.

Another important task for any leader is to develop a potential successor—someone who will be ready to step in and lead the team when the time comes for you to move on. Jack Rowe prepared me to become CEO when he left, and I in turn helped to recruit and train the man who eventually became my successor, a smart and talented executive named Mark Bertolini. In each case, the final choice was in the hands of the board, but providing the board with at least one great option is a job for the previous leader. In my case, the task of helping to prepare Bertolini to take my place as CEO led to one of the messiest political battles I had to referee during my years at Aetna.

Mark Bertolini is quite a character. A Detroit native, he worked for four years in the 1970s as a department coordinator of one of the city's trauma center emergency rooms. This painful experience left him vowing he would never work in our nation's dysfunctional health-care system again. But after earning an MBA from Cornell University, he got into the health insurance industry. I recruited him in 2003 to help manage our businesses in pharmacy, behavioral health, and dental coverage. Mark was a highly sought-after executive at the time, and from the moment I met him I viewed him as a potential successor.

Mark is also a student of philosophy, a practitioner of meditation and yoga, and a motorcycling enthusiast who sometimes comes to work decked out in leather riding gear. After a near-fatal skiing accident in 2004, he found alternative healing techniques so beneficial to his own pain management challenges that he later arranged to have classes in mindfulness and yoga made available to employees throughout Aetna.

Mark was a rising star at Aetna when I decided we needed to recruit a new executive to help with strategy. We conducted an exhaustive search among many of the best minds in our industry, and I interviewed several promising candidates. Eventually we settled on an executive whom I'll call Rich, who had served as CEO of a smaller regional insurance company and who seemed to have all the qualifications we were seeking, including a deep knowledge of the business and a creative mind. We wooed and won him, and Rich joined our team as a colleague—and a potential rival—of Mark's.

It soon became apparent that Rich and Mark were not playing well together. Part of the problem was personal. Rich had many strengths, but a talent for crisp, clear communication was not one of them. Whenever he spoke up in a meeting, he was so long-winded and repetitive that people would exchange glances and occasionally roll their eyes. (Remember that Rich had been a CEO before joining Aetna. One of the occupational hazards of being the "big boss" is that people may be reluctant to tell you when you are talking too much.) For the high-energy, let's-get-it-done Mark, Rich's long-windedness was a little hard to take.

More significant, as our strategy guru, Rich was supposed to develop innovative ideas for building our businesses—but the ideas he came up with lacked the sophistication and clarity of thought we'd expected. They also impinged on some of Mark's areas of responsibility as well as those of other executives. It would have helped if Rich's ideas had been brilliant, but most fell well short of that standard. The fact that Rich was not a good listener made Mark even more frustrated and upset.

Believing that Rich had some worthwhile ideas to contribute to Aetna's success, I wanted to figure out how to help him fit in to our organization. As CEO, I had a responsibility to find a way to help the mismatched team of Rich and Mark join forces productively. It wasn't easy. I spoke with both men, separately and together, in an effort to help them find common ground. I even enlisted the help of a smart and sensitive executive coaching consultant named Rusty O'Kelley to serve as a kind of "marriage counselor" for them.

Over time, it became increasingly clear to me—and to others at the company—that Rich had simply been a bad hire, a mistake on my part. In the end, Rich and Aetna had to part ways.

While Rich was clearly not up to our standards, Mark has never been one to suffer fools gladly, and he didn't make much effort to conceal his annoyance with Rich and his growing contempt for him. So I invested time in urging Mark to modify his at-times abrasive personal style.

Every leader behaves in a way that is a unique reflection of their character, upbringing, values, habits, and circumstances, and a wide range of leadership styles has been shown to be effective. Whereas Mark tends to be opinionated, brash, outspoken, and unconventional (wearing meditation beads in place of a necktie, for example), most people find me to be reserved, soft-spoken, deliberative, and rather conservative in my style. Those differences were certainly evident when Mark and I worked together, and they've persisted in the years since Mark succeeded me at Aetna. People who know us both use expressions like "night and day" to compare our leadership styles, and one of our joint friends describes Mark as "the anti-Ron" to emphasize the difference.

It would be interesting to trace the root causes for this divergence in personal style. There must be dozens of factors that have shaped both

Mark and me, dating back to our boyhoods and extending through-out our careers. Mark is younger than me, which means he grew up in an era when traditional business formalities were less restrictive and there was greater tolerance for wider variations in personal style. Mark also took the reins at Aetna at a time when the company was on sound business footing, as compared to a time of crisis when I took the helm; I suspect that people feel more relaxed and accepting of personal quirks when economic survival is not at stake.

It's also possible that race plays a part. I come from an ethnic background that is still unusual among the ranks of top executives. You might say that, in the executive suite, my color alone makes me stand out from the crowd; I have no need to do anything flashy or dramatic to draw attention to myself. On the other hand, in the eyes of some people, a black executive probably needs to be especially well-prepared, detail-oriented, and thorough in order to demon-strate their mastery of the leadership role. (I'm not accusing anyone of conscious racism. But in a society that has been steeped for gen-erations in various forms of bias, it's almost impossible for anyone to be completely free of subtle, unconsciously prejudiced assumptions.) In reaction to this reality, I have developed a style that relies on logic, clarity, and quiet but firm self-expression rather than flamboyance, charm, or charisma to win and retain the respect of my colleagues.

Each of us must play the hand we are dealt. I sometimes joke that if I behaved like some other executives—deploying sharp elbows and a tongue to match—I would be practically unemployable! The lead-ership style I've gravitated to has worked well for me—just as Mark's very different style has worked well for him.

However, when Mark and Rich were butting heads, I was per-turbed over the fact that Mark was playing the competitive game a little too rough. Knowing that he was on track to one day be the

CEO of Aetna, I shared my concerns with him. I knew Mark had no desire to be seen as angry or uncooperative and that he wanted to develop a leadership style that, while authentic and reflective of his true personality, would also invite and encourage others to participate and contribute as much as possible. So I quietly suggested to him that he work on curbing his tendency to shoot from the hip at times of conflict. I shared with Mark a favorite mantra that I often use to guide my own behavior when I am tempted to strike out verbally against an opponent: "If it would feel good to say it, don't!"

Mark took my advice in the right spirit and agreed to work on sanding down his rough edges. Eventually, the two of us even developed a little code that I used to help him stay on track. "Someday," I told him, "I'm going to write a book about leadership. And in that book, I'm going to recount all the things you've said that would have been better left unsaid! It'll be a great primer for other leaders who need to learn to curb their tongues."

Thereafter, whenever I heard Mark let slip a remark that I considered a little too harsh, I would cock an eyebrow at him and say, "That's going in the book!" Mark would chuckle, nod, and make a mental note of my gentle, indirect reprimand.

To his credit, Mark has continued to work on making the adjustments necessary to ensure that his personal leadership style is as effective as possible. In interviews, he has spoken openly about his problem with anger management and about how his daily practice of meditation has helped him be a more positive, compassionate leader. And Mark has shown himself to be a caring, people-centered leader in many other ways—most dramatically in early 2015 when he announced a significant increase in wages for Aetna's lowest-paid employees. His objectives were several-fold: to improve the morale of Aetna employees and enhance their commitment to the company, to help attract and retain the highest-quality people, and to show by example how America's big companies can help foster economic growth by supporting the expansion of our beleaguered middle class. The move garnered a lot of positive publicity for Aetna, and shares of the company's stock rose in its wake, suggesting that doing the right thing for your employees can also bring benefits to your shareholders. During his tenure, Mark has continued the transformation of Aetna, creating enormous value for patients and shareholders in the process.

There's more than one effective way to lead people, and it takes a variety of talents and styles to build the most powerful organization. The wise leader recognizes this truth and learns to respect, appreciate, and foster the contributions that people with widely diverse qualities can bring to the team.

TAKEAWAYS FROM CHAPTER 13

- The leader of an entire organization—as a CEO, a top executive, or a board member—has a unique set of tasks to perform. They start with shaping a positive, high performance culture one in which high expectations of achievement are set and enforced, while at the same time recognizing employees as important and valuable in their own right, not simply as cogs in a machine.

- A positive, high-performance culture begins with defining the values that should guide decision making within your organization. Do not take this task lightly. Confer with people throughout your organization, get real buy-in for the values you select, and define them in concrete, practical terms.

- If you discover that some of the values to which you aspire are not being practiced, get tough. Identify the changes needed to match actions to words, and take steps to make sure they're implemented. When employees realize that the organization's values are real and not mere window dressing, their sense of pride and commitment will grow.

- Troubled organizations are often plagued with dysfunctional habits such as finger-pointing, concealing unpleasant truths, and jockeying for power. The leader must tackle such habits head-on, making it clear that this behavior won't be tolerated.

- As the organizational leader, you must also model the kind of behavior you expect, especially among those whom you directly supervise. The tone you set in your interactions with your direct reports is likely to trickle down through the organization.

14

The Leader's Vision:
From Today's Reality to an Inspiring Future

*A company CEO should not delegate the essential task
of defining and articulating the corporate vision. Such
an effort demands both a firm grasp of current reality
and a clear-eyed picture of a hopeful future.*

I NOTED IN AN earlier chapter that my friend Ken Chenault likes
to cite Napoleon's definition of leadership: "to define reality and to
give hope." This leadership two-step starts with defining reality for
your organization. That begins with getting a firm grasp on that
reality yourself—a much more difficult task than you may realize.
In today's complex, ever-changing world, if you think the problems
faced by any organization are simple and straightforward, you are

probably missing something important—something that is all too likely to come back and bite you before long.

DEFINING REALITY: FIGURING OUT WHAT'S *REALLY* HAPPENING IN AND AROUND THE ORGANIZATION

As you'll recall, one of my first and most important steps when I joined Aetna was to spearhead the creation of a new system for gathering, analyzing, and disseminating basic data about our multifarious health insurance businesses. The building of our executive management information system was about defining reality, in all its complexity, for the entire Aetna team—an essential preliminary step before we could set about making that reality better.

Getting a grasp on your organization's reality requires connecting with all of the organization's key constituencies—employees, suppliers, outside organizations, regulatory agencies, and, of course, customers. People with differing perspectives define reality differently. Since each of your organization's stakeholders can have a significant impact on your future, as a leader, you need to understand and respect their varying perspectives, even if you view some of their opinions as shortsighted or flawed.

The more data points a leader draws information from, the better. Beware the trap of choosing a handful of trusted advisors and listening only to them. You can easily miss important developments that way. Pay attention to what your closest associates tell you—but then perform a reality check by comparing their version of the truth with as many other versions as possible.

This philosophy was behind the "listening tour" I conducted shortly after joining Aetna. I spent several weeks delving deeply into the organization's complicated, troubled reality. I visited (in person or virtually) many of the sites where our operations were housed, ranging from our home offices in Connecticut to customer sites around the country. I met with people from every organizational department and management level, ranging from top executives with decades of experience to brand-new employees working on the bottom rungs of the corporate ladder. I made a special effort to talk just a little, but to listen a lot—suspending judgment, withholding criticism, and trying not to offer snap opinions or top-of-the-head solutions to the problems I heard about. Instead, I focused on simply absorbing what Aetna people had to say—including the stress-filled emotional outpourings that were inevitable under the circumstances.

It wasn't always easy to maintain my neutral, tell-me-everything attitude. Our team members naturally looked to me as "the answer man" who would be leading Aetna out of trouble and back to safety. They peppered me with questions: Will there be layoffs? How much will our budget have to be cut? Are there businesses we need to sell? Is this office going to close? Is my job safe? In those early weeks, I simply shook my head. "We'll tackle all those questions in time," I would say. "Right now, we're still trying to get a handle on the situation. It would be a mistake to make any big decisions before we understand what's *really* going on." It was a tough message to deliver to our understandably anxious team members—but I think they appreciated the fact that I was approaching the challenge in a deliberate, thoughtful fashion.

The detailed picture I gathered during the weeks of my listening tour helped me recognize the full scope of the dire problems the company faced—and allowed me and my team to begin formulating a plan to save Aetna from the potential disasters that threatened us.

Of course, getting a firm grasp on reality isn't a one-time-only exercise. Nor is it something you do only in times of crisis. Reality is constantly changing, and your vision of it needs to be constantly tested and refined.

In my later years at Aetna, with the company having returned to profitable growth, I continued to work hard to maintain my connections with people at every level of the organization. For example, every month I would visit one of Aetna's forty far-flung business locations to visit with frontline employees. Supervisors were respectfully excluded from these small-group meetings to ensure confidentiality and honesty. I'd ask questions like these, among others: What's it *really* like to work here? What do you love about your job, and what do you hate? What are the customers saying? What kinds of complaints are you getting? What's the toughest task you have to handle on a daily basis? What can we do to make your job easier, better, more rewarding? The eye-opening answers often led to improvements in Aetna policies and systems that no one in the home office could have dreamed up.

Making and maintaining one-on-one connections with people throughout your organization is a crucial leadership skill. But fully understanding the reality you must grapple with requires more than just management by walking around. It often demands deep, detailed analysis of the information you gather from every available source—since the most important underlying trends and patterns are often far from obvious.

For this reason, Aetna developed what we called our health analytics division, which I described briefly in a previous chapter. It's a team of specialists dedicated to rigorously and objectively analyzing the changing financial realities of our health insurance business. The division is headed by an actuary, a professional highly trained in the art and science of measuring and managing risk and uncertainty, a skill that embraces disciplines ranging from statistics and probability to computer modeling and financial analysis. In fact, health analytics is now a subject of graduate school study, and every major health insurance company has its own division dedicated to the practice.

Our health analytics team created a new, much more rigorous process for analyzing what you might call Aetna's "cost of goods sold." In the case of a health insurance company, that includes not just our administrative and sales expenses but also the costs of providing health-care coverage to customers through reimbursements to physicians, hospitals, clinics, and other providers. This is a complicated set of calculations, with thousands of data points that vary enormously from one population to another and that change continually as medical practice evolves and as the state of public health fluctuates.

As part of this new process, we matched various cost categories (physician services, hospital expenses, pharmaceuticals, behavioral health care, and so on) with the Aetna team members who were responsible for negotiating and managing those costs. For the first time, we began scheduling monthly meetings with these team members so we could analyze cost trends and take immediate action to respond to the latest changes.

To make those meetings as meaningful and effective as possible, we lined up the cost trends against specific medical conditions—maternity care, heart problems, hip or knee ailments, and so on. This enabled us to understand how Aetna's financial experiences were related to changes in the daily lives of our patient-customers and to the particular health-care problems they faced.

Having taken these steps, we finally had the right constellation of data points to develop a truly meaningful picture of Aetna's reality. Now we could ask and answer questions like these: What kinds of clinical interventions are driving today's cost trends? What factors are having the greatest impact on our clients and on Aetna's bottom line? Have we accurately forecast the costs our clients are experiencing? If not, why not? What can we do to improve our accuracy in the future?

Like other insurance companies, Aetna wasn't always in full command of these essential elements of our business reality. One of our team members might negotiate an insurance arrangement with a particular hospital system, basing the premiums charged to customers on a specific set of cost forecasts, which were based on such factors as change in volume, hospital usage trends, expanded membership, and so on. The forecast for health-care cost increases for a given year might be four percent. But after the fact, the actual increase might turn out to be less than that (which could benefit Aetna) or significantly more (which could cost Aetna millions). This uncertainty carried much uncontrolled risk for the company.

As you can imagine, the advent of health analytics brought a greater degree of understanding, clarity, and control to this process. You might say that Aetna was a pioneer in using "big data" years before that became a buzzword. Health analytics enabled us to examine health-care cost trends on a monthly basis as they unfolded in real time. When they differed from our forecast, we could examine the causes of the discrepancies. We could conduct monthly analyses by geography, population type, age of clients, and other factors, culminating in meetings with leaders of individual health insurance businesses to discuss the trends and implement our business responses quickly, before suffering major financial consequences.

In some cases, our analysis of cost trends revealed circumstances in which we could intervene in ways to benefit care providers and consumers alike. For example, medical researchers agree that MRIs are one of the most overused tests for headaches and back pain. Aetna could analyze the use of MRIs, CT scans, and numerous other tests by region and provider. The findings could then be used in a variety of ways. We might have one of our on-staff physicians meet with the providers who had abnormally high rates of using MRI tests. We could evaluate whether they had an ownership stake in an MRI facility. Perhaps they could benefit from adopting different protocols or systems. We might implement a change in our negotiating tactics with suppliers or modify the pricing of our insurance products to customers. As a last resort, we might consider dropping a specific provider from the coverage network—a step we reserve only for the most extreme cases.

Most crucially, our decisions regarding coverage were always based on data. And we strictly avoided telling doctors how to practice medicine. Our job was simply to inform them about how their decisions were affecting costs—something their patients cared about a lot. Most doctors are scientists at heart, and they generally appreciated receiving reality-based information they could use to improve their patient care.

As this example illustrates, defining reality has become more complicated for leaders today than it was in Napoleon's time. We are fortunate to have access to much more powerful tools for analyzing reality than the great general enjoyed. Insurance isn't the only industry that is being transformed by the discipline of data analytics. Digital tools for analyzing information are enabling organizational leaders in every field to conduct in-depth studies of customers, markets, products, and services, harvesting valuable insights that can be used to make business operations more efficient, effective, and profitable.

GIVING HOPE: A VISION FOR THE FUTURE

Once a leader has a solid, three-dimensional understanding of today's reality based on continually refreshed reconnaissance and scientifically based analysis, the next job is to build a bridge to the future—an inspiring vision of where the leader, the organization, and its people can go together.

The power of Napoleon's definition of leadership is that it *links* "defining reality" with "giving hope." The two concepts are indeed closely connected. To define reality, you need to have a clear, coherent, graspable image of what your world is like today. Without an honest picture of reality, your vision of the future is just idle daydreaming. But if you can clearly and deeply grasp the nature of today's reality, you will be able to see where the seeds of hope for tomorrow are hiding. So defining reality and giving hope—which a cynic might consider conflicting concepts—are actually deeply intertwined.

Ken Chenault applied these principles throughout his years as a leader at American Express. For example, during the financial crisis of 2008–2009, the company was under tremendous economic stress (along with virtually every other major financial firm). Many wondered whether Amex could even survive. Chenault led his leadership team through a detailed, intensely fact-based analysis of the company's financial difficulties. This was the "defining reality" part of the process.

Then he shifted to the "giving hope" stage by asking which differentiating attributes of the business would be critical to its future success. In other words, against the backdrop of a clear, honest appraisal of the company's current condition, which positive factors could be identified that could lead to a financial turnaround for Amex? And what steps should be taken to protect and maximize those strengths? From the discussions that followed, three key ideas emerged, which ultimately became the three elements of a mantra that Chenault used to guide the company through the tough times. Chenault declared that American Express must always:

- *Stay liquid*—in other words, make sure Amex has enough solid assets to avoid the risk of being unable to meet its obligations and having to declare bankruptcy;

- *Continue to remain profitable*—that is, make sure Amex's ongoing operations are bringing in more money than the firm is spending; and

- *Selectively invest in growth*—that is, even as Amex works hard to overcome today's short-term financial troubles, the firm must look for smart opportunities to build programs and projects that will lead to successful new businesses tomorrow.

This short, simple, fact-based mantra defined the key challenges American Express faced during the financial crisis and also described what it needed to do to turn the page to a brighter future. In short, it defined reality and gave hope. And it did so in a succinct, understandable, memorable fashion that every employee of the company could use as a guide to making daily business decisions.

Chenault applied the Napoleonic approach to leadership in everyday situations as well as in times of crisis. "While meeting with my people throughout the day," he says, "I liked to ask them questions that would enable us to define the reality we're in—for example, in relation to a particular line of business or customer segment that we're discussing. Then I'd ask, 'Based on our long-term strategy for this business and the short-term tactics we're using, what reasons do we have to feel hopeful?' If the honest answer was 'none,' then we knew it was time to rethink our strategy!"

Operations and Strategy—Two Sides of the Same Coin

Chenault's way of linking reality with hope says a lot about how leaders need to develop their vision for the future. It's not about "being a visionary" in some mystical sense—someone with a prophetic gift or the fantastic imagination of a science-fiction writer. Rather, it's about having such a strong, realistic understanding of the nuts and bolts of your current situation that you can clearly picture what the next steps in the naturally unfolding reality are likely to be—as well as the key pressure points where smart leadership, deftly applied, can make a difference, transforming a potentially negative outcome into a positive one.

At Aetna, we had an intense focus on the facts, and I believed in the value of building strong plans to guide us. Regular deep dives gave us a thorough understanding of our industry, adjacent industries, and the economy, and helped us devise clear pathways forward that enabled us to define our vision. Based on this vision, we put in place detailed annual operating plans, along with three-year strategic plans with yearly updates.

This level of deliberative planning made a huge difference for Aetna. It guided the fundamentals of our acquisition strategy and our international expansion plans. It enabled us, after our turnaround, to pioneer a new product category, when we became the first national player to market consumer-directed health plans that incorporated transparency tools for consumers. It also helped guide us through the complex and convoluted health-care reform process that resulted in the Patient Protection and Affordable Care Act, providing us with a set of guiding principles and a thorough plan to execute.

The concept of planning can make people's eyes cross, but without a plan, you are like an acrobat trying to walk a high wire without a net.

When you think about "the vision thing" (as President George

H.W. Bush once called it) as a plan based on analysis of today's reality, it becomes less daunting and more down-to-earth—a skill that any leader with a firm grasp of facts can (and should) begin to practice. Some find it hard to operate on different levels—operational and strategic. Truly effective leaders can do both.

This helps to answer a question I am sometimes asked: How did I make the transition from being a technical problem-solver, as I was during the early years of my career, to being the kind of "visionary" leader many people considered me to be at Aetna? The answer is that these two kinds of leadership are not as far apart as they might seem. I believe that both are manifestations of *systems thinking*—a way of looking at organizations that I first learned at MIT and then practiced throughout my business career.

Systems thinking is a management discipline that focuses on understanding how a system works by examining the linkages and interactions between the components of the system. Throughout my management career, I've relied on systems thinking as a way of getting a handle on the problems faced by organizations. The main difference over the years has just been the expanding scope of the system. As a middle manager, the system I helped to run was relatively small, involving only a few people and a modest amount of money. As a CEO, it was much larger, involving more than forty thousand employees, millions of customers, and budgets in the billions of dollars. And, as I discuss in a later chapter, becoming the leader of the giant system known as Aetna ultimately enabled me to help shape the future of health care for the entire nation.

Yet while the systems I handled grew enormously over time, the underlying principles remained much the same. Focusing on operational details while developing a strategic vision for an organization as a whole is not paradoxical. These activities are two sides of the same coin. Or, as I sometimes like to say, *operational activity builds the bridge to a strategic future.*

The development of Aetna's health analytics division illustrates what I mean. Having invented big data before the world had heard of big data, we soon turned our attention to figuring how we could use that data to benefit people in getting or staying healthy. The data became a crucial tool, even a secret weapon, in our effort to become an industry leader in helping people lead healthier lives.

We invested heavily in an integrated clinical strategy, which drove much of our strategic work and even our acquisition strategy. Clinical integration—which means integrating data across multiple health-care venues, including medical, pharmacy, behavioral, and dental—gave us a more accurate, holistic view of how to improve or maintain member health. It was a fundamental underpinning of our medical and care management strategy, guiding us toward acquisitions such as Active-Health Management, iTriage, and Goodhealth Worldwide.

Integrated clinical data was also a fundamental element of our consumer-directed health plan, Aetna HealthFund. We used the data to evaluate how people were using health-care services and to design health plans that would let them take advantage of preventive health-care services and understand the real costs of elective services such as X-rays. These new data-driven capabilities offered concrete benefits both to our members and to Aetna.

Bringing the power of big data to bear on the business model of health insurance certainly had major strategic implications for our company and, indeed, for our industry. But the concept arose out of specific operational concerns. In short, our drive to get the details right opened our eyes to a range of strategic opportunities that might otherwise have eluded us—at least for a time.

TAKEAWAYS FROM CHAPTER 14

- Former American Express CEO Ken Chenault summarizes the job of the leader as "to define reality and to give hope."

- Defining reality" means that the leader must have a firm grasp on the current situation of the business and its place in the economic environment.

- To define reality accurately, the leader must be in touch with people from every level of their organization. This will give the leader access to multiple sources of information that can shape a rich, detailed image of current reality.

- In today's business world, the leader must also take advantage of the power of digital analytic tools for monitoring, measuring, and drawing connections among myriad data points, as Aetna does through its health analytics division. Big data can greatly enhance the image of reality that the leader will share with their team.

- "Giving hope" means that the leader must articulate a clear vision of a positive, successful future for the organization, together with a well-thought-out strategy that can help make the vision a reality.

- The elements of that strategy should be simple and clear enough to serve as guideposts for employees in making their daily business decisions.

- Operations and strategy, when they are done right, are two sides of the same coin—mutually supportive rather than conflicting.

15

Making Connections:
Communication as a Team Sport

As the leader of an organization, you'll have access to communication tools that can greatly amplify the reach of any message you need to send. These tools can make communication more powerful—but also more complicated.

WHEN YOU NEED TO turn around a troubled organization or guide one through a complex change process—two of the toughest challenges any leader can face—you need to engage the support of a critical mass of team members. You don't necessarily need to capture the hearts and minds of one hundred percent of your people, although of course you'll want to get as close to that goal as possible. But if you can get a solid ten percent firmly in your corner—five out of fifty in a small company, a hundred out of a thousand in a bigger organization—you can begin to make progress. Your first cadre of supporters will help spread your message through their daily words and actions. And over time, as signs of progress begin to appear, the remainder will gradually follow.

The first challenge for any leader in stressful times is to win over that critical ten percent. That requires working hard to get your message clear in your mind and to communicate it as accurately and compellingly as possible.

Fortunately, you shouldn't have to manage the messaging process completely on your own. I've always relied on the help of my closest advisors to help me improve my communication abilities. For example, before giving an important speech, I like to review the key points with a few staff members. Their honest advice has often helped me avoid needless missteps—for example, using language that would alienate or confuse the audience, delving into excessive detail, or omitting information that's essential to make my ideas clear.

When Kim Keck was my chief of staff, she was especially good at helping me explain Aetna's latest business results for lay audiences by translating numbers into words or images. Those of us with financial training who work every day immersed in figures and formulas can easily forget that the language of mathematics is not second nature to everyone; we need the help of people like Keck to show us how to bridge the divide.

In your early days as a business leader, you probably won't have a chief of staff to lean on. Instead, identify a colleague or friend, inside or outside the organization, who can give you frank, specific, intelligent advice about how your messaging efforts are coming across. Practicing your speech in front of an advisor of this kind can help you lift your performance from the B-minus level to an A or even A-plus.

Equally important is getting feedback after a speech, presentation, or meeting—the sooner the better, while memories are still fresh. After I give an important talk, I like to get reviews from two or three trusted friends who observed my performance. I ask questions like: What did I say that I shouldn't have said? Are there things I didn't say that I should have? When and how did I lose the audience? What did I say that really hit home? What can I do better next time? I emphasize that I need honest, objective feedback, not praise or flattery—and, of course, I work hard *not* to respond defensively or angrily when I hear negative feedback. As I've said, if people get the impression that you aren't comfortable hearing bad news, they quickly stop delivering it!

MULTI-CHANNEL COMMUNICATION AND FEEDBACK

Giving speeches is not the only communication skill that an organizational leader needs to master. In fact, CEOs probably give fewer speeches now than they ever have. For maximum impact, you need to convey crucial strategic concepts through multiple channels. Psychologists and learning experts tell us that people differ greatly in the ways they absorb information. Some find it easier to grasp ideas presented visually; others like messages conveyed orally; still others need an interactive, hands-on experience to fully understand a concept's meaning. When you have a message that *everyone* in your organization must understand, try to communicate it through every possible means—and keep repeating the message, even past the point when you are certain that everyone has been exposed to it.

Over the years, I've used some unorthodox tools to achieve this kind of "saturation messaging." For example, both at WellPoint and at Aetna, we hired professionals to design posters to make the complex workings of the health insurance industry vivid and clear to every employee. The posters were displayed in every corridor and used as the centerpiece in events to increase business literacy that employees at every level took part in.

The illustration on page 276 shows one of the posters or "knowledge maps" that we created. (For a closer look, visit www.RonWilliams.net.) Each knowledge map took some component of the health insurance business and brought it vividly to life. Sketched out by a team of my direct reports, who were our subject matter experts, the knowledge maps were then reviewed by the executive committee before being turned over to a team of graphic artists for final rendering. This process ensured that the artwork would accurately reflect our company's vision of the industry and our role in it—a job too important to be outsourced to anyone else.

To ensure that all employees benefited from the knowledge maps, we developed interactive workshops that brought them to life through questions, answers, and discussion. Each map was supplemented with three sets of cards like those you might use in a Monopoly game—except that these cards illustrated the Learning Goals for the workshop, the Value We Provide to our constituents, and the Aetna Values that we seek to embody in each of these interactions.

A bit corny? Maybe. But Aetna team members enjoyed the activities. Many said it was the first time they'd really understood how health insurance works—which means it was the first time they fully grasped the purpose of their work.

Combining visualization with verbal explanations gave everyone the same model, or mental image, for Aetna's operations. It helped to ensure that everyone was finally on the same page. Having everyone at Aetna participate in one of these workshops gave us a set of common ideas, images, and tools that we could refer to while developing and implementing business strategies.

I'd learned the importance of defining and communicating mental models from two main sources. One was my early academic training in psychology and organizational development. These fields use numerous models—for example, psychologist Abraham Maslow's famous hierarchy of needs, which captures the varying levels of human motivation from the most basic (physiological needs such as food and water) to the most advanced (the need for "self-actualization"). This hierarchy is typically presented as a pyramid, a visual aid that everyone immediately understands and remembers. My study of these fields impressed on me the simple truth that whenever you are trying to express a complex idea in an easily understood manner, you need a model for it—preferably one that takes a vivid visual form.

This insight was reinforced when I studied business at MIT's Sloan School of Management. Like all MBA students, I studied a host of financial and management models—varying ways to depict complex business relationships in a clear, memorable form. I even took a course in new business venturing that included a useful model for validating any new business idea. By the time I earned my degree, my brain was stuffed with an array of business models. Some were not particularly valuable, but many were useful in guiding and shaping my own thinking while also making it easier for me to share my ideas with colleagues.

A helpful corollary that I learned from my lifelong use of models is this rule: *If you have an idea that you can't model, it probably has too much clutter.* Go back to the drawing board (literally) and simplify, simplify, simplify!

Jill Griffiths, then Aetna's vice president for corporate communications, played a major role in helping me and my team members communicate our vision in a clear, actionable fashion. During my early years at the company helm, we launched a number of communications campaigns under the overall rubric of "back to basics." These were designed to refocus our people on insurance industry fundamentals, some of which the company had lost sight of during the years immediately preceding my arrival. We provided educational materials for all employees, covering such crucial questions as: What is an actuary, and how does the work of the actuary affect our bottom line? What is underwriting? What is a medical loss ratio, and why does it matter?

Some people at Aetna arguably didn't need to understand matters like these, but we made no exceptions. We wanted *everyone* at the company to understand what our business was, who our customers were, how we met their needs, and how we made money in the process. The better everyone understands the purpose of an organization, the better equipped they are to make smart decisions in their daily work that will help to advance the organization's goals—and the more likely they will be able to improve, innovate, and enhance their efforts so that the company's performance steadily improves.

CREATING A COMMON LANGUAGE

Another valuable communication skill for any organization leader is to establish shared definitions for important terms, ideas, and concepts. When these are missing, everyone in the organization is speaking a different language, with the most common result being that they start talking louder and louder—like tourists in a foreign country—trying to make themselves understood. True understanding is often a casualty.

Creating a common language is especially complicated, and important, when an organization is made up of people from many different backgrounds and with widely varying forms of training, education, and experience. At Aetna, we had thousands of employees who'd joined the corporation when their companies were acquired by Aetna, each now representing an Aetna division with a somewhat different culture and communication style. So my leadership team and I worked hard to identify instances in which our shared language was not consistent and clear, and to overcome those differences through dialogue, discussion, repetition, and practice.

In many cases, the differing definitions of key terms remained unnoticed and unconscious until some conflict forced the discrepancy into the open. One small but important example: During our regular meetings to review divisional and departmental performance, I discovered that many managers defined the term "goal achievement" to mean something like "ninety-five percent or better." This definition was vague and also prone to gradual expansion over time: If ninety-five percent counts as goal achievement, why not ninety-four percent? Or ninety?

When an issue of definition like this would arise in a meeting, I would pause the conversation and say, "Let's have a moment of clarity." I would explicitly point out the confusion and ask that we all agree to use terms in a consistent, clear fashion: "From now on, goal achievement means one hundred percent or better. That doesn't mean we will punish you for coming in at ninety-five or ninety-six percent. We'll examine and discuss the circumstances and figure out what you can do better next time. But it does mean that we are going to be clear and straightforward about how we use words—and we won't use the words 'goal achievement' unless the goal has *actually* been achieved."

In other cases, communication differences among people arise not due to terminological inconsistencies but due to variations in style. These can be subtle and easy to overlook if you don't consciously strive to notice them.

When I was at WellPoint, I worked with a colleague (I'll call him Zach) who was smart and talented, but with whom I constantly ran into communication problems. Zach and I often misunderstood each other, leading to needless errors and confusions. ("You thought I was going to handle that job? I thought you said you were going to do it!" "We agreed on Plan A? No way—I distinctly remember we decided to follow Plan B instead!")

I was at a loss to explain these difficulties until one day, in the middle of a conversation with Zach, I had an epiphany. Listening to Zach talking through his ideas about a project, I suddenly realized the difference between us: *Zach thinks and talks at the same time—in fact, he* uses *talking to work out his ideas and to figure out what he thinks. But I always think first, decide on my ideas, and* then *talk.*

I shared my observation with Zach, and we each realized that the communication style we practiced was the one that seemed natural to us. In fact, I found Zach's way of communicating confusing and practically inconceivable—and he felt exactly the same way about mine! Recognizing the difference made it much easier for us to work together. I now understood that, when Zach talked about an idea, he was offering not a polished proposal but rather musings and observations, generally leading to a conclusion that would emerge only at the end. And Zach now understood that I was doing just the opposite. I learned to simply ask Zach to repeat his conclusion at the end of the discussion.

From that moment on, misunderstandings between the two of us practically ceased.

MAKING HUMAN CONNECTIONS

Leading an organization isn't only about sharing big strategic insights and goals. It's also about being present as a person and making connections with your team members as individuals. You'll find you can do a much better job of motivating people if they feel they know you and sense that you truly care about them, their needs, and their concerns.

One way I tried to do this at Aetna, with the help of my communications team, was through "Ask Ron," a question-and-answer column that appeared on Aetna's intranet every two to three weeks. We invited employees to send in their questions, ideas, or concerns, and for each column I would receive twenty to twenty-five letters on average. I read each one and sometimes I agonized over how to respond appropriately. I didn't want to answer with airy generalizations but rather with meaningful, concrete details, which often required significant research by my staff.

One of the most common questions people asked was typically phrased something like this: "My sister works for such-and-such organization and gets better health insurance benefits than I do—even though I work for a health insurance company! How come?" In many cases, the sister (or brother-in-law or best friend) worked for a local government or federal agency.

In response, I tried to explain the realities of our industry. I might say, "If I had taxing authority (like the state government), I could give you better health-care benefits! But our customers will only pay us so much for the services we provide. The cost of the health insurance we provide to our employees reflects what we pay doctors for your health care. And since we can't do much to drive down those costs, we can only provide the level of care that our profits will pay for."

An answer like this didn't always completely satisfy the questioner. But I did my best to respond truthfully and to provide a real-world analysis that would help people understand the context in which their issue arose. Ninety-five percent of the challenges we face in life result not from anyone's malice or incompetence but from the sheer complexity of the interactions in our world, in which competing interests must somehow be balanced and satisfied. It would be nice if problems like these were easy to solve . . . but they almost never are.

I tried to make myself available in other forums to help educate, inform, and connect with our employees. I would attend a town hall meeting from time to time with one of my executives and participate in the question-and-answer session with employees. Occasionally, the local manager's response to an employee question would be on the abstract or technical side, explaining the *what* accurately but without the *why*. When I noticed this, I might chime in with my own contribution to connect the topic squarely with what I thought was the employee's underlying concern. (A crucial listening skill is learning to hear what people are *really* worried about, even when it isn't expressed explicitly in their words.) So I would interject an explanation using language like "the reason this is important is that . . ." or "solving this problem will enable us to help our customers better in the following way . . ." or "if we get this right, it will make your job easier because . . ."

You can nurture these *personal* connections with the people you want to lead in a number of ways. One simple rule to follow: Never eat alone. Don't hole up in your office with a sandwich at lunchtime or order a room service dinner while on a business trip. Instead, use meal times as opportunities to socialize with colleagues, customers, industry partners, or anyone else you'd like to know a little better. Breaking bread with people is a powerful way to move beyond a "strictly business" relationship and get to know what really makes them tick. The sense of connection established through small gestures like this one will come in handy when you need to call someone to ask for advice, information, or a favor. Any message you need to deliver will be more compelling when people feel they know you and consider you real, caring, and authentic.

My successor at Aetna, Mark Bertolini, is an outspoken person who wears his emotions, and his opinions, on his sleeve. He works hard to complement these traits with intense listening skills. Bertolini prides himself on spending plenty of time with Aetna employees from every level of the organization, striving to learn what makes them tick. For him, this is an essential requirement for leading. As he puts it, "You have no right to challenge someone else's point of view without understanding it first."

Making close personal connections with people can be a challenge for me. I'm a reserved man, unaccustomed to showing my emotions in public. In my judgment, too many leaders act as if they're the most important person in any room. I've always tried to behave in the opposite way—as if the focus should be on the job at hand, and never on me. So I've developed the habit of playing down my personal feelings. Maybe I went a little too far, since some of the people I worked with began to wonder whether I *had* any feelings in the first place!

But there were moments when circumstances broke down my reserve and revealed my softer side to my colleagues. My longtime communications director Jill Griffiths recalls one of the rare times I teared up in public. It happened while I was paying tribute to a longtime Aetna colleague upon his retirement. People who knew me were somewhat stunned at this rare show of emotion—and some assumed it must have been planned in advance. "Afterward," Jill says, "I received dozens of emails complimenting me: 'It was brilliant of you to get Ron to cry in a meeting! How on earth did you do it?' It was hard to convince them that it had happened spontaneously!"

If I had it to do over, I'd probably reveal my emotions a little more on a daily basis. My friend, former Xerox CEO Ursula Burns, offers this advice to ambitious young people:

> Some people say that a leader should never let people see her sweat. I think that's wrong. You *have to* let them see you sweat! People need to see that you're human . . . that you have weaknesses, flaws, and vulnerabilities. That you don't necessarily have all the answers. When they see this, it motivates them to contribute more—to step up with solutions to the problems you are grappling with. It helps them realize you're all in this together, a team of mere mortals working together to make big things happen . . . We need more *personal* leadership in America.
>
> I think that being a real person on the job, and sharing that real personality with the people around you, helps keep you on an even keel. I think it can help keep you from falling into the trap that some CEOs have fallen into—the trap of making bad decisions or violating the law because of hubris or an exaggerated sense of self. I want to always remember that I am just Ursula Burns, an ordinary person with my strengths and weaknesses—not some kind of Powerful Person moving pieces around on a chessboard.

I admire Burns, and I suspect her advice makes very good sense. But it would be hard for me to follow it while remaining true to myself. You are who you are, and you can't force yourself to be vulnerable, even though that might be a sound strategy for deepening your connections with people.

The truth is that my reserved nature is a limitation of mine.

My only defense is to say that I've worked on it, and I think I've improved over time. Through my years as a leader, I've softened my "strictly business" façade and loosened up a bit. I've learned to spend more time relating to people as people—asking about their personal lives, their families, and their interests, and paying attention to the answers, hopefully making my colleagues and associates a little more comfortable with me in the process.

In this, as in other ways, I remain a work in progress!

IN THE PUBLIC ARENA

Every business leader is called on sometimes to be a public spokesperson for their company. It's not a responsibility you can slough off or ignore, but it creates special communications challenges and poses some unusual risks that you must be careful to avoid.

It helps to be cognizant of the interests, goals, and needs of the media—what writers, editors, and producers are looking for. If you can cooperate and provide them with the kind of content they need, you are likely to get a fair shake from them.

Many times, it's a simple matter of helping them meet a deadline. As CEO, I used to say to my management team members, "If I can return calls from the PR team regarding a news reporter on deadline within thirty minutes, so can you." Even if you don't have any exciting news or groundbreaking insights to share with reporters, you can respond promptly to their requests for your time. They will probably appreciate it and perhaps treat you and your organization a little more favorably in their coverage.

Leaders can encounter certain communication pitfalls when they become public spokespeople for their company or industry. One mistake that's easy to make is to forget that everything you say is fodder for analysis—fair or unfair—by the media and by the general public. This reality underscores the importance of remembering and following my rule, "If there's something that will make you feel really good to say—something you are *itching* to say—*don't say it.*"

One of my predecessors at Aetna was punished severely for violating this rule. In 1999, during the period when Aetna was struggling financially and strategically, chairman and CEO Richard Huber had to deal with the widespread public perception that his company, along with other health insurers, was exploiting consumers. I'm sure he was frustrated by what he must have felt was unfair and one-sided media coverage of the issue, as well as lawsuits brought by dissatisfied customers and health-care providers. Huber's frustration boiled over when a California jury awarded a woman, whose husband, an Aetna subscriber, had died of a rare form of stomach cancer, with a $120.5-million verdict against Aetna—$4.5 million to cover medical expenses and $116 million in punitive damages. Huber unloaded to the press, providing his own bitter explanation of the trial's outcome: "You had a skillful ambulance-chasing lawyer, a politically motivated judge, and a weeping widow."

The emotion underlying Huber's statement may have been understandable, but his sarcastic reference to a woman who had lost her husband guaranteed that the public would recoil in horror. Huber was also sued for defamation by the woman's attorney over the "ambulance-chasing lawyer" remark. While the case was dismissed, Huber was forced to publicly apologize for his rash statement. The story was widely quoted in the press the next year when Huber resigned as CEO.

Once I became president of Aetna, I found myself playing the same role of public spokesperson. And I quickly discovered how easy it can be to become the unintentional center of controversy.

An easy trap to fall into is to use insider jargon when communicating with the general public. In the world of insurance, we sometimes speak about "culling members." A company may engage in this process when it discovers that it has mispriced its services to a particular set of customers, thereby putting itself in a position to consistently lose money on them. Obviously, an insurer can't remain in that position year after year. To fix the problem, it raises premium charges when the time comes for an annual policy renewal. Customers then can choose whether to pay the higher premiums or to leave and get coverage elsewhere. Most customers take the latter route, which is why the practice has come to be called "culling members"—it generally leads to a reduction in the number of covered individuals, while boosting the company's overall profitability.

As you can see from this description, there's nothing terribly sinister about culling members. But the term isn't an attractive one—it sounds as if insurance companies are cancelling members' policies for no good reason, leaving them bereft of coverage and without access to medical care. So smart insurance executives avoid using the term when talking with the public.

Unfortunately, I hadn't learned that lesson before I took part in one of my first Aetna "earnings calls" with members of the financial analyst community. I mentioned that Aetna would be culling members as part of its strategy to return to overall profitability—and some of the investment advisors who heard the phrase repeated it in their reporting about our company. People without expert knowledge of insurance were aghast. Over the next few days, Aetna and I, and the insurance industry in general, were subject to a number of attacks in the media over our alleged ruthlessness in pursuit of profit—all because of my careless choice of phrasing.

It was a valuable lesson to me in the importance of watching your language and thinking hard about how to translate industry jargon into terminology that ordinary people will understand.

TAKEAWAYS FROM CHAPTER 15

- An organizational leader has to transmit crucial messages throughout all layers of the business—a complex task that often requires a team approach to communication.

- Because different people respond differently to various forms of communication, an important message should be transmitted through a saturation approach that uses many different media—speeches, memos, posters, videos, online messaging, and so on.

- Use your personal presence as a communication tool. There's no substitute for the human connections that a leader makes through one-on-one encounters with team members and others.

- Take responsibility for making sure that all team members are using a shared language, with terms whose meaning everyone understands. When words and phrases are ambiguous, costly misunderstandings can occur.

- Another job that the organizational leader can't easily delegate is that of representing the organization in public—before the news media, among other business leaders, to customers, and in many other venues. In today's hot-wired, politically polarized, short-attention-span world, this creates a whole new set of challenges for a leader, who must work hard to master the communications challenges of the twenty-first century.

16

Shaking Up an Industry:
The Health-Care Reform Challenge

*Few experiences test the skills of a CEO like finding their
industry thrust into the spotlight of national controversy.
The story of Aetna's role in the health-care reform battles
of 2009–2010 vividly illustrates some of the toughest
challenges of business leadership in today's world.*

MY YEARS AT AETNA culminated with the biggest vision challenge of all. The push for national health-care reform in 2009–2010
under President Barack Obama called for creating and communicating an industry-wide vision for one of the nation's biggest and most
complex businesses.

I first met the then-senator Obama during the 2008 presidential
campaign, at the invitation of Penny Pritzker, a successful business
leader who later served as President Obama's secretary of commerce.

It was fascinating to have a chance to talk with a rising star of national politics who was rapidly positioning himself to become the first black president in our history. We discussed a range of economic topics. One of the points I raised was the idea of providing government financial help to people being laid off from their jobs to help them pay for extended health insurance coverage under the COBRA program. Senator Obama liked the concept, and after his election he implemented it during the massive worldwide recession then affecting millions of people around the United States.

I consider Obama's election as president in 2008 a turning point in American history—a huge milestone in the long journey toward creating a society in which the founders' dream of freedom and equality for all is truly realized. While, like practically everyone, I agreed with some of President Obama's policies and disagreed with others, I found him to be a person of high character, intelligence, and integrity—a fine role model for young people everywhere and a man I was proud to have leading our nation.

For all these reasons, I was honored to serve as an informal advisor to President Obama when he made health-care reform the signature initiative of his administration.

During the debate over the plan that became the Affordable Care Act (ACA)—sometimes referred to as Obamacare—I realized that Aetna had a unique opportunity to help shape the national health-care agenda. My executive team and I devoted countless hours to defining a values-based approach to health-care reform. We decided that Aetna should stand for certain core principles:

The goal of health-care reform should be that all Americans should be insured at reasonable cost, making it possible for them to receive access to decent health care while avoiding the devastation of unaffordable bills.

No one should be denied coverage because of a preexisting condition or other health problem.

The practice of "medical underwriting"—that is, adjusting health insurance risks to strictly reflect individual health status—should not be permitted to raise insurance prices for some individuals beyond the realm of affordability. Instead, rates should be banded and regulated so that insurance for the sickest patients would generally cost no more than three times as much as for the healthiest patients.

In the insurance industry, these principles were considered quite progressive for the time, which means they stirred up some controversy, both inside and outside Aetna. But they reflected the values we believed our company should uphold as well as the values we felt a majority of Americans were prepared to embrace. So we were proud to advocate them throughout the health-care reform debate. Whenever I had the chance to speak with President Obama or one of his staffers, I emphasized these values and worked to explain the likely impact of particular policy options on the prospects for achieving them.

My team and I also took on the challenge of educating congressional leaders and staffers about the nuances of the health-care and insurance systems. Aetna's government affairs advisor Steve Kelmar had many connections in Washington, which meant he usually heard about proposed amendments to the administration's reform program almost as soon as they were formulated. Using the intelligence Kelmar fed us, we modeled the likely impact of the proposed changes on the health insurance industry and the health-care marketplace, as well as the effects on consumers, and fed this information back to members of Congress and their staffers. "If you adopt this proposed change," we would say, "here are the likely impacts on consumers, employers, health-care providers, and the national economy." Folks on Capitol Hill soon recognized that we were trying to be honest brokers offering unbiased, accurate information about the realities of our complex industry, something they found quite valuable.

However, I quickly learned the dangers of wading into a highly charged political controversy, even when your motives are purely positive. My advocacy efforts were criticized by leaders of various consumer groups as well as by certain writers of newspaper columns and editorials. I worked quietly behind the scenes with influential senators and representatives on both sides of the aisle, many of whom expressed gratitude for my guidance—only to find myself publicly demonized by some of the same leaders as representing an industry they considered "greedy" and "immoral."

Naturally, any debate over important, complex issues like health care generates controversy and even acrimony. In today's highly polarized political environment, some policy advocates can succumb to the temptation to demonize their opponents, sometimes using factual distortions and even outright lies. This certainly happened during the debate over the ACA. Washington operatives shrug this off as "just politics," but I could never get away with such tactics as a CEO. Politicians, I learned, have greater leeway to communicate contradictory messages than business executives—a disillusioning realization that spelled an end to any thoughts I might have had of getting into politics myself!

I was particularly disappointed when *The Wall Street Journal*, a respected and highly influential publication known for its pro-business positions, carelessly mischaracterized my position on the individual mandate, one of the key provisions of the Obama administration's health insurance reform program. An op-ed article I wrote for the *Journal* was given the headline, "Why I No Longer Support the Health Insurance Mandate," which was a misleading and over-simplified summary of my position. My purpose in the article was to say that the financial penalty assessed by the law on individuals who failed to buy health insurance should be described as a tax, which in fact it is. As I've noted, I'm a big believer in the importance of using language clearly and accurately, and in this case I think the Obama team and its supporters in Congress were guilty of fudging their terminology for political reasons, which is usually a mistake. In fact, my point was ultimately supported by none other than the US Supreme Court, which upheld the constitutionality of the individual mandate in the ACA on the grounds that it actually levies a tax—which the administration was well within its rights to do.

The lesson I took from this incident: Try to avoid letting somebody else control the way in which your message is framed. If at all possible, at least reserve the right to critique the headline before it appears in print. When you serve as a public spokesperson for any position, always try to own and control your own words. That way, you can minimize the chance that others will distort and misuse them.

On another occasion, I was participating in a live televised forum about health-care reform with President Obama and other leaders, when I was suddenly ambushed by a question from the moderator, a prominent broadcast journalist. She demanded, "When so many Americans can't afford health care, how can you justify the huge salaries paid to insurance executives like you?"

Taken aback, I was momentarily tempted to respond, "And how much money do *you* make?" But then I recalled my own rule: "If it would make you feel good to say it—*don't!*" Instead, I seized the opportunity to explain the place of health insurance companies in a free market economy. The experience underscored for me the brutal nature of public controversy in a bitterly polarized society, where hit-and-run attacks that do little to advance the national understanding are par for the course.

Any change in health insurance (as in any complex industry) is bound to create winners and losers. In the case of Obamacare's passage in 2010, the roster of winners was different than most people think. Millions of people bought insurance through the newly created government-run health-care exchanges—a positive effect, though one that I believe could have been achieved in other, simpler ways. At the same time, Medicaid coverage expanded by seventeen to eighteen million people, which for political reasons could otherwise never have been done. In effect, the ACA was essentially a Medicaid expansion act, with a host of complicated additional provisions affecting private health insurance. It did provide millions of people with the peace of mind that health insurance brings, which is important—though the political acrimony and the economic disruption caused were a high price to pay.

Getting the ACA done, as imperfect as it was, was a major legislative and societal accomplishment for President Obama. In my view, it was also a powerful affirmation of the principle that health care is a right rather than a privilege.

I also regard Barack Obama's presidency as a phenomenal moment in the history of our country. President Obama faced an enormous set of challenges. He didn't necessarily fully understand the business world, but he did his best to listen and learn about it using input from a variety of sources, while balancing what he learned against political realities. Obama's willingness to listen and learn is an important value all leaders need to embrace.

My experiences in the public arena, positive and negative, have convinced me that more business leaders should be engaged public citizens. They owe it to themselves and to their companies to speak up when they have something of value to contribute to important national debates. If you are an aspiring leader, don't assume that your voice is important only within your own organization. Remember that you have a part to play in the broader community that makes your success possible—and make a commitment to play that role with integrity, decency, and effectiveness.

REFRAMING HEALTH CARE: HOW TO FIX A DYSFUNCTIONAL INDUSTRY

Everyone knows that the American health-care industry still has big problems. We have many of the finest physicians, nurses, and health-care facilities in the world, as well as medical research institutions, pharmaceutical makers, and scientific innovators who are unsurpassed in their expertise and creativity. But the costs we incur for care are unsustainably high and continuing to rise, too many people are uninsured or underinsured, and Americans suffer from needlessly high rates of many chronic health conditions, including obesity, diabetes, asthma, and heart disease, that cause avoidable suffering, disability, and premature death.

It would take a book as long as this one to detail the causes and the possible cures for this unfortunate state of dysfunction. Suffice it to say that US health care is in dire need of reframing. The reforms instituted by the ACA are a step in the right direction; at least they have made health insurance available to millions of people who formerly couldn't afford it. But more fundamental changes are still needed. Some worthwhile ideas are outlined in the 2007 report *Adjusting the Prescription*, created by the Health Care Reform Subcommittee of the nonprofit Committee for Economic Development, which I co-chaired.

For example, we need to find ways to ensure that every American— young or old, rich or poor, healthy or sick—has health insurance coverage in some form. One of the chronic problems with our piece-meal system is the inevitable creation of incentives for some people to become "free riders," relying on care that is paid for, directly or indirectly, by others. This is especially common among healthy young people, who often think of themselves (unconsciously) as "immortal" and therefore with no need for insurance—until, of course, the need suddenly arises. When I was CEO of Aetna, I had a recurring night-mare about the "fan letter" I dreaded receiving from a young health insurance customer:

Dear Mr. Williams,

I want to thank you for the amazing coverage Aetna provided to me after my recent skiing accident. I had to have two major surgical operations, I spent three weeks in the hospital, and I went through months of rehabilitative therapy. Nearly all of the cost was covered by my Aetna policy! Your company is the best.

Now that I am fully recovered, I am writing to cancel my policy. Enclosed you will find my final premium payment. Because I am young and healthy—and have given up ski-ing—I feel I am no longer in need of coverage. But I promise that the next time I suffer a serious injury or illness I will definitely choose Aetna as my insurance company!

Gratefully,
A Happy Customer

This problem of "adverse selection," in which only high-risk cus-tomers buy health insurance while low-risk customers go without, is a fundamental challenge that policy makers in Washington must face head-on if a real solution to our health-care problems is going to be achieved.

Today, US health care continues to evolve, experimenting with new business models that may help improve the economic viability of the industry while making care more affordable for larger numbers of people. In October 2018, while the final edits were being done on this book, Aetna and drug store giant CVS Health received approval from the Justice Department for a planned merger—the latest in a series of consolidations that have happened in recent years. In the years to come, we'll see the impact of this merger on the American public. Like most such moves, it will probably have some consequences that no one can yet foresee.

One way that Aetna, along with some other firms in the health insurance industry, is trying to contribute to a solution to the US health-care dilemma is through new programs designed to alter the business structures that shape the behavior of doctors, hospitals, and other health-care providers. Aetna's effort in this area is a new business called Healthagen. It was launched on my watch as part of our company's reframing effort and is one of the first health-care businesses of its kind. Having realized, thanks in part to our strategic planning process, that US health care was due for a shakeup, we wanted to get ahead of the curve. I asked Joe Zubretsky, one of my top executives who had previously worked on mergers and acquisitions and corporate strategy, to head up the project.

Healthagen uses new technologies—particularly the ability, in our digital age, to amass and analyze vast quantities of data—to reverse the traditional incentives of the health-care industry. The fee-for-service health-care system we're familiar with is focused on what's called "episodic acute care." Essentially, this means that patients visit the doctor when they are sick or hurt, and they pay the provider for helping to make them well through a prescription, an operation, or some other form of intervention.

The new approach that Healthagen exemplifies focuses on what's called "population health"—the overall health outcomes of everyone in a particular population group, including the distribution of outcomes throughout the group. It's based on the understanding that good health is a product of many interconnected factors. An individual's genetic inheritance is one factor. Others include the various lifestyle choices we make—the foods we eat, the kinds of exercise we practice, and our use of tobacco, alcohol, and other drugs. Environmental factors, both physical and psychological, are also significant: air and water quality, our social relationships, the level of stress we experience on the job, and the ways we cope with that stress. The last major factor is the quality of the medical care we receive and the rigor with which we adhere to the guidelines provided by our caregivers.

In a population health system, doctors and other providers attempt to positively influence all of these health factors. Caregivers are paid for their contributions to the well-being of the population, not merely for the interventions they provide in cases of illness or injury. Thus, the interests of the system are aligned with those of the patient. People don't want to visit the doctor and have procedures done; they want to feel well and to get on with their lives. Population health rewards health-care providers for helping to make that happen.

Data analytics plays a key role in empowering this approach. Sophisticated software algorithms informed by the latest medical research enable caregivers to identify patients who are at risk of serious problems, making it possible to help them stay well through preventive measures, such as diet and exercise counseling, targeted testing including advanced biometric measures, intelligently customized use of prescription drugs, and better management of chronic conditions that often lead to acute episodes. Population health also relies on well-managed information technology systems and consistent communications protocols to establish clear, timely connections among all caregivers involved with a particular patient—primary care physicians, clinical specialists, nurses, therapists, hospitals, clinics, testing facilities, and so on. This helps to avoid duplication of services, over- or undertreatment, misdiagnoses, and conflicting advice that ends up confusing and frustrating patients.

The goal of population health programs is to help people get the information, advice, and medical help they need *before* they get seriously ill, so they can avoid time away from work, home, and the people they love. When illnesses or injuries are unavoidable, a population health team should be able to identify the most effective treatments based on the latest data-driven research, to ensure a more rapid, more complete, and less costly recovery for both the patient and society as a whole.

If it works as planned, population health will yield wins for everyone involved. Health-care companies that run hospitals and clinics will be able to operate more efficiently, focusing their efforts on patients who truly need intensive care and maximizing the value of the services provided. Health-care professionals like doctors and nurses will be more satisfied with their work, knowing that they are helping patients achieve a better quality of life rather than simply providing palliative or restorative care after needless suffering has already occurred. Employers, government agencies, and others who foot the bill for health care will find that costs have stopped their dramatic, unsustainable escalation and that a clearer relationship between patient outcomes and money spent has been achieved.

And patients themselves will be able to enjoy longer, happier lives while experiencing less frustration with inefficient, disorganized, and needlessly expensive health care.

The early results from Healthagen have been promising. But expanding the program and others like it to provide care for hundreds of millions of Americans will be a big job. You might call it one of the biggest reframing projects in business history, and it's one on which the future health of our nation may well depend.

TAKEAWAYS FROM CHAPTER 16

- The leader of a major corporation has no choice but to represent their organization on the national stage—and when the entire industry becomes the center of a heated political debate, the pressure to communicate with integrity, courage, and clarity becomes greater than ever.

- Participating as Aetna's CEO during the health-care reform debate of 2009–2010 taught me many tough lessons—about the polarized nature of today's political world, about the cynicism of some of today's news media, and about the difficulty of getting government to adopt policies that reflect the complex economic realities of a vast, dynamic arena like health care.

- Some of my encounters during the health-care debate were disheartening. But the educational experience left me more convinced than ever of the necessity for business leaders to take an active role in helping to inform and shape the public debate about important economic challenges.

Epilogue:
Keep Breaking Barriers

The leadership challenge never ends. To ensure that you keep growing, set your personal achievement bar higher every year.

IF YOU STUDY AND practice the leadership techniques described in the preceding chapters, you and your organization are likely to enjoy success significantly greater than you may have expected—new products launched, failing business units turned around, organizational cultures transformed.

It's not magic. My personal experience and life observations have shown me that ordinary people—people like you and me—can achieve great things if they learn how to recognize and understand the barriers that limit them and then start overcoming them, deliberately, creatively, and persistently.

In your climb, remember and make use of recommendations offered in this book:

- When making career choices, seize every opportunity to learn and grow, even when there is no immediate or obvious payoff in sight.

- Volunteer to take on the toughest challenges. The daunting tasks others shun often hold special potential for achievement.

- When you feel boxed in by circumstances, try reframing the situation. A fresh perspective can offer an unforeseen, creative solution.

- Don't overlook the extraordinary power of simply finding the facts. Gathering data points from many perspectives can help untangle seemingly impossible quandaries.

- When those around you pose obstacles, don't jump to conclusions about their motives. Assuming positive intent can often enable you to turn apparent enemies into allies.

- To build a team of effective supporters, don't look for people like you but rather those with different skills and perspectives that complement your own.

- Master the art of managing two up and two down, so you can understand and respond to the objectives and needs of people at all levels of your organization.

- Learn how to define reality for the members of your team and to give them hope for the future—the two most crucial tasks any leader must undertake.

- Use artfully crafted questions to challenge the assumptions and overcome the misunderstandings that limit what you and your team can accomplish.

- Find ways to connect your dream of the future with the deepest values of the people you work with, so they can be motivated to help you make the dream a reality.

- Instill an appropriate sense of commitment into your team members—not through threats or punishment, but by energizing their highest aspirations.

- Work to discover your voice, and use it to communicate crucial insights clearly and persuasively to those around you—including people in the community at large.

None of these leadership strategies require extraordinary gifts. You don't need to be a mathematical Einstein, a creative Jobs, a financial Buffett, or a charismatic Kennedy. Your own abilities can suffice to make you an effective leader—provided you focus on the daily challenges around you and then work doggedly, thoughtfully, and positively with the people around you to overcome them.

If you do this, I predict you'll be surprised and delighted to find that barriers you once assumed were insurmountable are beginning to fall, enabling you to achieve goals that once appeared unreachable:

The project others couldn't get off the ground is completed on time and under budget.

The department some considered "unmanageable" becomes a high-achieving team of cooperative, energetic professionals.

The business that once appeared headed for bankruptcy returns to profitability, then begins to grow again—faster than ever.

But don't be satisfied with your first one or two "impossible" achievements. In the volatile business and social environment we find around us now, every triumph is short-lived. The personal breakthrough you enjoy today simply gives you permission to pursue an even more ambitious goal tomorrow.

The same is true on an organizational level. I've found that any team, in business or elsewhere, is capable of forgetting all the good lessons they have learned within two years. I call this the space-age plastic effect: Once you stop bending a piece of plastic, it reverts to its prior form. The same is true of muscles when you stop training them. Celebrating triumphs as if they are permanent, resting on your laurels, and becoming complacent represent enormous dangers that every leader and organization must constantly guard against.

You can avoid this danger by focusing on continual growth, both personal and organizational. Get into the habit of setting short-term and longer-term goals for yourself and reviewing your progress toward them regularly.

Various goal-setting systems are available. One that I like involves setting aside thirty to forty-five minutes at the same time every week with a pen and a pad to make a list of "key deliverables" for myself. These deliverables are things I have made a commitment to achieve in the three key areas of my life—my job, my family, and myself. My weekly list includes deliverables over four time periods—the next week, the next month, the next quarter, and the next year.

The kinds of deliverables you'll identify as crucial to your growth will vary, depending on the nature of your life and your work and the biggest challenges you currently face. Deliverables for your job might include an important project plan, a report your boss has requested, a decision concerning a new marketing campaign, or the selection of a candidate to fill a vacant position in your department. Deliverables for your family might include planning a family trip, decorating your home for the holidays, teaching your teenaged son to drive, or volunteering to help coach your daughter's soccer team. Deliverables for yourself might include starting a workout program at the gym, signing up for a class at the local Y, or reading a few chapters from that important new book on management you've been meaning to tackle.

Choosing your deliverables is a personal decision. But one category I think everyone ought to include is taking steps to stay current on changing technology. No matter what kind of work you do or what industry you're employed in, digital information and communications systems, along with other rapidly evolving technologies, are probably in the process of transforming the activities of your organization and the competitive landscape it faces. Depending on your business, the fields you need to stay abreast of may range from artificial intelligence, machine learning, and blockchain technology (which underlies so-called cryptocurrencies like Bitcoin) to genomic sequencing, 3-D printing, and nanotechnology (which lets engineers build materials and devices one molecule at a time).

I'm not suggesting that you need to learn how to write computer code or manipulate genetic code. But you do need to understand how new technologies like these are affecting the world we live in and the changes they may be triggering in your own business. When you craft your list of key deliverables for personal growth, include at least one or two items related to learning about technology. It's essential to ensure you won't find yourself left behind in our rapidly changing world.

Each week, review the list from the week before and note the progress you've made. Modify your plans as appropriate. You'll derive a real sense of satisfaction from the goals you've met.

Another important part of my personal growth formula is promising myself that I will strive each year to become fifteen percent better at what I do.

Why fifteen percent? In truth, the number is somewhat arbitrary. Many of the goals you'll pursue in your career can't be measured in precise mathematical terms. So applying a number to an annual level of improvement may feel slightly artificial. But I like challenging myself—and others—to get better in concrete, specific ways, not to pursue vague, general aspirations. Affixing a quantity to the goal helps create that feeling.

I also think that fifteen percent "feels" like the right sort of number. I suspect that setting a goal of improving by ten percent would feel a bit too easy—as if it translates into "just be a little better." By contrast, fifteen percent implies a bit more "stretch." And that's what I want to feel every year—as if I am challenging myself to tackle new skills and new heights of performance that are somewhat intimidating, even a bit scary.

You can make the general objective of improving by fifteen percent concrete and actionable in many ways. It's about setting higher goals, mastering new skills, learning new technologies, conquering new territories, and becoming a subtler, deeper, and more creative thinker. As a new year approaches, sit down and review what you've accomplished in the past year and think about some of the ways you can build on that in the coming twelve months—or branch out into new directions.

The following include some fifteen percent goals you might consider adopting:

- If you are in sales or in any leadership position in an organization where sales revenues are an important measure of success: Calculate your average sales increase rate over the past three years, then aspire to boost your sales by an extra fifteen percent *above* that average rate.

- If you help to run an organization that measures productivity in terms of products shipped, customers or clients served, or any similar, tangible metric: Calculate the average growth in your productivity metric over the past three years, then aim to increase it by an extra fifteen percent.

- Identify any personal skill area in which you need improvement. (If none come to mind, ask colleagues and team members for suggestions—I'm sure they will have some!) It could involve public speaking, team building, motivating others, hiring talent, or listening perceptively. Then make a specific skill-building plan that will stretch and enhance your abilities by fifteen percent. The plan might call for taking a challenging seminar, working on targeted assignments with a mentor, or joining a club of like-minded people who will push one another to get better.

- Volunteer to take on a tough outside project at work, in your industry, or in the community—one that will force you to develop new talents and apply them to a worthwhile cause. Think in terms of a project that you can complete in a year and that will leave you feeling as if you have accomplished at least fifteen percent more than what your regular "day job" demands.

Notice what all of these fifteen percent goals have in common. They all reach "above and beyond the call of duty" to embrace personal growth that exceeds the kind of goals typically set in a traditional management-by-objectives performance-planning meeting. And why not? Ordinary goals may be fine for ordinary people. But if your life objective is to become extraordinary, you need to stretch higher. That's what fifteen percent thinking is designed to help you do.

As an aspiring leader at any job level, the mindset of fifteen percent improvement will help you accelerate your path to success and keep you on top once you've arrived. Living in fifteen percent territory is inherently challenging; it means constantly tackling activities that you're uncomfortable doing. But that sense of discomfort tells you that you're taking on new risks and therefore have the potential to enjoy new rewards—and achieve even greater levels of performance beyond those you once considered impossible.

Acknowledgments

I STARTED WRITING THIS book quite some time ago. I soon realized how hard it was to tell the story in a way that others might benefit from. For this reason, it's appropriate for me to acknowledge all the people who made this book possible.

First and foremost, I want to express appreciation to my wife, Cynthia. I volunteered for the journey we have been on; Cynthia is part volunteer and part draftee. But without her support, encouragement, and objective counsel, my career success—and this book—would not have been possible. I will always be grateful to her.

Thanks to my son, Chris, who carefully reviewed numerous drafts of the manuscript and provided wise criticism and counsel.

Thanks to all my colleagues at Aetna who "took the trip" as we transformed the company's mission, values, culture, financial performance, and reputation. This was the biggest and most rewarding challenge of my career. It was a true privilege to help create a values-based, high-performance organization with outstanding financial performance, and to have it recognized as the most admired company in our sector. The people of Aetna made it possible.

Thanks to all the friends and associates who so generously shared their wisdom and experiences. My appreciation to Mark Bertolini, Ursula Burns, Ken Chenault, Ian Davis, Jerald Gooden, Jill Griffiths,

JD Hoye, Kim Keck, Pam Kehaly, Kathy Mentus, Kay Mooney, Dr. John "Jack" Rowe, Pat Russo, Elease Wright, and Joe Zubretsky. I believe the stories they've allowed me to recount in this book have made it much more valuable.

A special thank you to Vernon Jordan, who convinced me that my leadership journey held lessons that could help many others.

Finally, thanks to my co-author, Karl Weber, whose years of experience as a writer and editor helped me find my voice as a first-time author.

Index

About the Authors

RONALD A. WILLIAMS is chairman and CEO of RW2 Enterprises, LLC, as well as the former chairman and CEO of health insurance giant Aetna Inc. He focuses his energy on private equity, values-based leadership and transformational change, and health-care value creation. Through his firm, RW2 Enterprises, Williams counsels C-suite corporate executives on strategy and transformational leadership. He is the operating advisor to private equity firm Clayton, Dubilier, & Rice, and serves as chairman for portfolio companies agilon health and naviHealth. He is a director of American Express, The Boeing Company, and Johnson & Johnson.

Williams became president of Aetna and joined its board in 2002; in 2006, he became chairman and CEO. Under his leadership, Aetna was named *Fortune* magazine's "Most Admired Company" in the "Health Care: Insurance and Managed Care" category for three consecutive years. In 2011, the year he retired, Aetna had full-year operating earnings of $5.17 per share. Its market capitalization grew from $4.7 billion in 2001 to $15.3 billion in 2011, when the company also ranked 77th on the *Fortune 100* list.

Williams is a member of The MIT Corporation, vice chairman

of The Conference Board, and a member of the President's Circle of the National Academies. He was elected to the American Academy of Arts and Sciences and is a trustee of the Committee for Economic Development. He served on President Obama's Management Advisory Board from 2011 to 2017. He is a graduate of Roosevelt University and holds an M.S. in management from the Sloan School of Management at the Massachusetts Institute of Technology.

You can learn more about Ron Williams by visiting
www.ronwilliams.net.

KARL WEBER is a writer and editor who specializes in topics from business and politics to current affairs, history, and social issues.

Among other works, Weber has co-authored three books with Muhammad Yunus, founder of Grameen Bank and winner of the 2006 Nobel Peace Prize, including the *New York Times* bestseller *Creating a World Without Poverty*. Weber also edited three best-selling books by former President Jimmy Carter, as well as the number one bestseller *What Happened: Inside the Bush White House and Washington's Culture of Deception*, by former White House Press Secretary Scott McClellan.